BYRON

CHILDE HAROLD

TEXTE ANGLAIS

PUBLIÉ AVEC UNE NOTICE, DES ARGUMENTS
ET DES NOTES, EN FRANÇAIS

PAR ÉMILE CHASLES
Inspecteur général de l'instruction publique.

PARIS
LIBRAIRIE HACHETTE ET Cᴵᴱ
79, BOULEVARD SAINT-GERMAIN, 79

1883

BYRON

—

CHILDE HAROLD

A LA MÊME LIBRAIRIE :

Byron : *Childe Harold*, traduction française, par M. H. Bellet, avec le texte anglais. 1 vol. in-16.................. .... 3 fr.

Le même ouvrage, expliqué par deux traductions françaises, l'une littérale et *juxtalinéaire*, présentant le mot à mot français en regard des mots anglais correspondants, l'autre correcte et précédée du texte anglais, par M. H. Bellet. 1 vol. in-16... 6 fr.

Chacun des trois premiers chants............... 1 50
Le quatrième chant............................ 2 50

Motteroz, Adm.-Direct. des Imprimeries réunies, A, rue Mignon, 2, Paris.

NOTICE

SUR LORD BYRON ET SUR " CHILDE HAROLD "

LA VIE DE BYRON

La vie de lord Byron a été souvent écrite, et par des auteurs du premier ordre, sans qu'on soit aujourd'hui d'accord sur le jugement qu'il faut porter de lui. Quand il s'agit d'un écrivain puissant, aucune biographie ne vaut jamais l'autobiographie involontaire qu'il a donnée lui-même en laissant échapper de sa plume toutes ses pensées; il livre sa vie intime et la livre au monde entier.

L'apparition de lord Byron dans la littérature anglaise a fait époque, non seulement en Angleterre, mais encore en Europe. L'éclat et l'influence de ses poèmes, la lutte qu'il engagea et qu'il soutint contre la société de son pays, furent alors des événements publics, et sont aujourd'hui encore, à la distance des temps, les événements essentiels de la vie de lord Byron, ceux qui la racontent et l'expliquent mieux que personne ne pourrait le faire. S'il est vrai que la vie d'un poète est dans son œuvre, que l'homme se montre dans ses écrits, plus vivant et plus vrai que les portraits divers tracés plus tard par ses panégyristes ou par ses détracteurs, cela peut se dire surtout de lord Byron, le prince des poètes personnels, qui a jeté en même temps dans ses vers et dans le public l'écho sonore des pensées, des colères, des amours de sa vie. Avant lui, Jean-Jacques Rousseau avait ainsi fait, en publiant ses *Confessions* qui remuèrent le dix-huitième siècle. Byron eut la même hardiesse lorsqu'il donna *Childe Harold*, qui remua le dix-neuvième siècle, et dont la publication devint une date historique.

L'émotion fut grande lorsque parut, le 12 mars 1812, *Childe Harold*, poëme admirable, étincelant de lyrisme et d'ironie, d'enthousiasme et de colère, ouvrage étrange, dont on ne connaissait pas de modèle, car il mêlait le ton hardi d'une jeunesse frondeuse et sceptique au ton mélancolique de ce désenchantement qui n'appartient qu'à l'âge mûr; livre prismatique où brillaient capricieusement toutes les contradictions, fait de mépris et d'amour, de verve et de tristesse, de plaintes douloureuses et de bravades ardentes. L'auteur signait hardiment les défis qu'il adressait à son temps et à son pays. C'était un jeune lord, entré de la veille à la Chambre haute. Déjà placé par sa naissance, ses origines, son titre, à un rang élevé dans la société anglaise, il prenait, par son poème bizarre et puissant, la physionomie originale d'un révolté de génie. Le succès, qui d'un coup le mit en pleine lumière, fit de lui l'idole des hommes et des salons. Chose étrange! ce contempteur de la société anglaise en devint l'enfant gâté.

L'écho de ses triomphes et la popularité de son œuvre dépassèrent presque aussitôt les limites de son propre pays et devinrent, à travers l'Europe, comme le signal d'une révolution littéraire. Il semblait que le jeune auteur eût créé un mouvement d'idées, un genre, un style, inconnus jusqu'alors. Comme écrivain, il fut chef d'école, sans vivre au milieu des écrivains de son pays; comme homme, il devint le point de mire de la curiosité publique.

Plus tard, quand on sut que le poète, qui avait quitté l'Angleterre à jamais, venait de mourir, à trente-sept ans, à Missolonghi, où il s'était mis au service de la guerre de l'Indépendance, il s'ajouta à sa réputation un reflet nouveau de gloire et d'étrangeté. Une si courte et si brillante carrière a laissé dans l'histoire du siècle une trace lumineuse, et autour du nom de lord Byron une auréole, qui resteront comme la marque d'une époque littéraire, malgré les jugements que la sévérité de l'histoire ou la malignité des hommes pourra opposer à ce triomphe du scepticisme poétique.

Byron a été l'objet d'accusations extrêmes comme aussi d'éloges exagérés. Un concert d'admirations et d'anathèmes a salué chacun de ses ouvrages de son vivant, et poursuivi plus tard sa mémoire. Pour les uns, c'est un ardent et lyrique promoteur de la liberté qu'on ne saurait placer trop haut; pour d'autres, c'est un cynique, doué de tous les talents et souillé de toutes les fautes. Aujourd'hui encore, la critique, après l'avoir jugé mille fois, reste indécise, car tous les jugements sont cassés les uns après les autres par des faits nouveaux, et il manque à ce procès la pièce capitale, c'est-à-dire les *Mémoires* de Byron, qui ont été supprimés.

En réalité, Byron, dont on fait un homme tout d'une pièce, absolument funeste ou entièrement admirable, était le plus varié et le plus variable des caractères; une nature violente, inégale, richement douée, livrée à elle-même, ou plutôt la *nature* elle-même, quand rien ne la contient et quand personne ne la dirige. Lisez le IIIe chant de *Childe Harold;* là, il résume d'un mot l'histoire de son caractère, qui fit l'histoire de sa vie. *Untaught,* pas de discipline première! « On ne m'a pas appris, dit-il, quand j'étais jeune, à dompter mon cœur: ainsi ma vie fut-elle empoisonnée dans ses sources mêmes. »

.....Untaught in youth my heart to tame,
.....My springs of life were poisoned [1].

Et un peu plus loin il répète le même aveu avec le même mot. « On ne m'a appris à conformer ma pensée à celle des autres hommes;... se dérobe toujours à la contrainte... »

.....Untaught to submit
His tought to others ,..... still uncompelled [2].....

George Gordon Noël Byron naquit en Angleterre, à Londres, le 22 janvier 1788, d'une famille qui n'avait jamais connu le repos. Issu des Stuarts par sa mère et des conquérants normands par son père, il tient à une race que les aventures et les agitations ont tour à tour élevée et abattue.

Les *Burun* avaient figuré parmi ces envahisseurs scandinaves qui firent le désespoir de Charlemagne mourant, qui s'établirent malgré tout en France, puis en Angleterre, à l'époque de l'invasion normande. Ils donnèrent à la France ces *Biron* qu'on retrouve toujours dans la vie des camps, et parmi eux celui dont Henri IV n'a jamais pu fixer le caractère; ils donnèrent à l'Angleterre les *Byron* qui apparaissent d'abord dans les combats de terre ou de mer, et plus tard, en la personne de notre poète, dans les batailles

---

1. *Childe Harold,* chant III, strophe VII.
2. *Childe Harold,* chant III, strophe XII.

littéraires ou sociales. Les Byron anglais sont représentés au seizième siècle par sir John Byron qui, au moment où les réformés se partagent les biens du clergé, se fait donner l'abbaye de Newstead. Au dix-septième siècle, ils conquièrent la noblesse en combattant pour les Stuarts. Au dix-huitième, le chef de la famille est William Byron, grand-oncle du poëte; il vit à Newstead, seul et sauvage comme un sanglier, détestant ses voisins, détesté d'eux. S'étant pris de querelle avec un M Chaworth, il le tue dans un duel qui ressemble à un assassinat. Pendant que « le méchant lord », comme on l'appelle, mène cette vie dans son domaine, son frère cadet, John Byron, court les mers; il est distingué, il devient amiral, mais les marins disent que sa figure sombre attire la tempête, car il fait toujours naufrage, et ils le surnomment Jean Mauvais-Temps. L'amiral a un fils, John Byron, qui, lui, sera surnommé « Byron le fou ». En effet, il se jette dans toutes les aventures et dans tous les scandales, jusqu'au jour où il épouse, pour refaire sa fortune, miss Catherine Gordon de Gight, riche héritière d'Écosse, qui tenait par sa famille aux Stuarts, et qui sera la mère du poëte. Cela se passait en 1785. Cinq ans plus tard, le capitaine abandonnait sa femme et son pays, et, se sauvant devant ses créanciers, il passait en France, où il mourut l'année suivante. De la famille il restait une veuve, un enfant, qui fut notre poëte, et là-bas, à Newstead, le grand-oncle William, enfermé dans son égoïsme farouche.

Les dix premières années de la vie de Byron (1788-1798) sont des années d'agitation. Il naît dans une pauvre maison de Londres, où les désordres de son père et la ruine imminente assombrissent avant l'heure les premiers horizons de sa vie. A cinq ans, il va avec sa mère habiter un modeste réduit à Aberdeen, accompagné déjà par les soucis et les blessures d'amour-propre qui hantent les demeures des gentilshommes pauvres. A huit ans, il fait une maladie qui décide sa mère à l'emmener dans les Highlands, et là il trouve en pleine nature une liberté et des impressions vives qui paraissent avoir été sa première et sa seule éducation.

En effet, lady Byron ne comprenait guère pour son enfant que ce côté-là de l'éducation; elle aimait à le voir marcher et courir dans l'air libre. Mais c'était tout; elle ne songeait pas à ployer peu à peu aux exigences de la vie commune la nature vive et violente de son fils; et, pour tout dire, elle ne songeait pas davantage à se dominer elle-même, seul moyen de dominer l'enfant. Honnête femme, vivant d'une façon modeste, aimant ce fils unique avec tendresse, elle avait d'ailleurs, elle aussi, une nature capricieuse et violente qui se heurtait à celle de George Byron. Elle ne savait, dit-on, imposer aucun frein ni à ses tendresses, ni à ses colères envers lui. Bref elle ignorait que le premier moyen d'éducation est et sera éternellement l'exemple. On a raconté des détails singuliers sur les scènes orageuses qui se passaient entre la mère et l'enfant. Un jour, dit-on, après une de ces grandes querelles, chacun menaça l'autre de se tuer, et chacun s'en alla chez le pharmacien pour le prier de ne point livrer de poison à l'autre. Que faut-il en croire? Parmi les récits de toute sorte qui ont été faits après coup, j'en trouve un qui fait un grand éloge de lady Byron, et je trouve ailleurs des peintures qui, au contraire, la représentent comme incapable de se diriger. Quoi qu'il en soit, cette femme, jeune, riche, de grande maison, qui tout à coup se voit mariée à un fou, puis ruinée et chargée d'élever un orphelin indocile et fier, se trouvait en face d'une tâche singulièrement malaisée.

La destinée sembla s'adoucir pour tous deux lorsque, en 1798, George Byron devint le maître et l'héritier du titre et des biens des Byron. Le vieux lord William Byron était mort ; on salua *lord* le jeune George, on lui donna pour tuteur lord Carlisle, et il alla avec sa mère s'installer dans le vieux domaine de Newstead. Mais cette nouvelle situation ne changea rien à la nature de l'enfant, ni à la manière d'être de la mère, qui ne voulut pas s'entendre avec le tuteur. Le pli était déjà pris. On continua de vivre dans l'agitation, et les dix années qui s'écoulent (de 1798 à 1808) nous montrent le développement du caractère orgueilleux et sensible de lord Byron, qui est né bon, mais ingouvernable, qui a l'esprit élevé, mais toujours surexcité, qui, par noblesse d'âme, ne supporte pas la vue du mal, mais qui, par violence de tempérament, ne supporte pas davantage le joug du bien, ou la contradiction de qui que ce soit. Un accident de son enfance l'a d'ailleurs rendu plus susceptible qu'un autre. Il s'est foulé un pied dans une chute ; les efforts qu'on a faits pour le guérir ont rendu le mal irrémédiable. Il boitera légèrement, mais toute sa vie. Devenu un jeune homme, et très beau, il n'entrait pas dans un salon sans penser avec amertume à cette circonstance. De bonne heure il exagéra la dignité extérieure pour cacher son infirmité physique, et aussi l'infirmité morale de son caractère si vulnérable à la moindre atteinte.

Pendant cette période, il fit ses études à sa manière, préférant les exercices du corps aux *devoirs* qu'il trouvait fastidieux, et les lectures librement choisies à la suite régulière des travaux scolaires. Le cheval, l'escrime, la natation, la boxe, le passionnaient ; la poésie venait ensuite ; mais avant tout il tenait à ne pas être ou paraître l'élève de qui que ce fût (bien qu'il ait parlé avec reconnaissance d'un de ses professeurs, M. Drury). On le mit, en 1801, au collège de Harrow ; en 1805, il alla à Cambridge : partout il fut le même, un disciple mal commode, affectant les goûts d'un gentilhomme et les bizarreries d'un indépendant, se laissant dépasser par ses camarades dans les cours, mais ne souffrant pas que, dans les exercices du corps, personne le dépassât en force ou en adresse. Pour jouer un tour à quelque maître et l'effrayer, il nourrit un ours dans sa chambre ; mais cet espiègle n'est pas un méchant : s'il voit commettre une mauvaise action, il s'indigne et s'emporte. Un jour il voit, à l'école de Harrow, un *petit* battu par un *grand*. Il court à eux plein de colère et de larmes. « Combien de coups voulez-vous lui donner ? dit-il au grand. — Qu'est-ce que cela te fait ? répond le grand. — C'est que, s'il vous plaît, reprend Byron, j'en voudrais la moitié[1]. » Même vivacité, même émotion dans toutes les circonstances de la vie. Les moindres rencontres, les moindres impressions qu'il recevait du dehors bouleversaient son être. A l'âge de huit ans, il concevait une passion véritable pour une jeune Écossaise, Mary Duff ; un peu plus tard il s'éprenait de la beauté de miss Parker ; à quinze ans il voulait engager sa vie entière à Mary Chaworth, qui était précisément la petite-fille de ce voisin que son grand-oncle avait tué. Ses amitiés de collège, a-t-il dit lui-même, étaient des passions. Ses indignations et ses accès de générosité allaient jusqu'au paroxysme, comme ses caprices jusqu'à la fureur.

---

1. Le *petit* dont nous venons de parler devint plus tard le grand homme d'État, sir Robert Peel.

Il est évident que ses lectures, et les rêveries qui les suivaient, devaient lui donner aussi des moments d'enthousiasme, bien qu'il affectât l'insouciance. Il s'exerçait à faire des vers, si bien qu'il sortit de Cambridge avec un volume tout prêt et qu'il le publia (1807). Mais il se garda bien de laisser croire qu'il eût imité un maître, ni qu'il pensât à suivre les règles de l'art poétique ou à s'imposer le travail subalterne d'un écrivain de profession. Il détestait toute discipline, celle de l'Université comme celle du tuteur qu'il lui fallait subir jusqu'à sa majorité. D'un air délibéré il intitula son recueil de vers : *Heures de paresse (Hours of idleness)*, et il ajouta : par *George Gordon, lord Byron, mineur*. Ainsi présenté, le livre tomba entre les mains des critiques redoutables qui faisaient alors de la *Revue d'Édimbourg* un tribunal très écouté. Brougham lui-même se chargea de railler, dans un article impitoyable, les prétentions aristocratiques de l'écolier qui avait bien voulu se donner la peine d'écrire.

Lord Byron fut outré de fureur ; il jura de se venger d'une façon terrible : il composa immédiatement le plan d'une satire contre *les Poètes anglais et les Critiques écossais*, se promettant de n'épargner personne et d'écrire son œuvre de telle sorte qu'elle le ferait prendre au sérieux. Pour ce faire, il étudia à fond les satires de Pope, lut et annota les vers ou la prose des écrivains contemporains, s'arma de toutes pièces, ne se hâta pas de publier, ajouta, retoucha, en un mot *composa*… Composer, c'était le talent qui lui manquait et que la dure critique de Brougham le força d'acquérir. Ainsi arriva-t-il que Brougham, en traitant Byron si mal, lui rendit un signalé service. Deux ans entiers se passèrent avant que Byron publiât ses *English Bards*, qui ne parurent qu'en 1809. Mais quand ils parurent, l'écolier était devenu un homme et le rêveur un écrivain. Non seulement Byron avait étudié les maîtres de plus près, mais encore il avait jugé la société dans laquelle il entrait, caractérisé les hommes et les institutions, démêlé les erreurs ou les vices des uns et des autres, et enfin dégagé le défaut capital de la nation, la faiblesse dominante d'un grand peuple, ce qu'il allait attaquer sans merci : je veux dire cette pruderie, cette sévérité rogue, ce *cant* anglais, qui est le produit hybride du puritanisme le plus sérieux et de l'hypocrisie la plus artificielle ; masque à la portée de tous et qui peut servir tour à tour à un faux sage comme à un philosophe véritable. Byron ne distingua pas les puritains des hypocrites ; les uns et les autres pratiquaient la même intolérance. Il les brava et les défia, d'abord comme un jeune homme, en donnant des fêtes qui les scandalisaient ; ensuite en homme, en réclamant les droits de la nature et de la vérité, en exaltant la liberté et tout ce qui rompt avec les conventions sociales ou les servitudes politiques. C'est dans ces dispositions qu'il recommença ses débuts.

La même année (1809), on vit Byron entrer à la Chambre des lords, publier sa grande satire et déclarer qu'il quittait l'Angleterre pour voir autre chose et mieux. En effet, il partit au mois de juillet avec son ami Hobhouse, pour ne revenir que deux ans après, en juillet 1811. Il visita d'abord le Portugal et l'Espagne ; puis traversant la Méditerranée, il se rendit en Albanie, où les touristes n'allaient pas, voulut voir le célèbre Ali-Pacha et, de voyage en voyage, arriva la veille de Noël à Athènes. Ses rencontres, les spectacles que lui offrirent et les peuples en guerre, et les mœurs des pays différents, et le caractère des hommes, et les diversités infinies de la nature, et les ruines des civilisations disparues, exercèrent sur son esprit une puissante influence.

En même temps Byron lisait tout ce qu'on a écrit sur les contrées qu'il traversait, et les impressions d'autrui se joignant aux siennes, il se formait dans son imagination un panorama mouvant du monde de l'antiquité et du monde contemporain. Il voulut voir l'Orient, passa à Smyrne, à Éphèse, dans la Troade, traversa l'Hellespont à la nage, s'arrêta à Constantinople, puis revint à la ville des grands souvenirs, à Athènes. C'est de là qu'il repartit pour l'Angleterre, où il arriva la tête pleine de choses nouvelles, mais sans intention de publier les notes et les vers que lui avait dictés son voyage. Il voulait reprendre la querelle et la satire qui devaient forcer le respect de la critique. Il allait imprimer ses *Hints from Horace*, lorsqu'un de ses amis, Dallas, lui conseilla de publier au contraire ce qu'il avait écrit avec plus d'inspiration, au milieu des montagnes de l'Albanie ou des villes grecques, dans un sentiment plus vrai et sous le coup d'une émotion sincère. Byron suivit le conseil de son ami, et rassembla les morceaux qui forment les deux premiers chants de *Childe Harold*.

On était au commencement de 1812. Byron venait de prendre la parole à la Chambre des lords, au mois de février; il avait prononcé un discours libéral en faveur des ouvriers que l'on appelait « les briseurs de métiers », lorsque tout à coup, et de la façon la plus inattendue, on vit paraître le poème étrange et hardi qu'il intitulait *Childe Harold*. La surprise et l'admiration furent universelles; le succès fut immense. On salua le voyageur comme le premier poète de l'Angleterre. Pendant trois ans, la vie de Byron fut un triomphe. Il donna en 1813 le *Giaour* et la

Fiancée d'Abydos, en 1814, le *Corsaire* et *Lara*. En même temps il jouissait de toutes les satisfactions de la gloire et de tous les plaisirs du monde. Sa fortune ne suffisait guère à une pareille existence, surtout après des voyages dispendieux. Ses amis pensèrent à le marier, et l'on négocia son alliance avec une riche héritière. Le 2 janvier le mariage se fit : Byron, qui avait autrefois juré de mourir célibataire, épousa miss Isabella Milbank Noël.

Miss Milbank était une jeune fille intelligente, d'un caractère élevé, qui apportait avec elle toutes les facultés nécessaires en apparence pour être la compagne d'un poète et d'un lord. Elle se connaissait en poésie, elle savait la vie du monde. Byron, de son côté (ses lettres du moins l'attestèrent alors), entreprit d'être un bon mari. « J'aime Bell (Isabelle), écrivait-il à Thomas Moore, autant que vous aimez Bessy, votre femme. » Mais lord et lady Byron manquaient l'un et l'autre d'une qualité nécessaire dans toutes les alliances et les affections, aussi bien dans l'amitié et la camaraderie que dans la vie conjugale, la tolérance. Ils ne savaient pas supporter les différences de goûts et de caractère. Byron fut las dès le premier jour des récits de son beau-père, de l'intervention de sa belle-mère, de la présence d'une suivante de milady. A son tour lady Byron, qui était entourée de ce personnel et excitée, ne voulut pas accepter les caprices d'esprit ou de conduite de son mari. D'ailleurs elle paraît avoir été déçue dans une espérance secrète, qui était de ramener dans une voie de régularité et de calme cette fougueuse nature. Byron, que l'on avait oublié de discipliner quand il était enfant, se trouvant soumis dans son ménage à la discipline d'une femme honorable, ne se fit jamais à ce nouveau rôle. Une rupture était imminente entre les deux époux, lorsque la naissance d'un enfant sembla cimenter leur union : le 10 décembre naquit Augusta-Ada Byron. Un mois plus tard, lady Byron voulut porter son enfant à ses parents, à Kirby-Mellory. De cette résidence elle venait d'écrire à son mari une lettre affectueuse, lorsque tout changea : Byron reçut une seconde lettre, celle-là de sir Ralph Milbanke déclarant que sa fille n'était plus la femme de lord Byron et ne le reverrait jamais.

On tint parole : le poète ne revit jamais ni sa femme, ni son enfant, et on lui refusa toute explication. Cet événement, rendu public, fut le signal d'un véritable déchaînement contre lui. On se vengea alors de ses dédains, de ses triomphes, de sa supériorité. Ce fut la revanche des moralistes et du *cant*, qui ne manquèrent pas de signaler Byron comme un mauvais citoyen, qui avait outragé en même temps l'honneur conjugal et l'honneur britannique. Toute la presse s'en mêla, et le monde fit son métier en racontant mille anecdotes qui établissaient que Byron était criminel, dépravé, infâme, et même coupable d'inceste. « Si cela est vrai, répondit le poète, je suis indigne de l'Angleterre ; si cela est faux, l'Angleterre n'est pas digne de moi. » Et il quitta de nouveau son pays : le 26 avril 1816, il était en mer.

De 1816 à 1824, c'est-à-dire jusqu'à sa mort, la vie de Byron n'est plus qu'une suite de voyages ou de séjours à l'étranger. Il se rend d'abord, par Waterloo et les bords du Rhin, en Suisse ; là il habite Diodati, avec le poète Shelley, vivant sur le lac de Genève ou dans la montagne, visitant le pays de Clarens, illustré par Rousseau, et s'abandonnant aux rêveries et aux lectures. Il est alors, dit-il, à demi fou, c'est-à-dire qu'il livre son esprit blessé à toutes les colères que lui cause le passé et à toutes les admirations que lui apporte cette vie de libres voyages. Dans cette atmosphère tour à tour délicieuse ou grandiose, il vit avec une intensité qui surmène toutes ses facultés.

Deux ans après, en novembre 1818, il est en Italie, nouveau milieu qui exerce sur lui une influence toute différente. Tout d'abord la désinvolture ironique et souple du génie italien, qui mêle aux satires sociales tant d'art et de grâce coquette, lui rappelle qu'il peut faire la guerre avec d'autres armes que celles de la colère : c'est en 1818 qu'il publia *Don Juan*, le plus osé, le plus jeune et le plus gracieux de ses poëmes contre le *cant*. Ensuite l'esprit politique de l'Italie, la terre classique des conspirations, le frappe et le saisit. Il rencontre une femme, la comtesse Guiccioli, qui personnifie cet esprit politique. Elle devient la seconde femme de Byron ; elle le pousse à agir et à jouer un rôle dans les luttes de cette époque, qui ont pour but l'affranchissement de l'Italie où l'affranchissement de la Grèce. Byron écrit alors la *Prophétie du Dante* (1820). Il s'engage et se compromet dans l'insurrection des Romagnes (1821). La même année, il fonde avec Leigh Hunt le journal *le Libéral*. En 1822, il reçoit du comité philhellène, établi à Londres, l'invitation de s'associer à la révolte de la Grèce contre les Turcs. Il accepte ; il prépare tout pour cette véritable expédition, qu'il entreprend avec le pressentiment d'une fin prochaine et à laquelle il veut consacrer le reste de sa fortune et de sa vie. Le 14 juillet 1823, il part de Gênes. En 1824, il est à Missolonghi, où il a le titre de général en chef ; il rêve une action puissante et décisive, dans laquelle on rassemblerait toutes les forces désorganisées de ces pays pour opérer de concert une révolution sérieuse. Mais il s'impatiente de tout retard, il souffre de voir quelles mœurs et quelles idées barbares se mêlent à un grand mouvement national. D'ailleurs sa santé est épuisée, et il ne fait rien pour la ménager. Il suffit d'une imprudence pour l'achever, et il en commettra toujours. Son vieux domestique, Fletcher, qui l'a vu naître, qui l'a suivi partout, le voit mourir peu à peu, tombant et se relevant, comme une lampe qui finit de brûler.

« Le 9 avril fut un jour fatal, écrit Fletcher; mylord fut très mouillé dans sa promenade à cheval.... Dans la matinée du 10, il se plaignit de douleurs dans les membres et du mal de tête.... Ce ne fut que le troisième jour, le 13, que je commençai à concevoir des alarmes.... Le jour suivant je ne pus m'empêcher de supplier mylord d'envoyer chercher le docteur Thomas, de Zante. » Le 18, Byron apprit que tout était fini pour lui; il chargea Fletcher de ses dernières volontés. « Oh! mon enfant, s'écria-t-il, oh! ma chère fille, ma chère Ada! Oh! mon Dieu! » Et après deux journées entrecoupées de paroles d'adieu et d'accès de léthargie, il mourut le 19 avril 1824, à six heures du soir. On tira trente-sept coups de canon pour annoncer la fin de ce poète de trente-sept ans. Son corps fut transporté en Angleterre, où la nouvelle de sa mort devait causer des impressions si diverses. Le pays qu'il a tour à tour illustré et raillé ne pouvait pas lui faire des obsèques triomphales. La dépouille de lord Byron fut portée et ensevelie à Newstead : lui, qui avait si vivement signalé le sort des poètes toscans dont les cendres ne sont pas à Florence, il ne fut pas admis à avoir sa sépulture à Westminster.

ROLE, INFLUENCE ET ÉCOLE DE BYRON

Si Byron n'est pas encore à Westminster, c'est que la bataille engagée sur son nom n'est pas encore terminée : elle durera autant que le siècle et sera jugée par l'histoire. En effet, de 1820 à 1880, un mouvement immense s'est fait dans la littérature européenne, mouvement préparé avant Byron, mais que Byron détermina dans la poésie. A peine parut-il, que l'ancienne école fut éclipsée. Ceux mêmes qui venaient de renouveler les sources de la poésie, tels que Crabbe et Walter Scott, furent si violemment dépassés par le nouveau venu, qui brisait systématiquement toutes les barrières, qu'ils parurent rejetés dans l'époque antérieure. L'originalité des allures de Byron, le décousu volontaire du style, le défi jeté aux idées reçues, l'ardeur extraordinaire et la sève juvénile qui se faisaient jour dans chaque vers et dans chaque mot de son œuvre, parurent des nouveautés admirables. On imita Byron, même quand on paraissait le combattre. Lamartine l'adjura en vers magnifiques : « Mortel, ange ou démon, s'écriait-il, qui es-tu ? » Tel était le prestige du démon, que, tout en l'exorcisant, Lamartine le suivit. Lui aussi, il demanda à la mélancolie une source nouvelle d'inspiration lyrique ; mais, en s'attachant aux pas de ce maître, qui est violent, Lamartine, l'élégance même, tempère le rêve et la tristesse par l'harmonie de l'âme. A son tour, Victor Hugo, qui avait débuté comme un classique, changea de route pour devenir le chef français du romantisme, qui se confondit avec l'école byronienne. Puis Alfred de Musset, plus sensible aux vers de *Don Juan* qu'à tout le reste, s'empara de la strophe voluptueuse et railleuse de l'auteur anglais. Tandis que les poètes subissaient ainsi, dans leur originalité même, l'influence de Byron, la grande puissance du dix-neuvième siècle, la critique, s'essayait à caractériser et à juger Byron et son école. Des études profondes étaient publiées par Villemain, par Macaulay, par Philarète Chasles, études continuées et renouvelées dans des livres comme ceux de M. Taine. Ce ne fut pas tout : non seulement on étudia l'écrivain, mais on imita l'homme et les types qu'il a créés. Dans l'histoire de nos mœurs, le personnage byronien, avec sa misanthropie, son air fatal, sa liberté de pensée, son indépendance sociale, son divorce universel, fut un modèle tout trouvé pour les gens qui voulaient créer une mode ; et quand on copia le personnage dans le roman, le drame et le mélodrame, il se répandit encore davantage dans le public, si bien que ce type d'exception devint un type vulgaire, et que l'originalité primitive de la création aboutit à un lieu commun.

La postérité dégagera Byron de ces dernières descendances qui le compromettent. Au lieu de suivre l'école jusque dans ces extrêmes transformations, elle rattachera le poète anglais à ses origines, c'est-à-dire aux philosophes du dix-huitième siècle. Déjà on a fait justice des Byroniens et placé Byron à sa vrai place.

Il n'est pas si difficile qu'on le croit, dit Philarète Chasles, en parlant des excès des Byroniens, d'exagérer la passion, de hausser la voix, de chausser le cothurne, de pleurer sa misère, de chanter la désespérance, de maudire l'univers. La nature byronienne, nature de convention et de théâtre, se parodie aisément. On s'est donc fait misanthrope ; on a verni sa misanthropie d'une couche de fatuité ; on a médit des femmes et de Dieu, de la société et de la foi, du despotisme et de la liberté. Le scepticisme aigu et destructeur qui règne dans cette admirable épopée satirique que l'on nomme *Candide* avait déjà frayé la route. Avant Candide, nous avions Bayle, sceptique érudit; tout à côté de Candide, Werther le panthéiste, qui se tuait, non en philosophe amoureux, mais en artiste; non parce que Lolotte se mariait, mais faute de pouvoir s'associer assez intimement à la nature universelle, aux ondes du torrent qui bondit et aux rafales du vent qui souffle. Werther et Candide combinés et réunis dans un seul personnage couvert d'une draperie élégante, éclatante, armé de poésie, étincelant de nouveauté dans l'expression, et d'énergie dans le style, — voilà Byron.

A ce jugement sur l'écrivain, il faut joindre le jugement de M. Taine sur l'homme. Après avoir parlé de la manière de vivre du poète et des excès alternatifs de sobriété et de plaisir qu'il commettait, M. Taine ajoute :

Ainsi vivent ces âmes véhémentes, incessamment heurtées et brisées par leur propre élan, comme un boulet arrêté qui tourne et semble tranquille, tant il va vite, mais qui, au moindre obstacle, saute, ricoche, met tout en poudre, et finit par s'enterrer. Le plus pénétrant des observateurs, Beyle, qui vécut avec lui plusieurs semaines, dit qu'à certains jours il était fou; d'autres fois, en présence des belles choses, il devenait sublime. Quoique contenu et si fier, la musique le faisait pleurer. Le reste du temps, les petites passions anglaises, l'orgueil du rang par exemple, la vanité du dandy, le mettaient hors des gonds : il ne parlait de Brummel qu' « avec un frémissement de jalousie et d'admiration ». Mais, petite ou grande, la passion présente s'abattait sur son esprit comme une tempête, le soulevait, l'emportait jusqu'à l'imprudence et jusqu'au génie. Son journal, ses lettres familières, toute sa prose involontaire est comme frémissante d'esprit, de colère, d'enthousiasme; le cri de la sensation y vibre aux moindres mots : depuis Saint-Simon, on n'a pas vu de confidences plus vivantes. Tous les styles semblent ternes, et toutes les âmes semblent inertes à côté de celle-là.

C'est là, en effet, le secret de la vie et de la gloire de Byron. Il a impressionné, par l'énergie troublée de sa nature de feu, un siècle qui était préparé par la Révolution à toutes les audaces. Il se placera, dans l'histoire littéraire, après Jean-Jacques Rousseau, dont il est l'élève et l'enfant. Mais ici le fils a un autre tempérament que le père. Là même où le souvenir de Rousseau est vivant, par exemple sur les rivages du lac Léman, le souvenir de Byron se présente à l'esprit avec un caractère à part. Tandis que la rêverie de Rousseau est tendre et décevante, celle de Byron est mêlée d'éclairs orageux. Lamartine s'écrie, en s'adressant au lac Léman :

> Byron, comme un lutteur fatigué du combat,
> Pour saigner et mourir, sur tes rives s'abat ;
> On dit que, quand les vents roulent ton onde en poudre,
> Sa voix est dans tes cris et son œil dans ta foudre.

Byron lui-même a essayé à plusieurs reprises de marquer la différence entre lui et l'auteur de la *Nouvelle Héloïse*. Il l'a fait dans une lettre, qui est un jeu d'esprit, sophistique par le raisonnement et le détail, mais curieuse au fond ; car le poëte, en signalant les dissemblances de caractère qu'il tient à souligner, et en insistant, avoue lui-même que, dès le premier jour, on le comparait à Rousseau.

Ma mère, dit-il, avant que je fusse âgé de vingt ans, voulait absolument que je ressemblasse à Rousseau, et Mme de Staël faisait la même comparaison en 1813. L'*Edinburgh Review* a dit quelque chose de semblable dans sa critique du IVe chant de *Childe Harold*. Pour moi, je ne vois de ressemblance entre nous sur aucun point. Rousseau écrivit en prose, moi j'ai écrit en vers. Il était du peuple ; moi, je suis de l'aristocratie ; il était philosophe, je ne le suis nullement. Il publia son premier ouvrage à l'âge de quarante ans ; j'en avais dix-huit quand je fis paraître le mien. Son coup d'essai lui procura des éloges universels; le mien eut un sort tout contraire. Il épousa sa ménagère; je n'ai pu faire ménage avec ma femme. Il crut que le monde entier complotait contre lui; mon petit monde paraît croire que j'ourdis constamment des trames contre son repos : du moins si j'en puis juger d'après ce qui se dit et s'imprime sur mon compte. Il aimait la botanique; moi, j'aime les fleurs, les arbustes, mais sans rien comprendre aux genres, aux espèces, etc., etc. Il écrivit de la musique; je borne mes connaissances, sur cet art, à ce que l'oreille me met à portée de saisir. Je n'ai jamais voulu rien apprendre par principes, pas même une langue. J'ai appris par routine, par l'oreille et de mémoire. J'en avais une très bonne, au témoignage du poète Hodgson, qui, lui-même, en avait une excellente. Rousseau écrivait avec hésitation et labeur; moi avec rapidité, et généralement sans peine.

Il ne voulut jamais ni monter à cheval ni nager, et il n'entendait rien à l'exercice des armes; moi, je suis bon nageur, et, quoique je ne sois pas très hardi à cheval (m'étant enfoncé une côte dans une course que je fis à l'âge de dix-huit ans), je suis assez bon écuyer, et, de plus, je fais assez bien des armes, surtout à l'espadon, quand je sais me posséder, ce qui m'est difficile, mais ce que je m'efforce toujours de faire depuis le jour où, en 1805, luttant contre M. Purling, dans les salles d'Angelo et Jackson, à Londres, je le fis tomber et lui démis la rotule. J'ai été, en outre, très fort au jeu de *cricket*, et l'un des onze qui, en 1805, soutinrent une joute contre pareil nombre d'étudiants du collège d'Eton.

Rousseau, d'ailleurs, par son pays, son genre de vie, ses habitudes et son caractère, avait si peu de rapport avec moi, que j'ai peine à concevoir d'où est venue cette comparaison, qui a cependant été faite *à trois reprises différentes*, et toujours d'une manière remarquable.

J'ai oublié de dire qu'il avait la vue courte, et que la mienne est, au contraire, parfaite; elle l'est au point qu'étant un jour au grand théâtre de Boulogne, et placé dans une des loges les plus éloignées, j'ai pu lire des inscriptions qui étaient tout près de la scène, tandis que d'autres personnes occupant avec moi la même loge, et qui étaient jeunes et pourvues d'excellents yeux, n'y pouvaient démêler une seule lettre, et croyaient que tout ce que j'en faisais n'était que pour les mystifier. A tout prendre, je me crois fondé à dire que cette comparaison est inexacte de tout point. Ce n'est pas qu'elle ait rien dont je sois piqué. Rousseau était un grand homme, et, si la comparaison était juste, je ne pourrais que m'en tenir honoré. Mais je n'aime pas à me complaire dans une idée fausse.

Toutes ces différences sont réelles ; mais le point capital de la ressemblance, que le poète laisse dans l'ombre, c'est leur révolte commune contre la loi sociale. Byron et Jean-Jacques possédaient l'un et l'autre une personnalité puissante, toujours en éveil et toujours blessée. L'un et l'autre ils ont prétendu faire dominer la personnalité de l'homme sur les sociétés humaines. Tous deux ont concouru à la grande révolution qui a revendiqué plus de liberté pour l'homme, Rousseau portant l'éloquence dans la critique des institutions humaines, Byron portant dans la même œuvre la poésie, et je ne sais quelle séduction de jeunesse aventureuse. Leur rôle commun et la logique de leur rôle voulaient qu'ils fissent prévaloir l'individu sur la société, le tempérament et l'humeur sur la loi ; c'est là l'envers de leur gloire ; mais, avant de le leur reprocher, il faut se souvenir qu'ils ont payé de leur bonheur l'indépendance même de leur vie, — que les écrivains qui agitent l'humanité sont consumés par la flamme de leur génie — et que ce qui restera d'eux, en définitive, c'est l'éclat qu'ils ont jeté sur la cause éternelle de la liberté.

COMMENT FUT COMPOSÉ ET COMMENT IL FAUT LIRE " CHILDE HAROLD "

Il est impossible de lire *Childe Harold* si l'on ne se rend pas compte de la manière dont il fut composé. Ce n'est, dit l'auteur lui-même, ni un roman qui raconte les aventures de quelque héros, ni un poème proprement dit, qui se développerait sur un certain plan. Ce n'est même pas une œuvre venue d'un seul jet. C'est l'assemblage des notes d'un voyageur mêlées de descriptions, de souvenirs et de digressions personnelles.

Le premier chant est consacré au Portugal et à l'Espagne;

Le second, à l'Albanie et à la Grèce;

Le troisième, à Waterloo, aux bords du Rhin et à la Suisse;

Le quatrième, à l'Italie.

A travers cette espèce d'itinéraire poétique sont jetés et s'entre-croisent des fragments de poésie personnelle qui forment une autobiographie de Byron sous le masque de Childe Harold.

Deux thèmes principaux reviennent sans cesse dans le tissu de l'œuvre : le spectacle des choses humaines et le spectacle d'une âme de poète, puissante et maladive.

Le retour régulier de ces deux sujets et le plan même d'un itinéraire descriptif qui ne comporte ni aventures, ni incidents, deviendraient singulièrement monotones si l'auteur ne remédiait pas à ces défauts par la vivacité de l'expression, le mouvement imprévu de la pensée et la liberté capricieuse des changements de ton. Il se plaît à employer tour à tour toutes les formes rapides de la strophe lyrique et toutes celles de l'ironie triste ou joyeuse.

Pour éclairer la marche générale de l'ouvrage, nous donnons ici, avec le texte, non seulement des notes placées au bas des pages, mais encore des sommaires qui marquent d'étape en étape la route sinueuse que suit le poète. Ces arguments analytiques permettront aux maîtres de choisir les passages qu'ils voudront faire expliquer, choix nécessaire dans un livre de cette nature, qui, par son étendue même, ne peut guère être lu tout entier.

Néanmoins ni les notes, ni les arguments ne rendent compte de la difficulté principale que l'on va rencontrer, c'est-à-dire du détail du style, qui est plein d'images, d'allusions et de disparates, mêlant de parti pris les accents railleurs de la misanthropie au ton grave ou sublime de la poésie lyrique, et passant de l'un à l'autre subitement, comme pour déjouer et dérouter notre attention.

Ces allures décevantes de Byron sont particulièrement sensibles dans les deux premiers chants. On devra, dès le début, établir la différence profonde qui sépare ces deux premiers chants des deux derniers, et se rappeler qu'ils n'ont pas été publiés en même temps.

Chants I et II. — Ils répondent au premier voyage de lord Byron et sont faits de 1809 à 1812. A cette époque, le poète est toujours animé de l'idée de répliquer à ses critiques par une satire éclatante. Il part, le sourire aux lèvres; il improvise des vers brusques et moqueurs, dans lesquels il jette pêle-mêle les expressions archaïques des vieux contes, les locutions populaires, les noms propres des hommes qu'il raille, et la parodie des genres littéraires ou du style biblique dont on a ennuyé son enfance.

C'est par exemple avec une intention ironique et même bouffonne qu'il avait d'abord écrit le *Chant des adieux* (après la strophe XIII). Il parodiait les adieux larmoyants, les *Good night*, qui avaient servi de cadre à tant de poètes. S'emparant des modèles, il substituait à la tristesse des adieux, le bonsoir sarcastique qu'il adressait à l'Angleterre. Il se moquait de ses compagnons de voyage, de son ami Hobhouse, de son domestique Fletcher et du petit groom Robert (ou Bob) Rushton. Avec un éclat de joie brutal et trivial il révélait que son pauvre ami Hobhouse eut le mal de mer, que Fletcher eut peur, que Bob pleura, et que tous ils ne songeaient guère à la poésie, s'étendant comme des bûches sur le pont :

Stretch'd along the deck like logs.

Au moment où il voulut publier *Childe Harold*, au moment où il revit cette narration burlesque et peu originale, il convint avec ses amis qu'il fallait la récrire. Il supprima les grossièretés. Il opposa Childe Harold et son impassible figure à ses serviteurs qui pleurent la patrie et la famille. Le contraste de cette émotion des pauvres gens qui aiment quelque chose, et de l'indifférence suprême du sceptique qui n'aime plus rien, produisit un effet inattendu : l'auteur s'étudia alors à répéter, en le mesurant, un contraste qui était d'ailleurs dans la nature et surtout en lui-même.

Un second exemple des remaniements apportés au chant Ier est dans le morceau sur la *Convention de Cintra*. En l'écrivant, Byron n'avait pas assez d'injures pour bafouer l'Angleterre, la presse anglaise, les généraux anglais ; il nommait en toutes lettres ceux qui lui déplaisaient, et tombait dans l'invective pure et simple. On obtint de lui la suppression de plusieurs strophes qui se retrouvent aujourd'hui, dans les éditions complètes, à titre de variantes.

L'histoire de ces variantes ne laisse aucun doute sur ce qui se passa dans l'esprit de Byron. Il débuta d'une façon un peu légère, par des anathèmes étourdis, dans lesquels il entrait plus de verve sarcastique que de mélancolie réelle. Peu à peu ses dispositions se modifièrent. Il vit du pays ; il fut frappé de trouver, dans les mœurs, les guerres, les chants nationaux, les annales des divers peuples, autre chose que des sujets d'ironie facile et d'improvisation satirique. Il s'éleva graduellement vers des pensées plus hautes et plus humaines. En même temps le spectacle de la nature le portait dans des sphères plus dignes de son génie, et ses lectures continuelles lui montraient comment d'autres s'étaient inspirés tour à tour et de la contemplation de la nature, et de la méditation de l'histoire. Se transformant d'heure en heure, le poète eut quelque peine à arranger en poëme les deux premiers chants de *Childe Harold*. On s'apercevra, en les lisant, qu'ils ont été retouchés.

Chants III et IV. — Ce fut tout différent quand il écrivit les deux derniers chants, qui répondent à son second voyage. A cette époque, il était vraiment triste, et il emportait avec lui une blessure incurable, celle dont il parle dès le premier vers, celle dont il parlera à son lit de mort : il ne devait jamais revoir son enfant ! Séparé pour toujours de son pays, de sa famille, il hésita entre la colère qu'il éprouvait contre ses calomniateurs, la lointaine vision du bonheur envolé, et les diversions nouvelles que lui offraient le voyage, la littérature, la politique ou la guerre. Sa mère n'était plus, ses amis d'enfance avaient disparu ; il retrouvait à Waterloo la place où était tombé bravement Howard, le fils d'un homme qu'il avait raillé, et il saluait avec respect le nom qu'il avait tourné en ridicule. Bref, le poëte porta dans la seconde partie de son œuvre un sentiment plus profond de la vie et du malheur, une amertume plus sincère et une inspiration plus généreuse. Là il n'y a plus guère de variantes ; tout coule de source, et on lit plus aisément ces deux chants parce qu'ils ont été écrits avec plus d'émotion et parce qu'ils sont incontestablement les plus beaux.

PREFACE

TO THE

FIRST AND SECOND CANTOS

The following poem was written, for the most part, amidst the scenes which it attempts to describe. It was begun in Albania; and the parts relative to Spain and Portugal were composed from the author's observations in those countries. Thus much it may be necessary to state for the correctness of the descriptions. The scenes attempted to be sketched are in Spain, Portugal, Epirus, Acarnania and Greece. There, for the present, the poem stops; its reception will determine whether the author may venture to conduct his readers to the capital of the East, through Ionia and Phrygia; these two cantos are merely experimental.

A fictitious character is introduced for the sake of giving some connection to the piece; which, however, makes no pretension to regularity. It has been suggested to me by friends, on whose opinions I set a high value, that in this fictitious character, "Childe Harold," I may incur the suspicion of having intended some real personage: this I beg leave, once for all, to disclaim — Harold is the child of imagination, for the purpose I have stated. In some very trivial particulars, and those merely local, there might be grounds for such a notion; but in the main points, I should hope, none whatever.

It is almost superfluous to mention that the appellation " Childe," as " Childe Waters, Childe Childers," etc., is used as more consonant with the old structure of versification which I have adopted. The " Good Night," in the beginning of the first canto, was suggested by " Lord Maxwell's Good Night," in the Border Minstrelsy[1], edited by Mr. Scott.

With the different poems which have been published on Spanish subjects, there may be found some slight coincidence in the first part, which treats of the Peninsula, but it can only be casual; as, with the exception of a few concluding stanzas, the whole of this poem was written in the Levant.

The stanza of Spenser, according to one of our most successful poets, admits of every variety. Dr. Beattie makes the following observation: — " Not long ago, I began a poem in the style and stanza of Spenser, in which I propose to give full scope to my inclination, and be either droll or pathetic, descriptive or sentimental, tender or satirical, as the humour strikes me ; for, if I mistake not, the measure which I have adopted admits equally of all these kinds of composition." — Strengthened in my opinion by such authority, and by the example of some in the highest order of Italian poets, I shall make no apology for attempts at similar variations in the following composition; satisfied that if they are unsuccessfull, their failure must be in the execution, rather than in the design sanctioned by the practice of Ariosto, Thomson, and Beattie.

London, February, 1812.

ADDITION
TO THE PREFACE

I HAVE now waited till almost all our periodical journals have distributed their usual portion of criticism. To the justice of the generality of their criticisms I have nothing to object: it would ill become me to quarrel with their very slight degree of censure, when, perhaps, if they had been less kind they had been more candid. Returning, therefore, to all and each my best thanks for their liberality, on one

---

1. Les chants du Border, ou de la frontière d'Écosse.

point alone shall I venture an observation. Amongst the many objections justly urged to the very indifferent character of the " vagrant Childe " (whom, notwithstanding many hints to the contrary, I still maintain to be a fictitious personage), it has been stated, that, besides the anachronism, he is very *unknightly*, as the times of the Knights were times of Love, Honour, and so forth. Now, it so happens that the good old times, when " l'amour du bon vieux temps, l'amour antique," flourished, were the most profligate of all possible centuries. Those who have any doubts on this subject may consult Sainte-Palaye, *passim*, and more particularly vol. II. p. 69 [1]. The vows of chivalry were no better kept than any other vows whatsoever; and the songs of the Troubadours were not more decent, and certainly were much less refined, than those of Ovid. The " Cours d'amour, parlemens d'amour, ou de courtesie et de gentilesse, " had much more of love than of courtesy or gentleness. See Roland on the same subject with Sainte-Palaye. Whatever other objection may be urged to that most unamiable personage Childe Harold, he was so far perfectly knightly in his attributes — *No waiter, but a knight templar* [2]. By the by, I fear that Sir Tristrem and Sir Lancelot were no better than they should be, although very poetical personages and true knights " sans peur," though not " sans reproche." If the story of the institution of the " Garter " be not a fable, the knights of that order have for several centuries borne the badge of a Countess of Salisbury, of indifferent memory. So much for chivalry. Burke need not have regretted that its days are over, though Marie-Antoinette was quite as chaste as most of those in whose honours lances were shivered, and knights unhorsed.

1. Qu'on lise dans l'auteur du roman de *Gérard de Roussillon*, en provençal, les détails très circonstanciés dans lesquels il entre sur la réception faite par le comte Gérard à l'ambassadeur du roi Charles; on y verra des particularités singulières, qui donnent une étrange idée des mœurs et de la politesse de ces siècles aussi corrompus qu'ignorants. (*Mémoires sur l'ancienne chevalerie*, par M. de la Curne de Sainte-Palaye. Paris, 1781.)

2. Byron cite ici un passage d'une pièce en vers publiée dans l'*Anti-Jacobin*, journal de Canning et Frere.

Before the days of Bayard, and down to those of Sir Joseph Banks[1] (the most chaste and celebrated of ancient and modern times), few exceptions will be found to this statement: and I fear a little investigation will teach us not to regret these monstrous mummeries of the middle ages.

I now leave " Childe Harold " to live his day, such as he is; it had been more agreeable, and certainly more easy, to have drawn an amiable character. It had been easy to varnish over his faults, to make him do more and express less, but he never was intended as an example, further than to show, that early perversion of mind and morals leads to satiety of past pleasures and disappointment in new ones, and that even the beauties of nature, and the stimulus of travel (except ambition, the most powerful of all excitements) are lost on a soul so constituted, or rather misdirected. Had I proceeded with the poem, this character would have deepened as he drew to the close; for the outline which I once meant to fill up for him was, with some exceptions, the sketch of a modern Timon[2], perhaps a poetical Zeluco[3].

---

1. Sir Joseph Banks avait eu à Otahiti des aventures que l'on racontait en riant.

2. Timon, le misanthrope d'Athènes, est connu par l'histoire et par Shakspeare.

3. Zeluco est le héros d'un roman du docteur Moore, qui a peint sous ce nom le caractère d'un jeune homme bien doué, mais élevé sans direction et malheureux.

TO IANTHE[1]

Not in those climes where I have late been straying,
Though Beauty long hath there been matchless deemed,
Not in those visions to the heart displaying
Forms which it sighs but to have only dreamed,
Hath aught like thee in truth or fancy seemed:
Nor, having seen thee, shall I vainly seek
To paint those charms which varied as they beamed —
To such as see thee not my words were weak
To those who gaze on thee what langage could they speak?

Ah! may'st thou ever be what now thou art,
Nor unbeseem the promise of thy spring,
As fair in form, as warm yet pure in heart,
Love's image upon earth without his wing,
And guileless beyond Hope's imagining!
And surely she who now so fondly rears
Thy youth, in thee, thus hourly brightening,
Beholds the rainbow of her future years,
Before whose heavenly hues all sorrow disappears.

1. Dédicace à une enfant, Charlotte Harley, plus tard lady Charlotte Bacon. Elle n'avait pas douze ans; elle était la seconde fille du comte d'Oxford.

Lord Byron, qui admirait en elle la beauté naissante et sans artifices, fit faire son portrait par le peintre Westall, et traça lui-même le portrait en vers qu'on va lire. Placé en tête d'un poème plein de railleries, comme un emblème de pureté radieuse, il forme un vivant contraste avec les mensonges et les vices que l'auteur prétend flageller. Ainsi Dante nous montre-t-il, dès le début de la *Divine Comédie*, une lumière pure qu'il salue avec respect : c'est l'étoile de la vérité qu'il met au front de la jeune Beatrix Portinari, une enfant de Florence.

Young Peri[1] of the West!—'tis well for me
My years already doubly number thine;
My loveless eye unmoved may gaze on thee,
And safely view thy ripening beauties shine;
Happy, I ne'er shall see them in decline;
Happier, that while all younger hearts shall bleed,
Mine shall escape the doom thine eyes assign
To those whose admiration shall succeed,
But mixed with pangs to Love's even loveliest hours decreed.

Oh! let that eye, which, wild as the Gazelle's,
Now brightly bold or beautifully shy,
Wins as it wanders, dazzles where it dwells,
Glance o'er this page, nor to my verse deny
That smile for which my breast might vainly sigh
Could I to thee be ever more than friend:
This much, dear maid, accord; nor question why
To one so young my strain I would commend,
But bid me with my wreath one matchless lily blend.

Such is thy name with this my verse entwined;
And long as kinder eyes a look shall cast
On Harold's page, Ianthe's here enshrined
Shall thus be first beheld, forgotten last:
My days once numbered, should this homage past
Attract thy fairy fingers near the lyre
Of him who hailed thee, loveliest as thou wast,
Such is the most my memory may desire;
Though more than Hope can claim, could Friendship less require?

---

1. *Young Peri.* Byron, qui a écrit en Orient la première partie de *Childe-Harold*, compare Ianthe à une Péri, c'est-à-dire à ces beautés orientales qui, dans les légendes de la Perse, sont placées entre le ciel et la terre.

ARGUMENT ANALYTIQUE

DU CHANT PREMIER

EN PORTUGAL ET EN ESPAGNE

Non-invocation. — Le poète ne veut pas invoquer la Muse que les mauvais poètes ont fatiguée. (Strophe I.)

Portrait de Childe Harold. — Ses vices, sa noblesse, ses dégoûts précoces. Pourquoi il s'exila et quitta le vieux monastère qui lui servait de demeure. Son isolement moral. (Str. II à XI.)

Adieux à l'Angleterre. — Ode du départ. — Opposition entre les humbles qui ont des affections ici-bas, et les grands, qui sont sceptiques. (Str. XII à XIV.)

En Portugal, jusqu'à la strophe XXXI. — Admirable nature, nation misérable et asservie. A partir de cette strophe, on va voir de nombreuses allusions aux guerres dont la Péninsule fut le théâtre, et aux armées de la France. Il importe, pour les comprendre, de se rappeler l'époque. Lord Byron, qui donna en 1813 les deux premiers chants de son poème, les composa ou les refit pendant cette période de 1808 à 1813, durant laquelle Napoléon envahissait tour à tour le Portugal et l'Espagne, que soutenait l'Angleterre. Le Portugal, jadis si grand au temps de Vasco de Gama et d'Albuquerque, était devenu comme l'esclave, tantôt de la France, tantôt de l'Angleterre. C'est ce qui explique les vers cruels que l'on va lire. (Str. XV à XXIII.)

La convention de Cintra. — Junot, chargé d'envahir le Portugal, fut battu à Vimeiro par Wellesley (depuis Wellington). A la suite de cette affaire, Junot signa avec le général Dalrymple la convention de Cintra, par laquelle les Français s'engageaient à évacuer le Portugal. Cette convention mécontenta également les Anglais et Napoléon. Junot et Dalrymple furent disgraciés. (Str. XXIV à XXVI.)

Passage du Portugal en Espagne. — Le plan du poème correspond ici à la vie réelle de Byron, qui partit de Lisbonne pour Séville, envoyant ses bagages par mer à Gibraltar. (Str. XXVII à XXX.)

La frontière d'Espagne et de Portugal. — Contraste de deux nations. (Str. XXXI à XXXIV.)

En Espagne, jusqu'à la fin du chant. — Souvenirs illustres de la lutte de l'Espagne contre l'Islamisme pendant huit siècles. — Chants populaires qui consacrent ces souvenirs. (Str. XXXV à XXXVI.)

Appel de lord Byron à l'Espagne contre ses envahisseurs, c'est-à-dire contre Napoléon. (Str. XXXVII à XLIV.)

L'Andalousie. — Contraste singulier de la gaieté des villes et de l'inquiétude des campagnes, du cri « Vive le roi ! » et des malédictions contre le roi, des sérénades d'amour et de l'imminence de la guerre. (Str. XLV à LIII.)

Les femmes espagnoles. — L'héroïne de Saragosse. — La beauté des Espagnoles et leur liberté opposées à la pâleur des Anglaises et à l'esclavage des Orientales. (Str. LIV à LIX.)

Apostrophe au Parnasse. — Strophes sur la poésie antique et sur les poètes modernes. (Str. LX à LXIII.)

Retour à l'Espagne. — Cadix, héritière de Paphos. (Str. LXIV à LXVII.)

Les fêtes et les dimanches de l'Andalousie, en opposition aux fêtes et aux dimanches du Nord. (Str. LXVIII à LXXI.)

Les combats de taureaux. (Str. LXXII-LXXIX.)

Les mœurs espagnoles. — Les vengeances. — La liberté des femmes. — Harold est blasé. Stances désespérées à Inez. (Str. LXXX à LXXXIV.)

Adieux à l'Espagne. — Dernier salut à son génie indépendant. Dernier appel à la guerre. (Str. LXXXV à XC.)

Les morts. — Pensée de Byron pour ceux qu'il a perdus. (Str. XCI à XCIII.)

NOTE

SUR LE TITRE ET L'ÉPIGRAPHE DE CHILDE HAROLD

Lord Byron se plaît à donner à son œuvre une physionomie archaïque, comme Walter Scott à ses récits. Il fait de son héros un pèlerin, un *Childe*, et de son poème un *romaunt*. Le *Childe* (devenu plus tard *Child*) était l'enfant noble, en Espagne l'infant ; un *romaunt* était un de ces grands contes comme ceux que l'on traduisait jadis du breton en langue populaire ou *romane* : ils ont donné naissance au *roman* moderne. Ainsi le poème le plus imprégné des sentiments de notre époque et des idées d'un révolté se présente-t-il sous l'aspect d'une vieille légende.

En revanche, Byron met aussi à la première page l'épigraphe suivante :

« L'UNIVERS est une espèce de livre dont on n'a lu que la première page quand on n'a vu que son pays. J'en ai feuilleté un assez grand nombre, que j'ai trouvées également mauvaises. Cet examen ne m'a point été infructueux. Je haïssais ma patrie. Toutes les impertinences des peuples divers parmi lesquels j'ai vécu m'ont réconcilié avec elle. Quand je n'aurais tiré d'autre bénéfice de mes voyages que celui-là, je n'en regretterais ni les frais ni les fatigues. »

Cette épigraphe est une profession de foi sceptique empruntée au livre anonyme de Fougeret de Monbron. Celui-ci publia en 1750 le *Cosmopolite*, ouvrage satirique dans lequel il développe la maxime : *Patria est ubicunque est bene*. C'était un devancier plus hardi qu'illustre : comme lui, Byron, quittant l'Angleterre, se déclare citoyen du monde.

CHILDE HAROLD'S
PILGRIMAGE
A ROMAUNT

CANTO THE FIRST

Non-invocation. — Le poète ne veut pas invoquer la Muse, que les mauvais poètes ont fatiguée. (Strophe I.)

I

Oh, thou! in Hellas deemed of heavenly birth,
Muse! formed or fabled at the minstrel's will!
Since shamed full oft by later lyres on earth,
Mine dares not call thee from thy sacred hill[1] :
Yet there I've wandered by thy vaunted rill;
Yes! sighed o'er Delphi's long deserted shrine,
Where, save that feeble fountain, all is still;
Nor mote[2] my shell awake the weary Nine
To grace so plain a tale—this lowly lay of mine.

1. *Sacred hill*, le Parnasse. — *Vaunted rill*, la source de Castalie.
2. *Nor mote*, ma lyre ne pourrait pas. *Mote* est un archaïsme, comme *childe* et *romaunt*. Il est ici pour *might*.

Portrait de Childe Harold. — Ses vices, sa noblesse, ses dégoûts précoces. Pourquoi il s'exila et quitta le vieux monastère qui lui servait de demeure. — Son isolement moral. (Str. II à XI.)

II

Whilome[1] in Albion's Isle there dwelt a youth,
Who ne[2] in virtue's ways did take delight;
But spent his days in riot most uncouth,
And vexed with mirth the drowsy ear of Night.
Ah me! in 'sooth[3] he was a shameless wight,
Sore given[4] to revel and ungodly glee[5];
Few earthly things found favour in his sight
Save concubines and carnal companie,
And flaunting wassailers[6] of high and low degree.

III

Childe Harold was he hight[7] :— but whence his name
And lineage long, it suits me not to say;
Suffice it, that perchance they were of fame,
And had been glorious in another day :
But one sad losel[8] soils a name for aye,

---

1. *Whilome.* Archaïsme employé par Spencer pour *once*, jadis. C'est le *while* moderne avec sa forme anglo-saxonne. Byron avait d'abord commencé son poème par cette strophe de vieux conteur : « Jadis vivait... »
2. *Who ne... did.* Archaïsme, *ne* pour *not.*
3. *In sooth,* sur ma foi !
4. *Sore given.* Adonné jusqu'à la perdition aux vices de la jeunesse, aux festins, aux chants impies.
5. *Glee* marque l'éclat de la joie, de la parole, des chansons.
6. *Wassailers,* les porteurs de toasts, de santés.
7. *Was he hight.* Inversion pour *he was hight,* et archaïsme. Le mot *hight*, qui correspond à l'allemand *heissen*, est pour *called.*
8. *Losel.* Mot tombé en désuétude, que les uns traduisent par tache, les autres par homme déconsidéré et prodigue. Webster dit : « *Losel,* a wasteful fellow. » C'est tout simplement un libertin, un relâché, un débraillé.

However mighty in the olden¹ time;
Nor all that heralds rake from coffined clay,
Nor florid prose, nor honied lies of rhyme,
Can blazon evil deeds, or consecrate a crime.

IV

Childe Harold basked him in the noontide sun,
Disporting there like any other fly;
Nor deemed before his little day was done
One blast might chill him into misery.
But long ere scarce a third of his passed by,
Worse than adversity the Childe befell;
He felt the fulness of satiety :
Then loathed he in his native land to dwell,
Which seemed to him more lone than Eremite's sad cell.

V

For he through Sin's long labyrinth had run,
Nor made atonement when he did amiss,
Had sighed to many though he loved but one²,
And that loved one, alas! could ne'er be his.
Ah, happy she! to 'scape from him whose kiss
Had been pollution unto aught so chaste;
Who soon had left her charms for vulgar bliss,
And spoiled her goodly lands to gild his waste,
Nor calm domestic peace³ had ever deigned to taste.

---

1. *Olden*, archaïsme. Au temps jadis.

2. *He loved but one.* Il n'aima qu'une femme. Byron fait allusion à Maria Chaworth, et; comme d'autres poètes, il se persuade que cet amour d'enfance aurait pu être éternel.

3. *Domestic peace.* Ce vers explique mieux que tous les commentaires pourquoi lord Byron ne resta pas avec sa femme.

VI

And now Childe Harold was sore sick at heart[1],
And from his fellow bacchanals would flee;
'Tis said, at times the sullen tear would start,
But Pride congealed the drop within his ee[2] :
Apart he stalked in joyless reverie,
And from his native land resolved to go,
And visit scorching climes beyond the sea
With pleasure drugg'd, he almost longed for woe,
And e'en for change of scene would seek the shades below.

VII

The Childe departed from his father's hall :
It was a vast and venerable pile ;
So old, it seemed only not to fall,
Yet strength was pillar'd in each massy aisle.
Monastic dome[3] ! condemned to uses vile !
Where Superstition once had made her den
Now Paphian girls were known to sing and smile;
And monks might deem their time was come agen[4],
If ancient tales say true, nor wrong these holy men.

VIII

Yet oft-times in his maddest mirthful mood[5]
Strange pangs would flash[6] along Childe Harold's brow,
As if the memory of some deadly feud

1. *Sore sick at heart.* Le cœur douloureusement malade. Comparez à ce passage le cri du docteur de Shakspeare au IVe acte de *Macbeth*, lorsqu'il découvre que c'est le cœur de la reine qui est malade et non le corps. Rapprochez ensuite du passage de Shakspeare le vers d'Horace : *Mente minus validus quam corpore toto.*

2. *Ee* pour *eye.*

3. *Monastic dome.* Il s'agit évidemment ici de Newstead-Abbey, où Byron donna des fêtes destinées à faire quelque scandale.

4. *Agen* comme *again.*

5. *Mood* est littéralement *l'humeur*, ce que l'allemand exprime par *Muth* et le grec par θυμός.

6. *Flash*, luire rapidement, jaillir, passer comme un éclair.

Or disappointed passion lurked below:
But this none knew, nor haply cared to know;
For his was not that open, artless soul
That feels relief by bidding sorrow flow,
Nor sought he friend to counsel or condole,
Whate'er this grief mote [1] be, which he could not control.

IX

And none did love him: though to hall and bower [2]
He gathered revellers from far and near,
He knew them flatt'rers of the festal hour;
The heartless parasites of present cheer.
Yea! none did love him—not his lemans dear—
But pomp and power alone are woman's care,
And where these are light Eros finds a feere [3];
Maidens, like moths, are ever caught by glare,
And Mammon [4] wins his way where Seraphs might despair.

X

Childe Harold had a mother—not forgot,
Though parting from that mother he did shun [5];
A sister whom he loved, but saw her not
Before his weary pilgrimage begun [6]:
If friends he had, he bade adieu to none.

---

1. *Mote*, pour *might*, comme plus haut.
2. *To hall and bower*, la salle de festin et le boudoir. Byron oppose et réunit en même temps les fausses affections qui naissent entre compagnons de table et celles que la galanterie simule, les amis de table (*flatt'rers*, *parasites*), et les amantes, *lemans*: ce dernier mot est un archaïsme.

3. *Feere* pour *fere*, compagnon ami.
4. *Mammon*, le dieu syrien de la richesse; les Grecs l'appelaient Plutus.
5. *He did shun*. Cette strophe, dans laquelle Byron donne un souvenir à sa mère et à sa sœur, est un peu singulière. Il a fui l'une et il ne voyait pas l'autre depuis trois ans.
6. *Begun* pour *began*.

Yet deem not thence his breast a breast of steel :
Ye, who have known what 't is to dote upon
A few dear objects, will in sadness feel
Such partings break the heart they fondly hope to heal.

XI

His house, his home, his heritage, his lands,
The laughing dames in whom he did delight,
Whose large blue eyes[1], fair locks, and snowy hands,
Might shake the saintship of an anchorite,
And long had fed his youthful appetite ;
His goblets brimm'd with every costly wine,
And all that mote to luxury invite,
Without a sigh he left, to cross the brine,
And traverse Paynim[2] shores, and pass Earth's central line[3].

Adieux à l'Angleterre.—Ode du départ.— Opposition entre les humbles, qui ont des affections ici-bas, et les grands, qui sont sceptiques. (Str. XII à XIV.)

XII

The sails were filled, and fair the light winds blew[4],
As glad to waft him from his native home ;
And fast the white rocks faded[5] from his view,
And soon were lost in circumambient foam :

---

1. *Whose large blue eyes.* Byron résume en un vers le genre de beauté des jeunes Anglaises

2. *Paynim*, l'Orient. Expression archaïque tirée des romans français du moyen âge. Les pays étrangers, lointains, à travers lesquels on rêvait de s'aventurer, étaient surtout la champ de bataille des croisades, l'Orient, la terre des Gentils, le « paganisme, » comme on disait ; de là l'abréviation *Paynim.*

3. *Pass Earth's central line.* Le poète avait rêvé de faire le tour du monde, ce qu'il ne fit pas. Il voulait passer aux Indes et franchir l'équateur.

4. *Fair blew.* Les vents soufflèrent gentiment, favorablement.

5. *Faded*, perdirent leur couleur et leurs contours.

And then, it may be, of his wish to roam
Repented he, but in his bosom slept
The silent thought, nor from his lips did come
One word of wail, whilst others sate and wept,
And to the reckless gales unmanly moaning kept.

XIII

But when the sun was sinking in the sea
He seized his harp, wich he at times could string,
And strike, albeit with untaught melody,
When deemed he¹ no strange ear was listening:
And now his fingers o'er it he did fling,
And tuned his farewell in the dim twilight.
While flew the vessel on her snowy wing,
And fleeting shores rece ed from his sight,
Thus to the elements he poured his last " Good Night²."

1

ADIEU, adieu! my native shore
 Fades o'er the waters blue;
The night-winds sigh, the breakers roar,
 And shrieks the wild sea-mew³.
You sun that sets upon the sea
 We follow in his flight;
Farewell awhile to him and thee,
 My native Land—Good Night!

---

1. *When deemed he*, pour *when he deemed*, inversion. De même au vers suivant, on a imprimé quelquefois: *did he fling* pour *he did fling*.

2. *Good night*, son adieu. C'était une mode littéraire de composer des adieux dans lesquels les poètes répétaient, soit le mot français *adieu*, soit la locution anglaise *good night*. Byron imite et raille tour à tour cet usage.

3. *Shrieks the wild sea-mew*, inversion pour *the wild sea-mew shrieks*. Nous signalons au début du livre ces formes de style.

2

2

A few short hours and he will rise
  To give the morrow birth;
And I shall hail the main and skies,
  But not my mother earth.
Deserted is my own good hall,
  Its hearth is desolate;
Wild weeds are gathering on the wall,
  My dog howls at the gate.

3

"—Come hither, hither, my little page[1]!
  Why dost thou weep and wail?
Or dost thou dread the billows' rage,
  Or tremble at the gale?
But dash the tear-drop from thine eye;
  Our ship is swift and strong:
Our fleetest falcon scarce can fly
  More merrily along."

4

"—Let winds be shrill, let waves roll high,
  I fear not wave nor wind:
Yet marvel not, Sir Childe, that I
  Am sorrowful in mind;
For I have from my father gone,
  A mother whom I love,
And have no friend, save these alone,
  But thee—and one above[2].

---

1. *My little page.* L'auteur appelle ainsi un enfant, Robert Rushton, qu'il avait emmené à son service: c'était le fils d'un de ses tenanciers.

2. *One above.* J'ai un ami là-haut, Dieu.

5

"My father blessed me fervently,
    Yet did not much complain;
But sorely will my mother sigh
    Till I come back again."
"—Enough, enough, my little lad!
    Such tears become thine eye;
If I thy guileless bosom had,
    Mine own would not be dry.

6

" Come hither, hither, my staunch yeoman¹,
    Why dost thou look so pale?
Or dost thou dread a French foeman?
    Or shiver at the gale?"—
"—Deem'st thou I tremble for my life?
    Sir Childe, I'm not so weak;
But thinking on an absent wife
    Will blanch a faithful cheek.

7

" My spouse and boys dwell near thy hall,
    Along the bordering lake,
And when they on their father call,
    What answer shall she make?"

---

1. *My staunch yeoman*, mon fidèle écuyer; il s'agit du domestique de Byron, William Fletcher, qui accompagna partout son maître, le suivit en Grèce et reçut son dernier soupir.

"—Enough, enough, my yeoman good,
  Thy grief let none gainsay;
But I, who am of lighter mood [1],
  Will laugh to flee away."

8

For who would trust the seeming sighs
  Of wife or paramour?
Fresh feeres will dry the bright blue eyes
  We late saw streaming o'er.
For pleasures past I do not grieve,
  Nor perils gathering near;
My greatest grief is that I leave
  No thing that claims a tear.

9

And now I'm in the world alone,
  Upon the wide, wide sea:
But why should I for others groan,
  When none will sigh for me?
Perchance my dog will whine in vain,
  Till fed by stranger hands;
But long ere I come back again
  He'd tear [2] me where he stands.

---

1. *I who am of lighter mood.* Je suis d'une humeur plus légère. Primitivement Byron avait écrit, sous la dictée de cette bonne humeur, des vers joyeusement moqueurs sur son départ, sur ses compagnons, sur les accidents du voyage. Plus tard il mêla à l'expression de son scepticisme celle du chagrin d'autrui. Ce contraste est devenu le charme et l'originalité de la pièce présente.

2. *He'd tear*, pour *He would tear*. On a raconté que Byron, revenant un jour de voyage, ne fut pas reconnu par un de ses chiens. Un sceptique ne croit pas même à la fidélité des chiens.

CANTO THE FIRST.

10

With thee, my bark, I'll swiftly go
    Athwart the foaming brine;
Nor care what land thou bear'st me to,
    So not again[1] to mine.
Welcome, welcome, ye dark-blue waves!
    And when you fail my sight,
Welcome, ye deserts, and ye caves!
    My native Land—Good Night!

XIV

On, on the vessel flies, the land is gone,
And winds are rude in Biscay's sleepless bay.
Four days are sped, but with the fifth, anon,
New shores descried make every bosom gay;
And Cintra's mountain greets them on their way,
And Tagus dashing[2] onward to the deep,
His fabled golden tribute bent to pay;
And soon on board the Lusian pilots leap,
And steer 'twixt fertile shores where yet few rustics reap.

En Portugal, jusqu'à la strophe XXXI. — Admirable nature, nation misérable et asservie.

A partir de cette strophe, on va voir de nombreuses allusions aux guerres dont la Péninsule fut le théâtre, et aux armées de la France. Il importe, pour les comprendre, de se rappeler l'époque. Lord Byron, qui donna en 1813 les deux premiers chants de son

---

1. *So not again,* pourvu que tu ne me ramènes pas.
2. *Dashing,* se précipitant. Plus haut, dans la 3ᵉ stance des Adieux, Byron disait *dash the tear-drop,* sèche tes larmes. Les deux sens paraissent fort éloignés; ils se rapportent cependant à un même sens premier qui est : « faire un mouvement rapide », d'où : frapper vite, se précipiter, effacer vivement, etc., selon les compléments.

poème, les composa ou les refit pendant cette période de 1808 à 1813, durant laquelle Napoléon envahissait tour à tour le Portugal et l'Espagne, que soutenait l'Angleterre. Le Portugal, jadis si grand au temps de Vasco de Gama et d'Albuquerque, était devenu comme l'esclave, tantôt de la France, tantôt de l'Angleterre. C'est ce qui explique les vers cruels que l'on va lire. (Str. xv à xxiii.)

XV

Oh, Christ! it is a goodly sight[1] to see
What Heaven hath done for this delicious land!
What fruits of fragrance blush on every tree!
What goodly prospects o'er the hills expand!
But man would mar them with an impious hand:
And when the Almighty lifts his fiercest scourge
'Gainst those who most transgress his high command,
With treble vengeance will his hot shafts urge
Gaul's locust host[2], and earth from fellest foemen purge.

XVI

What beauties doth Lisboa first unfold!
Her image floating on that noble tide[3],
Which poets vainly pave with sands of gold,
But now whereon a thousand keels[4] did ride
Of mighty strength, since Albion was allied,
And to the Lusians did her aid afford:
A nation swoln with ignorance and pride,
Who lick yet loathe[5] the hand that waves the sword
To save them from the wrath of Gaul's unsparing lord.

---

1. *Goodly sight*, vue charmante.
2. *Gaul's locust host*, l'armée de sauterelles de la Gaule.
3. *Tide*, le flot, le fleuve.
4. *Keels*, les navires.

5. *Lick yet loathe*. Dans la poésie anglaise ces assemblages de mots commençant par la même consonne sont fréquents et même recherchés. On aime l'allitération.

XVII

But whoso entereth within this town,
That, sheening far, celestial seems to be,
Disconsolate will wander up and down,
'Mid many things unsightly to strange ee;
For hut and palace show like filthily:
The dingy denizens[1] are reared in dirt;
Ne personage of high or mean degree
Doth care for cleanliness of surtout or shirt;
Though shent with Egypt's plague, unkempt, unwashed, unhurt.

XVIII

Poor, paltry slaves! yet born 'midst noblest scenes—
Why, Nature, waste thy wonders on such men?
Lo! Cintra's glorious Eden[2] intervenes
In variegated maze of mount and glen.
Ah me! what hand can pencil guide, or pen,
To follow half on which the eye dilates
Through views more dazzling unto mortal ken
Than those whereof such things the bard relates,
Who to the awe-struck world unlocked Elysium's gates.

XIX

The horrid crags, by toppling convent crowned,
The cork-trees hoar that clothe the shaggy steep,
The moutain-moss by scorching skies imbrowned,
The sunken glen, whose sunless shrubs must weep,

---

1. *Denizens*, les naturels du pays. Le style de ce passage, dans lequel Byron se sert de mots populaires ou vieillis pour attaquer les Portugais, la négligence méridionale et la vermine (*Egypt's plague*), donne une idée de ce qu'était la poésie de *Childe Harold* dans sa première rédaction.

2. *Cintra's glorious Eden*. A 20 kilomètres environ de Lisbonne, apparaît le village de Cintra, situé sur la pente d'une montagne, formé de villas nombreuses et digne de la belle description du poète.

The tender azure of the unruffled deep,
The orange tints that gild the greenest bough,
The torrents that from cliff to valley leap,
The vine on high, the willow branch below,
Mixed in one mighty scene, with varied beauty glow.

XX

Then slowly climb the many-winding way,
And frequent turn to linger as you go,
From loftier rocks new loveliness survey,
And rest ye at " Our Lady's house of woe [1];"
Where frugal monks their little relics show,
And sundry legends to the stranger tell:
Here impious men have punished been, and lo!
Deep in yon cave Honorius [2] long did dwell,
In hope to merit Heaven by making earth a Hell.

XXI

And here and there, as up the crags you spring,
Mark many rude-carved crosses near the path:
Yet deem not these devotion's offering—
These are memorials frail of murderous wrath:
For wheresoe'er the shrieking victim hath
Pour'd forth his blood beneath the assassin's knife,
Some hand erects a cross of mouldering lath;
And grove and glen with thousand such are rife
Throughout this purple land, where law secures not life [3].

1. *Our Lady's house of woe.* Notre-Dame des Douleurs. Ici Byron a commis une méprise qu'il avoue lui-même. Le nom portugais *Nossa Senhora de Peña* veut dire : *Notre-Dame du Rocher.* Le mot *peña*, avec le tildé sur l'n, signifie rocher et se prononce *pegna*; sans accent, il devient *pena*, peine.

2. *Honorius.* Saint Honorius aurait creusé là une grotte qui fut son ermitage.

3. *Where law secures not life.* Byron a raconté qu'il fut attaqué à Lisbonne, et il ajoute que d'ailleurs les Maltais et les Siciliens commettent aussi de fréquents meurtres toujours impunis.

XXII

On sloping mounds, or in the vale beneath,
Are domes where whilome kings did make repair;
But now the wild flowers round them only breathe;
Yet ruin'd splendour still is lingering there.
And yonder towers the Prince's palace[1] fair:
There thou too, Vathek[2]! England's wealthiest son,
Once formed thy Paradise, as not aware
When wanton Wealth her mightiest deeds hath done,
Meek Peace voluptuous lures was ever wont to shun.

XXIII

Here didst thou dwell, here schemes of pleasure plan,
Beneath yon mountain's ever beauteous brow:
But now, as if a thing unblest[3] by Man,
Thy fairy dwelling is as lone as thou!
Here giant weeds a passage scarce allow
To halls deserted, portals gaping[4] wide:
Fresh lessons to the thinking bosom, how
Vain are the pleasaunces[5] on earth supplied;
Swept into wrecks anon by Time's ungentle tide!

La convention de Cintra. — Junot, chargé d'envahir le Portugal, fut battu à Vimeiro par Wellesley (depuis lord Wellington). A la

1. *Prince's palace.* Byron signale, au milieu de la nature toujours vivante, les ruines des choses humaines, le palais désert du prince Jean et le palais abandonné du riche William Beckford.

2. *Vathek.* C'était le titre d'un ouvrage, célèbre alors, du même William Beckford. A la fin du dix-huitième siècle on parlait beaucoup des singularités de ce Beckford, Anglais riche comme un nabab (au moins cent mille livres sterling de revenu), qui allait en Portugal s'acheter un palais près des rois du pays, qui écrivait en français un roman sceptique, et qui revenait en Angleterre pour y bâtir à Fonthill, sur son domaine patrimonial, une résidence merveilleuse sans pouvoir (selon Byron) trouver la paix nulle part.

3. *Unblest,* non béni, maudit.
4. *Gaping,* béants.
5. *Pleasaunces,* archaïsme.

suite de cette défaite, Junot signa avec le général Dalrymple la convention dite de Cintra, par laquelle les Français s'engageaient à évacuer le Portugal. Cette convention mécontenta également les Anglais et Napoléon. Junot et Dalrymple furent disgraciés. (Str. XXIV à XXVI.)

XXIV

Behold the hall where chiefs were late convened!
Oh! dome displeasing [1] unto British eye!
With diadem hight foolscap, lo! a fiend [2],
A little fiend that scoffs incessantly,
There sits in parchment robe arrayed, and by
His side is hung a seal and sable scroll,
Where blazon'd glare names known to chivalry,
And sundry signatures adorn the roll,
Whereat the Urchin points and laughs with all his soul [3].

XXV

Convention is the dwarfish demon styled
That foiled the knights in Marialva's dome [4]:
Of brains (if brains they had) he them beguiled,
And turned a nation's shallow joy to gloom.

1. *Oh! dome displeasing!* Pour bien saisir le sens, le ton, les images bizarres de tout ce passage, il faut se rappeler l'émotion causée alors par la convention de Cintra. Junot était enveloppé par l'ennemi et perdu. Il fit si bien qu'on lui acheta, pour ainsi dire sa retraite et qu'il partit avec armes et bagages sur les vaisseaux mêmes de l'Angleterre.

2. *A fiend.* Cette convention est une œuvre satanique, c'est le démon lui-même en parchemin.

3. *Laughs with all his soul* Après cette strophe ironique, lord Byron en avait écrit d'autres beaucoup plus violentes. Il y montrait les Anglais fous de joie à la nouvelle de la bataille de Vimeiro, puis fous de colère à la nouvelle de la convention, et tout le bruit qui se fit à Londres sans aboutir à rien. Sur les instances de ses amis, il retrancha ce passage.

4. *In Marialva's dome.* La convention avait été signée dans le palais du marquis de Marialva.

Here Folly dashed to earth the victor's plume,
And Policy regained what arms had lost:
For chiefs like ours in vain may laurels bloom!
Woe to the conqu'ring, not the conquer'd host,
Since baffled Triumph droops on Lusitania's coast.

XXVI

And ever since that martial synod met,
Britannia sickens, Cintra! at thy name;
And folks in office at the mention fret,
And fain would blush, if blush they could, for shame.
How will posterity the deed proclaim!
Will not our own and fellow-nations sneer,
To view these champions cheated of their fame,
By foes in fight o'erthrown, yet victors here [1],
Where Scorn [2] her finger points through many a coming year?

Passage du Portugal en Espagne. — Le plan du poème correspond ici à la vie réelle de Byron, qui partit de Lisbonne pour Séville, envoyant ses bagages par mer à Gibraltar. (Str. XXVII à XXX.)

XXVII

So deemed the Childe, as o'er the mountains he
Did take his way in solitary guise:
Sweet was the scene, yet soon he thought to flee,
More restless than the swallow in the skies:
Though here awhile he learned to moralize [3],

---

1. *Victors here.* Les vaincus prenaient figures de vainqueurs. Byron avait écrit d'abord : *Dull Victors! baffled by a vanquished foe.*

2. *Where Scorn.* On a remarqué plus haut *Folly,* la Folie; *Policy,* la Politique; *Triumph,* le Triomphe. Ici *Scorn,* le Mépris; plus loin encore, *Meditation,* sont des abstractions personnifiées, dans le style de Spenser. La suppression de l'article appartient ici à la forme littéraire plutôt qu'aux lois grammaticales anglaises.

3. *To moralize,* suivre une pensée morale.

For Meditation fixed at times on him;
And conscious Reason whispered to despise
His early youth, misspent in maddest whim;
But as he gazed on truth his aching eyes grew dim [1]

XXVIII

To horse! to horse [2]! he quits, for ever quits
A scene of peace, though soothing to his soul:
Again he rouses from his moping fits,
But seeks not now the harlot and the bowl.
Onward he flies, nor fixed as yet the goal
Where he shall rest him on his pilgrimage;
And o'er him many changing scenes must roll
Ere toil his thirst for travel can assuage,
Or he shall calm his breast, or learn experience sage.

XXIX

Yet Mafra [3] shall one moment claim delay,
Where dwelt of yore the Lusians' luckless queen;
And church and court did mingle their array,
And mass and revel were alternate seen;
Lordlings and freres—ill-sorted fry I ween!
But here the Babylonian whore hath built
A dome, where flaunts she in such glorious sheen,
That men forget the blood which she hath spilt,
And bow the knee to Pomp that loves to varnish guilt.

1. *Grew dim.* Son regard s'obscurcissait.
2. *To horse! to horse!* Byron partit à cheval et fit soixante-dix milles par jour.
3. *Yet Mafra.* Mafra, à 26 kilomètres de Lisbonne, frappa le poète par son étendue « prodigieuse », dit-il. Il y trouve un palais, un couvent, une très belle église et un parc immense. Le poète protestant et libéral maudit le tout ensemble, comme un mélange de vices et de superstition.

XXX

O'er vales that teem with fruits, romantic hills,
(Oh, that [1] such hills upheld a freeborn race!)
Whereon to gaze the eye with joyaunce fills,
Childe Harold wends through many a pleasant place.
Though sluggards deem it but a foolish chase,
And marvel men should quit their easy chair,
The toilsome way, and long, long league to trace,
Oh! there is sweetness in the mountain air,
And life, that bloated Ease [2] can never hope to share.

La frontière d'Espagne et de Portugal. — Contraste des deux nations. (Str. XXXI à XXXIV.)

XXXI

More bleak to view the hills at length recede,
And, less luxuriant, smoother [3] vales extend;
Immense horizon-bounded plains succeed!
Far as the eye discerns, withouten end [4],
Spain's realms appear whereon her shepherds tend
Flocks, whose rich fleece right well the trader knows—
Now must the pastor's arm his lambs defend:
For Spain is compassed by unyielding foes,
And all must shield their all, or share Subjection's woes.

---

1. *Oh, that...* Ah! si..., plût à Dieu que... Cette forme elliptique est devenue régulière en anglais.
2. *Ease*, l'Indolence. Nouvel exemple de ces personnifications que nous avons signalées.
3. *Smoother*, en pente douce.
4. *Withouten end*, sans fin. *Withouten*, archaïsme pour *without*:

XXXII

Where Lusitania and her Sister meet,
Deem ye what bounds¹ the rival realms divide?
Or ere the jealous queens of nations greet²,
Doth Tayo interpose his mighty tide?
Or dark Sierras rise in craggy pride?
Or fence of art, like China's vasty wall?—
Ne barrier wall, ne river deep and wide,
Ne horrid crags, nor mountains dark and tall,
Rise like the rocks that part Hispania's land from Gaul:

XXXIII

But these between a silver streamlet glides,
And scarce a name distinguisheth the brook,
Though rival kingdoms press its verdant sides.
Here leans the idle shepherd on his crook,
And vacant on the rippling waves doth look,
That peaceful still 'twixt bitterest foemen flow;
For proud each peasant as the noblest duke:
Well doth the Spanish hind the difference know
'Twixt him and Lusian slave³, the lowest of the low.

XXXIV

But ere the mingling bounds have far been passed⁴,
Dark Guadiana rolls his power along
In sullen billows, murmuring and vast,
So noted ancient roundelays⁵ among.

---

1. *Deem ye what bounds*, par quelles barrières pensez-vous que soient séparés les royaumes rivaux? *Deem ye* pour *what bounds do you deem*.

2. *Greet*, avant qu'elles ne se rejoignent. Ici *greet*, se saluer, est presque synonyme de *meet*, se rencontrer.

3. *Lusian slave*. Byron lui-même a trouvé sans doute son jugement trop dur pour un peuple malheureux; il l'a atténué plus tard dans une note.

4. *Pass'd*, à peine a-t-on franchi ces limites...

5. *Roundelays*. Les chansons ou ballades, allusion au *Romancero* et

Whilome upon his banks did legions throng
Of Moor and Knight, in mailed splendour drest:
Here ceased the swift their race, here sunk the strong;
The Paynim turban and the Christian crest
Mixed on the bleeding stream, by floating hosts oppressed.

En Espagne, jusqu'à la fin du chant. — Souvenirs illustres de la lutte de l'Espagne contre l'islamisme pendant huit siècles. — Chants populaires qui consacrent ces souvenirs. (Str. XXXV à XXXVI.)

XXXV

Oh, lovely Spain! renowned romantic land!
Where is that standard which Pelagio[1] bore,
When Cava's traitor-sire first called the band
That dyed thy mountain-streams with Gothic gore?
Where are those bloody banners which of yore

au *Cancionero*, les deux recueils de chants populaires dans lesquels on retrouve encore, parmi des récits d'aventures, de petites odes énergiques et sublimes rappelant les actes des libérateurs de l'Espagne. Ce sont les annales héroïques de la Castille et de l'Andalousie. Corneille les avait lues avant d'écrire le *Cid*. « Ces sortes de petits poèmes, dit-il, sont comme des originaux décousus de leurs anciennes histoires. » Victor Hugo a traduit la ballade fameuse qui représente le roi Roderick vaincu, errant et jetant des regards douloureux sur ce royaume où il ne possède plus « un créneau ». Schiller y a puisé le sujet du conte intitulé : *le Gant*. Walter Scott a écrit la *Vision de don Roderick*. A son tour, Byron, entrant en Andalousie, lit et rappelle les mêmes sources poétiques.

1. *Pelagio, Cava*. Ces deux noms rappellent deux épisodes de la lutte de l'Espagne contre les Maures : Pélage, la retraite et la résistance des chrétiens dans les montagnes des Asturies ; la Cava, l'aventure de la fille du comte Julien, qui fut outragée par le roi Roderick. On l'appelait tantôt Florinda, tantôt la Cava. Son père se vengea en ouvrant l'Espagne aux Maures. — Byron, en parlant ici du père traître, *traitor-sire*, répète les vers du *Romancero* :

> O cosa nunca pensada
> Que por sola una doncella
> La cual cava se llamaba,
> Causen estos dos traidores
> Que Espana sea domenada

Waved o'er thy sons, victorious to the gale,
And drove at last the spoilers to their shore?
Red gleamed the cross, and waned the crescent pale,
While Afric's echoes thrill'd with Moorish matrons' wail[1].

XXXVI

Teems not[2] each ditty with the glorious tale?
Ah! such, alas! the hero's amplest fate!
When granite moulders and when records fail,
A peasant's plaint prolongs his dubious date.
Pride! bend thine eye from heaven[3] to thine estate,
See how the Mighty shrink into a song!
Can Volume, Pillar, Pile[4] preserve thee great?
Or must thou trust Tradition's simple tongue,
When Flattery sleeps with thee, and History does thee wrong?

Appel de lord Byron à l'Espagne contre ses envahisseurs, c'est-à-dire contre Napoléon. (Str. XXXVII à XLIV.)

XVII

Awake, ye sons of Spain! awake! advance[5]!
Lo! Chivalry, your ancient goddess, cries,
But wields not, as of old, her thirsty lance,

---

1. *With Moorish matrons' wail.* Ce passage rappelle le *bella matribus detestata* du poète Horace.

2. *Teems not,* ellipse. Chacun des chants populaires n'est-il pas rempli de ce glorieux conte? Le poète n'emploie pas dans cette interrogation l'auxiliaire *do.*

3. *Bend thine eye from... to...* Abaisse et attache tes yeux. —

4. *Pillar, Pile.* L'histoire et les monuments historiques, les colonnes (*Pillar*) ou édifices (*Pile*), ne garantissent pas la grandeur à venir.

5. Pour comprendre cette espèce de chant de guerre, il faut signaler d'avance au lecteur la strophe XLI, dans laquelle il est dit : « Trois armées vont sacrifier au dieu de la guerre, trois cris retentissent : France! Espagne!

Nor shakes her crimson plumage in the skies :
Now on the smoke of blazing bolts she flies[1],
And speaks in thunder through yon engine's roar :
In every peal she calls—" Awake! arise ! "
Say, is her voice more feeble than of yore,
When her war-song was heard on Andalusia's shore?

XXXVIII.

Hark! heard you not those hoofs of dreadful note[2]?
Sounds not the clang of conflict on the heath?
Saw ye not whom the reeking sabre smote,
Nor saved[3] your brethren ere they sank beneath
Tyrants and tyrants' slaves?—the fires of death,
The bale-fires[4] flash on high :—from rock to rock
Each volley tells that thousands cease to breathe ;
Death rides upon the sulphury Siroc,
Red Battle stamps his foot[5], and nations feel the shock.

XXXIX

Lo! where the Giant on the mountain stands,
His blood-red tresses deep'ning[6] in the sun,

Angleterre ! » Il s'agit de la nouvelle guerre de l'indépendance ouverte en Espagne par l'avènement même de Joseph Bonaparte (1808-1813). « Ce qu'a fait l'Espagne contre les Maures, elle doit le faire contre la Gaule », dit Byron.

1. *Bolts.* Les traits de feu, s'applique ici à l'artillerie. Byron fait de la voix du canon, qui a détruit la chevalerie, la voix même de la chevalerie qui appelle les Espagnols au combat.

2. *Hoofs of dreadful note.* — Le bruit terrible des sabots des chevaux dans une charge de cavalerie.

3. *Nor saved.* Ellipse qui s'explique par le parallélisme de cette phrase avec les précédentes. — N'avez-vous pas entendu?... N'avez-vous pas vu?... N'avez-vous pas pensé à sauver?...

4. *Bale-fires.* L'éclair du canon est un *feu d'alarme* comme on en allumait en Espagne dans les *atalayas*, ou tours construites sur les hauteurs.

5. *His foot.* La bataille étant personnifiée, on considère *Battle* comme un masculin, et l'adjectif possessif qui s'y rapporte est *his*.

6. *Deepening.* Assombrissant. — *Deepen*, creuser, rendre plus pro-

With death-shot glowing in his fiery hands,
And eye that scorcheth all it glares upon;
Restless it rolls, now fixed, and now anon
Flashing afar,—and at his iron feet
Destruction cowers[1], to mark what deeds are done;
For on this morn three potent nations meet,
To shed before his shrine the blood he deems most sweet.

XL

By Heaven! it is a splendid sight to see
(For one who hath no friend, no brother there)
Their rival scarfs of mixed embroidery,
Their various arms that glitter in the air!
What gallant war-hounds[2] rouse them from their lair
And gnash their fangs, loud yelling for the prey!
All join the chase, but few the triumph share;
The Grave shall bear the chiefest prize away,
And Havoc[3] scarce for joy can number their array.

XLI

Three hosts[4] combine to offer sacrifice;
Three tongues prefer strange orisons on high;
Three gaudy standards flout the pale blue skies;
The shouts are France, Spain, Albion, Victory!
The foe, the victim, and the fond ally
That fights for all, but ever fights in vain,
Are met—as if at home they could not die—

fond, prend le sens de : rendre plus foncé, plus grave ou plus épais.

1. *Cowers*, s'accroupit à ses pieds.
2. *Gallant war-hounds*, vaillants chiens de guerre.
3. *Havoc*, la Dévastation. Peut-être ce mot se rapproche-t-il, quant à l'étymologie, de l'anglais *hawk* et de l'allemand *Habicht*.
4. *Three hosts*, trois armées. Le mot *host* est exactement le vieux français *host* (écrit souvent *ost*). Celui-ci vient de *hostis*, l'ennemi, puis rmée ennemie, puis l'armée

To feed the crow on Talavera's plain [1],
And fertilize the field that each pretends to gain.

XLII

There shall they rot—Ambition's honoured fools!
Yes, Honour decks [2] the turf that wraps their clay!
Vain Sophistry! in these behold the tools,
The broken tools, that tyrants cast away
By myriads, when they dare to pave their way
With human hearts—to what?—a dream alone.
Can despots compass aught that hails [3] their sway?
Or call with truth one span [4] of earth their own,
Save that wherein at last they crumble bone by bone

XLIII

Oh, Albuera [5]! glorious field of grief!
As o'er thy plain the Pilgrim [6] pricked his steed,
Who could foresee thee, in a space so brief,
A scene where mingling foes should boast and bleed!
Peace to the perished! may the warrior's meed

1. *On Talavera's plain.* Talavera de la Reina, ville sur le Tage, dans la Nouvelle-Castille, fut témoin d'une grande bataille livrée le 27 juillet 1809 aux Français par les Espagnols et les Anglais réunis. Elle demeura indécise, mais elle fut regardée comme une défaite des Français, parce qu'ils se retirèrent.

2. *Honour decks*, la gloire couvre et décore. — *To deck* signifie couvrir, puis orner. Les deux sens se réunissent ici, comme plus loin, dans la strophe XLIV.

3. *Hails.* Peuvent-ils obtenir qu'un être salue volontiers leur pouvoir? *To hail*, saluer, prend sa signification ici de l'ensemble du texte.

4. *One span*, un empan de terre. C'est la pensée des anciens : Combien faut-il de pieds de terre pour ensevelir un maître du monde?

5. *Albuera.* Autre champ de bataille, illustré, le 16 mai 1811, par une seconde rencontre des Français avec les Anglo-Espagnols, également malheureuse pour les premiers. Albuera est un village situé au sud-est de Badajoz.

6. *The Pilgrim.* Le pèlerin (Childe Harold ou Byron) passa par Albuera en 1809; la bataille n'eut lieu qu'en 1811.

And tears of triumph their reward prolong!
Till others fall where other chieftains lead
Thy name shall circle round the gaping throng,
And shine in worthless lays, they theme of transient song.

XLIV

Enough of Battle's minions[1]! let them play
Their game of lives, and barter breath for fame:
Fame that will scarce reanimate their clay,
Though thousands fall to deck[2] some single name.
In sooth 't were sad to thwart their noble aim[3]
Who strike, blest hirelings! for their country's good
And die, that living might have proved[4] her shame;
Perished, perchance, in some domestic feud,
Or in a narrower sphere wild Rapine's path pursued.

L'Andalousie. — Contraste singulier de la gaieté des villes et de l'inquiétude des campagnes, du cri « Vive le Roi », et des malédictions contre le roi, des sérénades d'amour et de l'imminence de la guerre. (Str. XLV à LIII.)

XLV

Full swiftly Harold wends[5] his lonely way
Where proud Sevilla triumphs unsubdued[6]:

---

1. *Battels minions.* Assez parler des *mignons* de la guerre. Ce mot, qui n'a pas de synonyme exact, signifie à peu près *les favoris*. C'est une expression française. Corneille, voulant dire que l'Académie l'a favorisé, s'appelle, un peu subtilement, un « indigne mignon de la fortune ». Sur l'origine de ce mot les linguistes sont partagés : les uns le font venir de l'allemand *Minne*, amour; les autres de *minor* ou *minimus*, petit, cher-petit.

2. *To deck,* illustrer, comme plus haut, strophe XLII.
3. *Their aim, who.* Le noble but de ceux qui...
4. *Might have proved,* seraient devenus.
5. *Wends,* il va son chemin. Byron affectionne ce verbe archaïque, dont aujourd'hui le prétérit seul, *went*, est usité comme un temps de *to go*.
6. *Unsubdued.* Séville est encore libre. Elle l'était quand Byron y

CANTO THE FIRST. 37

Yet is she free—the spoiler's wished for prey!
Soon, soon shall Conquest's fiery foot intrude,
Blackening her lovely domes with traces rude.
Inevitable hour! 'Gainst fate to strive
Where Desolation plants her famish'd brood
Is vain, or Ilion, Tyre might yet survive,
And Virtue vanquish hall, and Murder cease to thrive.

XLVI

But all unconscious of the coming doom[1]
The feast, the song, the revel here abounds;
Strange modes of merriment the hours consume,
Nor bleed these patriots with their country's wounds,
Nor here War's clarion, but Love's rebeck sounds;
Here Folly still his votaries inthrals[2];
And young-eyed Lewdness[3] walks her midnight rounds;
Girt with the silent crimes of Capitals,
Still to the last kind Vice clings to the tott'ring walls.

XLVII

Not so the rustic—with his trembling mate
He lurks, nor casts his heavy eye afar,
Lest he should view his vineyard desolate,
Blasted below the dun hot breath of war.

passa; elle ne l'était plus quand il publia son poème. C'est pourquoi il prophétise à coup sûr, en disant : La conquête y mettra le pied, *shall intrude.*

1. *Doom,* le destin. Ce mot signifie *condemnation,* sentence, arrêt, puis arrêt du destin, fatalité.

2. *Inthrals,* tient asservis. —

Le mot *thrall* veut dire : esclave ou asservir; de même son dérivé.

3. *And young eyed Lewdness...* Les trois vers qui terminent strophe présentent l'image du vice qui erre dans les murs d'une ville de plaisir, tandis que la guerre approche, qui renversera ces murs : contraste saisissant.

No more beneath soft Eve's consenting star [1]
Fandango twirls his jocund castanet:
Ah, monarchs! could ye [2] taste the mirth ye mar,
Not in the toils of Glory would ye fret;
The hoarse dull drum would sleep, and Man be happy yet!

XLVIII

How carols now the lusty muleteer?
Of love, romance, devotion is his lay,
As whilome he was wont the leagues to cheer,
His quick bells wildly jingling on the way?
No! as he speeds, he chants " Vivà el Rey [3]! "
And checks his song to execrate Godoy [4],
The royal wittol Charles, and curse the day
When first Spain's queen beheld the black-eyed boy,
And gore-faced Treason sprung from her adulterate joy.

XLIX

On yon long, level plain, at distance crowned
With crags, whereon those Moorish turrets rest,
Wide scatter'd hoof-marks dint [5] the wounded ground;
And, scathed by fire, the greensward's darken'd vest

---

1. *Consenting star*, étoile complaisante.
2. *Could you*, si vous pouviez.
3. *Viva el Rey!* mots espagnols : *Vive le roi!* Byron saisit ce trait naïf du caractère méridional, qui chante sans réflexion le refrain *Viva el rey!* et qui s'interrompt pour maudire le roi Charles IV.
4. *Godoy*. Don Manuel Godoï, né en 1764 à Badajoz, était un garde du corps de belle mine et de famille noble, qui devint, par la faveur de la reine, le maître de l'Espagne sous le règne de Charles IV (1788-1808). Ignorant et médiocre, mais séduisant, il arriva à tout, fut grand d'Espagne, généralissime, grand amiral, premier ministre, duc d'Alcudia et prince de la Paix. Il disparut d'Espagne à la chute du roi et vint mener une existence obscure à Paris, où il est mort en 1851.
5. *Hoof-marks dint...* La trace des chevaux marque le sol déchiré.

Tells that the foe was Andalusia's guest:
Here was the camp, the watch-flame[1], and the host,
Here the bold peasant storm'd[2] the dragon's nest;
Still does he mark it with triumphant boast;
And points to yonder cliffs, which oft were won and lost

L

And whomsoe'er along the path you meet
Bears in his cap the badge[3] of crimson hue,
Which tells you whom to shun and whom to greet:
Woe to the man that walks in public wiew
Without of loyalty[4] this token true:
Sharp is the knife[5], and sudden is the stroke;
And sorely would the Gallic foeman rue,
If subtle poniards, wrapt beneath the cloke,
Could blunt the sabre's edge, or clear the cannon's smoke.

LI

At every turn[6] Morena's dusky height
Sustains aloft the battery's iron load;
And, far as mortal eye can compass sight,
The moutain-howitzer, the broken road,
The bristling palisade, the fosse o'erflowed,

---

1. *Watch-flame*, le feu de bivouac.
2. *Stormed*, a donné l'assaut. Le mot *storm* veut dire orage, tempête, puis assaillir.
3. *Badge*, marque, insigne.
4. *Without of loyalty.* Exemple des libertés énergiques de style de Byron. Au lieu de: *this true token of loyalty*, il écrit par inversion: *of loyalty this token true.*
5. *Sharp is the knife*, et plus bas *wrapt beneath the cloke.* Allusion à la coutume des Espagnols qui portent sous leur vêtement le couteau long et affilé, connu sous le nom général de couteau catalan, et s'exercent à le lancer de loin avec une adresse extrême.
6. *At every turn...* À chaque détour de la Sierra-Morena, on voit sur les sommets sombres. Mot à mot: les sommets de la Morena...

The station'd bands, the never-vacant watch,
The magazine in rocky durance [1] stow'd,
The holster'd steed beneath the shed of thatch,
The ball-piled pyramid, the ever-blazing match,

LII

Portend the deeds to come:—but he whose nod [2]
Has tumbled feebler despots from their sway,
A moment pauseth ere he lifts the rod;
A little moment deigneth to delay;
Soon will his legions sweep through these their way;
The West must own the Scourger of the world.
Ah! Spain! how sad will be thy reckoning-day,
When soars Gaul's Vulture, with his wings unfurled,
And thou shalt view thy sons in crowds to Hades [3] hurled.

LIII

And must they fall? the young, the proud, the brave,
To swell one bloated [4] Chief's unwholesome reign?
No step between submission and a grave?
The rise [5] of rapine and the fall of Spain?
And doth the Power that man adores ordain
Their doom [6], nor heed the suppliant's appeal?

---

1. *Durance.* réduit, caverne. — Ce mot paraît être une ellipse des vieilles expressions qui, au moyen âge désignaient la prison, le *carceré duro*, la *robe de durance*, tout ce qui enferme durement. De là le sens de prison, cachot, puis caverne.

2. *He whose nod.* Celui qui d'un signe de tête renversa les rois. Il s'agit ici de Bonaparte, qui préoccupe alors toute l'Europe.

3. *Hades.* Tu verras les fils précipités aux enfers. Ici Byron, qui a lu les anciens comme les modernes, malgré sa prétention de ne suivre personne, répète non seulement un vers d'Homère, mais encore le nom mythologique des enfers employé par le poète : ψυχὰς δ'Ἄϊδι προΐαψεν.

4. *Bloated.* Gonflé d'orgueil.

5. *Rise,* le triomphe.

6. *Doom,* vu plus haut déjà, implique l'idée de condamnation fatale.

Is all that desperate Valour acts in vain?
And Counsel sage, and patriotic Zeal,
The Veteran's skill, Youth's fire, and Manhood's heart of steel?

Les femmes espagnoles. — L'héroïne de Saragosse. — La beauté des Espagnoles et leur liberté opposées à la pâleur des Anglaises et à l'esclavage des Orientales. (Str. LIV à LIX.)

LIV

Is it for this the Spanish maid [1], aroused,
Hangs on the willow her unstrung guitar,
And, all unsex'd, the anlace [2] hath espoused,
Sung the loud song, and dared the deed of war?
And she, whom once the semblance of a scar
Appall'd, an owlet's larum chilled with dread,
Now views the column-scattering bay'net jar,
The falchion flash, and o'er the yet warm dead
Stalks with Minerva's step where Mars might quake to tread.

LV

Ye who shall marvel when you hear her tale,
Oh! had you known her [3] in her softer hour,
Mark'd her black eye that mocks her coal-black veil,

---

1. *The Spanish maid.* Allusion à la célèbre Augustina. Pendant le siège de Saragosse, une batterie espagnole, balayée par notre feu, resta sans défenseurs. Cette femme s'élança sur les cadavres encore chauds (*the yet warm dead*) des artilleurs espagnols, saisit une mèche et mit le feu. Son exemple ramena ses hommes au combat. C'est pour ces actes que les pouvoirs publics lui décernèrent une récompense nationale.

2. *Anlace*, nom d'une arme ancienne qui paraît avoir été l'une de ces dagues courtes que l'on cache dans les vêtements.

3. *Had you known her.* « Je l'ai vue, dit Byron, se promener souvent au Prado, portant les décorations et les médailles que la Junte lui avait données. »

Heard her light, lively tones in Lady's bower,
Seen her long locks that foil¹ the painter's power,
Her fairy form, with more than female grace,
Scarce would you deem that Saragoza's tower
Beheld her smile² in Danger's Gorgon face,
Thin the closed ranks, and lead in Glory's fearful chase.

LVI

Her lover sinks—she sheds no ill-timed tear;
Her chief is slain—she fills his fatal post;
Her fellows flee—she checks their base career³;
The foe retires—she heads the sallying host:
Who can appease like her a lover's ghost?
Who can avenge so well a leader's fall?
What maid retrieve⁴ when man's flush'd hope is lost?
Who hang so fiercely on the flying Gaul,
Foiled by a woman's hand, before a battered wall?

LVII

Yet are Spain's maids no race of Amazons,
But form'd for all the witching arts of love:
Though thus in arms they emulate her sons,
And in the horrid phalanx dare to move,
'Tis but the tender fierceness of the dove,
Pecking the hand that hovers o'er her mate:
In softness as in firmness far above
Remoter females⁵, famed for sickening prate⁶;
Her mind is nobler sure, her charms perchance as great.

---

1. *Foil*, met en faute, déjoue, le pouvoir du peintre.
2. *Smile in...* sourit à la face du Danger, face de Gorgone.
3. *Their base career*, leur course, leur fuite honteuse.
4. *What maid retrieve.* — Sous-entendez *can*, exprimé plus haut.
5. *Remoter females.*—Les femmes de là-bas, les Anglaises.
6. *Sickening prate*, leur bavardage écœurant.

LVIII

The seal Love's[1] dimpling finger hath impressed
Denotes how soft that chin which bears his touch :
Her lips, whose kisses pout to leave their nest,
Bid man be valiant ere he merit such :
Her glance how wildly beautiful! how much
Hath Phœbus[2] woo'd in vain to spoil her cheek,
Which glows yet smoother from his amorous clutch!
Who round the North for paler dames would seek?
How poor their forms appear! how languid, wan, and weak!

LIX

Match me, ye climes! which poets love to laud;
Match me, ye harems of the land! where now
I strike my strain, far distant, to applaud
Beauties that ev'n a cynic must avow;
Match me[3] those Houries, whom ye scarce allow
To taste the gale lest Love should ride the wind[4],
With Spain's dark-glancing daughters—deign to know
There your wise Prophet's paradise we find,
His black-eyed maids of Heaven, angelically kind.

Apostrophe au Parnasse. — Strophes sur la poésie antique et sur les poètes modernes. Byron explique qu'il a écrit *Childe*

1. *The seal Love's finger*, pour *the seal that...* le sceau que le doigt de l'Amour y a marqué. Ici encore Byron se souvient de ses lectures. Aulu-Gelle avait parlé de la fossette du menton dans les mêmes termes : *Sigilla in mento impressa amoris digitulo vestigio demonstrant mollitudinem.*

2. *Hath Phœbus...* Sens général : leur teint brûlé (courtisé) du soleil amoureux n'en a que plus de charme.

3. *Match me... with..!* Comparez-moi avec ces Espagnoles les Houris orientales!

4. *Ride the wind*, chevaucher le vent.

Harold en Grèce, en Turquie : "*where now I strike my strain*" (str. LIX) ; "*Parnassus whom I now survey*" (str. LX). Il est à Delphes en 1809, et il ne résiste pas à la pensée qui l'écarte un moment de la péninsule espagnole (Str. LX à LXIII.)

LX

Oh, thou Parnassus! whom I now survey,
Not in the phrensy of a dreamer's[1] eye,
Not in the fabled landscape of a lay,
But soaring snow-clad through thy native sky
In the wild pomp of mountain-majesty!
What marvel if I thus essay to sing?
The humblest of thy pilgrims passing by
Would gladly woo thine Echoes with his string,
Though from thy heights no more one Muse will wave her wing.

LXI

Oft have I dreamed of Thee! whose glorious name
Who knows not[2], knows not man's divinest lore :
And now I view thee, 'tis, alas, with shame
That I in feeblest accents must adore.
When I recount thy worshippers of yore
I tremble, and can only bend the knee ;
Nor raise my voice, nor vainly dare to soar,
But gaze beneath thy cloudy canopy
In silent joy to think at last I look on Thee!

---

1. *Dreamer.* Les poètes casaniers ne voient le Parnasse qu'en rêve. Byron l'a vu en rêve (*I have dreamed*, stance LXI) et en réalité. Les stances qu'on lit ici sont émues, pleines d'un sentiment vrai et grave, c'est l'éloge passionné de la poésie antique. Byron lutte avec Virgile, se disant comme lui *Musarum ingenti percussus amore*.

2. *Whose..... who knows not.* Quiconque l'ignore, ignore la plus divine des sciences humaines. — Construction tout anglaise.

LXII

Happier in this than mightiest bards have been,
Whose fate to distant homes confined their lot,
Shall I unmoved behod the hallow'd scene,
Which others rave of, though they know it not?
Though here no more Apollo haunts his grot,
And thou, the Muses' seat art now their grave,
Some gentle spirit still pervades the spot,
Sighs in the gale, keeps silence in the cave,
And glides with glassy foot o'er yon melodious wave.

LXIII

Of thee hereafter[1].—Even amidst my strain
I turned aside to pay my homage here;
Forgot the land, the sons, the maids of Spain;
Her fate, to every freeborn bosom dear;
And hail'd thee, not perchance without a tear.
Now to my theme—but from thy holy haunt
Let me some remnant, some memorial bear;
Yield me one leaf[2] of Daphne's deathless plant,
Now let thy votary's hope be deemed an idle vaunt.

Retour à l'Espagne. — Cadix, héritière de Paphos (LXIV à LXVII).

LXIV

But ne'er didst thou, fair Mount! when Greece was young
See round thy giant base a brighter choir,

---

1. *Of thee hereafter.* De toi (je parlerai) plus loin encore.
2. *One leaf.* Le poète ne veut qu'une feuille de laurier, mais il rêve l'immortalité et l'avoue. (Voy. la *Biographie.*)

Nor e'er did Delphi, when her priestess sung
The Pythian hymn with more than mortal fire,
Behold a train[1] more fitting to inspire
The song of love, than Andalusia's maids,
Nurst in the glowing lap of soft desire :
Ah! that to these were given such peaceful shades
As Greece can still bestow, though Glory fly her glades.

LXV

Fair is proud Seville; let her country boast
Her strength, her wealth, her site[2] of ancient days;
But Cadiz, rising on the distant coast,
Calls forth a sweeter, though ignoble praise[3].
Ah, Vice! how soft are thy voluptuous ways!
While boyish blood is mantling, who can 'scape
The fascination of thy magic gaze?
A Cherub-hydra[4] round us dost thou gape,
And mould to every taste thy dear delusive shape.

LXVI

When Paphos fell by Time—accursed Time!
The Queen[5] who conquers all must yield to thee –
The Pleasures fled, but sought as warm a clime;
And Venus, constant to her native sea,
To nought else constant, hither deign'd to flee,

---

1. *Behold a train.* Byron revient à l'Espagne par une transition un peu forcée.
2. *Her site,* sa situation prospère.
3. *Ignoble praise.* Cadix mérite qu'on la chante sans l'ennoblir, car le Vice y règne. On a souvent traduit sans exactitude ces vers, dans lesquels le poète, qui admire la Beauté, marque si bien qu'il n'admire pas le vice vulgaire.
4. *A Cherub-hydra.* Tu es en même temps un chérubin et une hydre; tu changes de forme, selon le goût de chacun.
5. *The queen.* Vénus. D'ailleurs il la nomme plus bas.

And fix'd her shrine within these walls of white;
Though not to one dome circumscribeth she
Her worship, but, devoted to her rite,
A thousand altars¹ rise, for ever blazing bright.

LXVII

From morn till night, from night till startled Morn²
Peeps blushing on the revel's laughing crew,
The song is heard, the rosy garland worn;
Devices quaint, and frolics ever new,
Tread on each other's kibes. A long adieu
He bids to sober joy³ that here sojourns :
Nought interrupts the riot, though in lieu
Of true devotion monkish incense burns,
And love and prayer unite, or rule the hour by turns.

Les fêtes et les dimanches de l'Andalousie, en opposition aux fêtes et aux dimanches du Nord. (Str. LXVIII à LXXI.)

LXVIII

The Sabbath⁴ comes, a day of blessed rest :
What hallows it upon this Christian shore?
Lo! it is sacred to a solemn feast :

1. *Though...* et plus bas *a thousand altars.* Traduisez : D'ailleurs la volupté a des autels sans nombre, ailleurs et à Cadix.

2. *Startled Morn...* L'aurore étonnée voit revenir la bande rieuse des gens de plaisir, dans cette ville où les folies se suivent de si près qu'elles marchent les unes sur les autres (mot à mot sur les cors ou les engelures, *kibes,* les unes des autres). Expression vulgaire, comme Byron en avait mis beaucoup dans la première façon de son poème satirique.

3. *Sober joy.* Le plaisir sage, celui qui est délicat et contenu.

4. *The Sabbath,* doit être ici entendu comme le dimanche, jour de repos.

Hark! heard you not the forest-monarch's[1] roar?
Crashing the lance, he snuff's the spouting gore
Of man and steed, o'erthrown beneath his horn;
The throng'd arena shakes with shouts for more;
Yells the mad crowd o'er entrails freshly torn,
Nor shrinks the female eye, nor ev'n affects to mourn.

LXIX

The seventh day this; the jubilee of man.
London! right well thou know'st the day of prayer:
Then thy spruce citizen, wash'd artizan,
And smug apprentice gulp their weekly air[2]:
Thy coach of hackney[3] whiskey, one-horse chair,
And humblest gig through sundry suburbs whirl;
To Hampstead, Brentford, Harrow[4] make repair;
Till the tired jade the wheel forgets to hurl,
Provoking envious gibe from each pedestrian churl.

LXX

Some o'er thy Thamis row the ribbon'd fair[5].
Others along the safer turnpike[6] fly;
Some Richmond-hill ascend, some scude to Ware,
And many to the steep of Highgate hie.

---

1. *The forest-monarch.* Le taureau, roi des forêts. Byron annonce qu'il va parler, plus loin, des fameux combats de taureaux, qui sont le jeu de l'Espagne.

2. *Their weekly air.* Ils ont un jour par semaine pour humer l'air « hebdomadaire » de la campagne.

3. *Thy coaches of hackney.....* Fiacres, whiskis (cabriolet léger), cabriolets et le petit gig (cabriolet sans capote), roulent vers les villages voisins, et l'on rit quand une haridelle ne peut plus avancer.

4. *Hampstead, Brentford, Harrow, Ware,* etc. Noms de la banlieue de Londres.

5. *The ribboned fair,* les beautés enrubannées.

6. *Turnpike,* les barrières à péage des routes anglaises. Ils suivent la route, ce qui est plus sûr.

Ask ye, Bœotian shades[1]! the reason why?
'T is to the worship of the solemn Horn[2],
Grasped in the holy hand of Mystery,
In whose dread name both men and maids are sworn,
And consecrate the oath with draught, and dance till morn.

LXXI

All have their fooleries—not alike are thine,
Fair Cadiz, rising o'er the dark blue sea!
Soon as the matin bell proclaimeth nine,
Thy saint adorers count the rosary:
Much is the VIRGIN teased to shrive them free
(Well do I ween the only virgin there)
From crimes as numerous as her beadsmen be;
Then to the crowded circus[3] forth they fare:
Young, old, high, low, at once the same diversion share.

Les combats de taureaux. (Str. LXXII à LXXIX.)

LXXII

The lists are oped[4], the spacious area clear'd,
Thousands on thousands piled are seated round;
Long ere the first loud trumpet's note is heard,

---

1. *Bœotian shades*. Byron écrivait cette stance à Thèbes, dans la ville traditionnelle des énigmes.
2. *The solemn Horn*. La corne traditionnelle. Dans les cabarets, on conservait l'usage de jurer sur une paire de cornes, que l'on s'ascrait le plus et le mieux possible. Ces facéties, venues du moyen âge, avaient l'air d'un mystère bachique.
3. *Circus*. L'enceinte destinée aux combats de taureaux.
4. *Oped.* La lice est ouverte. *Oped*, de *ope* qui a été remplacé par *open*, d'où *opened*.

Ne vacant space for lated wight is found:
Here dons, grandees, but chiefly dames abound[1],
Skill'd in the ogle of a roguish eye,
Yet ever well inclined to heal the wound;
None through their cold disdain are, doom'd to die,
As moon-struck bards complain, by Love's sad archery[2].

LXXIII

Hush'd is[3] the din of tongues—on gallant steeds,
With milk-withe crest, gold spur, and light-poised lance,
Four cavaliers prepare for venturous deeds,
And lowly bending to the lists advance;
Rich are their scarfs, their chargers featly prance:
If in the dangerous game they shine to-day,
The crowd's loud shout and ladies' lovely glance,
Best prize of better acts, they bear away,
And all that kings or chiefs e'er gain their toils repay.

LXXIV

In costly sheen and gaudy cloak array'd,
But all afoot, the light-limb'd Matadore[4]
Stands in the centre, eager to invade
The lord of lowing herds; but not before
The ground, with cautious tread, is traversed o'er,

---

1. *Dons, grandees..... abound.* Ici abondent les *dons*, les *grands*... Don (*dominus*, seigneur) est un titre d'honneur qui se place devant le prénom. Il est aussi commun en Espagne que le mot monsieur en France ; la *Grandeur* est la première distinction en Espagne.

2. *Sad archery*, les flèches meurtrières. Parodie du style langoureux.

3. *Hushed is.* On fait silence ; le bruit des langues s'apaise.

4. *Matadore.* Le *matador*, c'est-à-dire le tueur, de *matar*, tuer (*mactare*). Le *matador* agit le dernier ; c'est celui qui, dans une course de taureaux, est chargé d'achever d'un coup l'animal blessé.

Lest aught unseen should lurk to thwart his speed :
His arms a dart, he fights aloof, nor more
Can man achieve without the friendly steed—
Alas! too oft condemn'd for him to bear and leed.

LXXV

Thrice sounds the clarion; lo! the signal falls [1],
The den expands, and Expectation mute
Gapes round the silent circle's peopled walls.
Bounds with one lashing spring the mighty brute,
And, wildly staring, spurns, with sounding foot,
The sand, nor blindly rushes [2] on his foe :
Here, there, he points his threatening front, to suit
His first attack, wide waving to and fro
His angry tail; red rolls his eye's dilated glow.

LXXVI

Sudden he stops; his eye is fixed : away,
Away thou heedless boy! prepare the spear :
Now is thy time to perish, or display
The skill that yet may check his mad career.
With well-timed croupe the nimble coursers veer [3];

Byron se préoccupe peu de distinguer ici les divers *toreros*. Il y a les *picadores*, les *chulos*, les *banderilleros*, qui excitent et percent le taureau ; puis un seul homme, le tueur. Le poète se trompe lorsque plus loin il parle de plusieurs *matadores;* mais il pense à peindre les mœurs d'une nation plutôt que les usages des *toreros*.

1. *The signal falls*. Le signal tombe, on donne le signal. Le président de la course, qui est ordinairement l'*alcade* (maire), jette de sa loge dans l'arène la clef de l'écurie où est enfermé le taureau.

2. *Not... rushes*. Mais il ne se rue pas.

3. *With well-timed croupe... veer*. — Le cheval vire avec un mouvement de croupe qui ramasse l'arrière-train et qui est bien réglé, appris au manège, dit Byron. Comparez Webster : *Croupade*, « *a leap in which the horse pulls up his hind legs toward his belly*. »

On foams the bull, but not unscathed he goes;
Streams from his flank the crimso torrent clear:
He flies, he wheels, distracted with his troes;
Dart follows dart; lance, lance; loud bellowings speak
   his woes.

LXXVII.

Again he comes; nor dart nor lance avail
Nor the wild plunging of the tortured horse [1];
Though man and man's avenging arms assail,
Vain are his weapons, vainer is his force.
One gallant steed is stretch'd a mangled corse;
Another, hideous sight! unseam'd appears,
His gory chest unveils life's panting source;
Though death-struck, still his feeble frame he rears;
  Staggering, but stemming all, his lord unharm'd he
   bears.

LXXVIII

Foil'd bleeding, breathless, furious to the last,
Full in the centre stands the bull at bay [2],
Mid wounds, and clinging darts, and lances brast [3],
And foes disabled in the brutal fray:
And now the Matadores around him play,
Shake the red cloak, and poise the ready brand:
Once more through all he bursts his thundering way—
Vain rage! the mantle quits the conynge [4] hand,
  Wraps his fierce eye—'tis past—he sinks upon the sand!

---

1. *The tortured horse.* Le malheureux cheval, monté par un *picador* et destiné à mo rir, est réellement torturé par de forts éperons du cavalier et par le taureau, qui souvent le soulève sur ses cornes.

2. *At bay,* aux abois.

3. *Brast,* archaïsme pour *burst.*

4. *Conynge,* pour *cunnings* habile. Comparez *keen,* pénétrant.

LXXIX

Where his vast neck just mingles with the spine,
Sheathed in his form the deadly weapon dies.
He stops—he starts—disdaining to decline[1]:
Slowly he falls, amidst triumphant cries,
Without a groan, without a struggle dies.
The decorated car appears—on high
The corse is piled—sweet sight for vulgar eyes—
Four steeds that spurn[2] the rein, as swift as shy,
Hurl the dark bulk along, scarce seen in dashing by[3].

Les mœurs espagnoles. — Les vengeances. — La liberté des femmes. — Harold est blasé. Stances désespérées à Inez. (Str. LXXX à LXXXIV.)

LXXX

Such the ungentle sport that oft invites
The Spanish maid, and cheers[4] the Spanish swain[5].
Nurtured in blood betimes, his heart delights
In vengeance, gloating on another's pain.
What private feuds the troubled village stain!
Though[6] now one phalanx'd host should meet the foe.
Enough, alas! in humble homes remain,
To meditate 'gainst friends the secret blow,
For some slight cause of wrath, whence life's warm stream must flow.

---

1. *Decline*, se détourner, battre en retraite.
2. *Spurn*, dédaigner. — Sens premier, frapper du pied (voy. str. LXXV): *and, wildly staring, spurns with; sounding foot.* — Sens dérivé, repousser du pied, puis rejeter, dédaigner.

3. *In dashing by*, en passant comme un trait.
4. *Cheers*, ravit.
5. *Swain*, le jeune homme.
6. *Though... etc.* Ils sont à l'armée, mais il en reste dans les chaumières.

LXXXI

But Jealousy[1] has fled: his bars, his bolts,
His wither'd sentinel, Duenna sage!
And all whereat the generous soul revolts,
Wich the stern dotard deemed he could encage,
Have passed to darkness with the vanish'd age,
Who late so free as Spanish girls were seen
(Ere War uprose in his volcanic rage),
With braided tresses bounding o'er the green,
While on the gay dance shone Night's lover-loving[2] Queen?

LXXXII

Oh! many a time and oft, had Harold loved,
Or dream'd he loved, since rapture is a dream;
But now his wayward bosom was unmoved,
For not yet[3] had he drunk of Lethe's stream;
And lately had he learn'd with truth to deem
Love has no gift so grateful as his wings:
How fair, how young, how soft soe'er he seem,
Full from the fount of Joy's delicious springs
Some bitter[4] o'er the flowers its bubbling venom flings.

---

1. *But jealousy.* — Cette stance, qui est une transition un peu forcée à un autre sujet, peut être comprise comme une allusion au *Barbier de Séville.* Les femmes espagnoles, dit Byron, ne sont plus, comme Rosine, enfermées sous les verrous de Bartolo.

2. *Lover-loving.* La reine de la Nuit aimant ceux qui aiment.

3. *For not yet...* Il n'avait pas encore oublié ses récentes déceptions. Le poète se contredit : son héros est changeant.

4. *Some bitter*, quelque chose d'amer. Rapprochez de ces mots le *amari aliquid* de Lucain, dans ces vers : ...*medio de fonte leporum Surgit amari aliquid quod in ipsis floribus angat.*

LXXXIII

Yet to the beauteous form he was not blind,
Though now it moved him as it moves the wise;
Not that Philosophy on such a mind
E'er deign'd to bend her chastely-awful eyes:
But[1] Passion raves itself[2] to rest, or flies;
And Vice, that digs her own voluptuous tomb,
Had buried long his hopes, no more to rise:
Pleasure's pall'd victim! life-abhorring gloom
Wrote on his faded brow curst Cain's unresting doom.

LXXXIV

Still he beheld, nor mingled with the throng[3];
But view'd them not with misanthropic hate:
Fain would he now have join'd the dance, the song;
But who may smile that sinks beneath his fate?
Nought that he saw his sadness could abate:
Yet once he struggled 'gainst the demon's sway,
And as in Beauty's bower[4] he pensive sate,
Poured forth this unpremeditated lay.
To charms as fair as those that soothed his happier day.

---

1. *Yet... On* remarquera ici surtout ces particules restrictives *yet. Though... Not that... But...* — Byron, faisant ici son propre portrait, multiplie les nuances et les restrictions. C'est le défaut de la poésie personnelle.

2. *Raves itself to rest*, s'emporte jusqu'à épuiser ses forces et s'arrêter.

3. *The throng*, la foule. Ce mot est le complément tout à la fois du verbe *beheld* et de la préposition *with*.

4. *In Beauty's bower*, dans le salon d'une femme. Voir *bower* employé dans un sens analogue (strophe IX). Byron intercale ici un chant composé plus tard.

TO INEZ.

1

Nay, smile not at my sullen brow;
　　Alas! I cannot smile again:
Yet Heaven avert[1] that ever thou
　　Shouldst weep, and haply weep in vain.

2

And dost thou ask what secret woe
　　I bear, corroding joy and youth?
And wilt thou vainly seek to know
　　A pang, even thou must fail to soothe[2]?

3

It is not love, it is not hate,
　　Nor low Ambition's honours lost,
That bids me loathe my present state,
　　And fly from all I prized the most:

4

It is that weariness which springs
　　From all I meet, or hear, or see:
To me no pleasure Beauty brings;
　　Thine eyes have scarce a charm for me.

---

1. *Heaven avert...* Que le ciel écarte... C'est la formule latine: *Di omen avertant!*

2. *Fail to soothe.* Tu ne réussirais pas à calmer la douleur; tu faillirais à la tâche.

5

It is that settled, ceaseless[1] gloom
  The fabled Hebrew[2] wanderer bore,
That will not look beyond the tomb,
  But cannot hope for rest before.

6

What Exile from himself can flee?
  To zones though more and more remote,
Still, still pursues where'er I be,
  The blight of life—the demon Thought[3].

7

Yet others rapt in pleasure seem,
  And taste of all that I forsake;
Oh! may they still of transport dream,
  And ne'er, at least like me, awake!

8

Through many a clime 'tis mine[4] to go,
  With many a retrospection curst;
And all my solace is to know,
  Whate'er betides, I've known the worst.

---

1. *Settled, ceaseless*, définitive et constante.
2. *The fabled Hebrew*, l'Hébreu légendaire. C'est le Juif errant.
3. *The demon Thought*. Le démon (qu'on appelle) la Pensée me poursuit en quelque lieu que je puisse aller. Ici l'inversion est destinée à faire porter toute la phrase sur le dernier mot.
4. *'Tis mine.* C'est mon destin, mon lot.

9

What is that worst? Nay do not ask—
In pity from the search forbear:
Smile on—nor venture to unmask
Man's heart, and view the Hell that's there.

Adieux à l'Espagne. — Dernier salut à son génie indépendant. Dernier appel à la guerre. (Str. LXXXV à XC.)

LXXXV

Adieu, fair Cadiz! yea, a long adieu!
Who may forget how well thy walls have stood?
When all were changing thou alone wert true,
First to be free, and last to be subdued:
And if amidst a scene, a shock so rude,
Some native blood was seen thy streets to dye,
A traitor [1] only fell beneath the feud:
Here all were noble, save Nobility;
None hugg'd a conqueror's chain, save fallen Chivalry!

LXXXVI

Such be [2] the sons of Spain, and strange her fate!
They fight for freedom who were never free,

---

1. *A traitor.* Solano, gouverneur de Cadix, fut assassiné comme traître au moment où Cadix résolut de résister aux étrangers.

2. *Such be.* On sait que *be* s'emploie, dans Shakspeare et parmi le peuple, pour tous les modes du présent du verbe. — Byron peint ici l'étrange histoire de l'Espagne, la première des nations pour défendre son indépendance contre l'étranger, et l'une de celles qui ont compris le plus tard la liberté véritable.

A kingless[1] people for a nerveless state;
Her vassals combat when their chieftains flee,
True to the veriest slaves of Treachery:
Fond of a land which gave them nought but life,
Pride points the path that leads to Liberty;
Back to the struggle, baffled in the strife,
War, war is still the cry, " War even to the knife[2]!"

LXXXVII

Ye, who[3] would more of Spain and Spaniards know,
Go, read whate'er is writ of bloodiest strife:
Whate'er keen Vengeance urged on foreign foe
Can act, is acting there against man's life:
From flashing scimitar to secret knife,
War mouldeth there each weapon to his need—
So may he guard the sister and the wife,
So may he make each curst oppressor bleed—
So may such foes deserve the most remorseless deed!

LXXXVIII

Flows there a tear of pity for the dead?
Look o'er the ravage of the reeking plain;
Look on the hands with female slaughter red[4];
Then to the dogs resign the unburied slain,
Then to the vulture let each corse remain,

---

1. *Kingless.* — L'Espagne était sans roi, Charles IV étant prisonnier.

2. *Even to the knife.* « Nous ferons la guerre au couteau », disait Palafox, le défenseur de Saragosse, quand on lui représentait qu'il était sans armée.

3. *Ye, who.* Vous qui voulez connaître l'Espagne...Cette strophe noble a remplacé les premiers vers que Byron avait écrits contre un certain Carr, lequel publiait alors un mauvais livre sur l'Espagne. Ces vers étaient mauvais et pleins de personnalités stériles.

4. *Female slaughter*, les mains rougies en massacrant des femmes.

Albeit unworthy of the prey-bird's maw;
Let their bleach'd bones, and blood's unbleaching stain
Long mark the battle-field with hideous awe:
Thus only may our sons conceive the scenes we saw!

LXXXIX

Nor yet, alas! the dreadful work is done;
Fresh legions [1] pour adown the Pyrenees:
It deepens still, the work is scarce begun,
Nor mortal eye the distant end foresees.
Fall'n nations gaze on Spain; if freed, she frees
More than her fell Pizarros once enchain'd:
Strange retribution! now Columbia's ease
Repairs the wrongs that Quito's sons [2] sustain'd,
While o'er the parent clime prowls Murder unrestrain'd.

XC

Not all the blood at Talavera [3] shed,
Not all the marvels of Barossa's fight,
Not Albuera lavish of the dead,
Have won for Spain her well asserted right.
When shall her Olive-branch [4] be free froom blight?
When shall she breathe her from the blushing toil?
How many a doubtful day shall sink in night,

---

1. *Fresh legions...* Les Français descendent des Pyrénées!.. De même le poète italien Boiardo, qui avait écrit tout un ouvrage burlesque contre la France et Roland, le héros français, s'arrête tout à coup et s'écrie : « Pendant que je raille, les Français descendent des Alpes!... »

2. *Quito's sons.* Les colonies espagnoles s'entr'aident, tandis qu la mère patrie est déchirée.
En 1809 et 1810, Quito, le Mexique, la Plata, se révoltèrent presque ensemble.

3. *Talavera, Barossa, Albuera*, noms de batailles livrées par l'Espagne.

4. *Olive-branch.* Les oliviers de la terre espagnole.

Ere the Frank robber turn him from his spoil,
And Freedom's stranger-tree grow native of the soil!

Les morts. — Pensée de Byron pour ceux qu'il a perdus. (Str. xci à xciii.)

XCI.

And thou[1], my friend!—since unavailing woe
  Bursts from my heart, and mingles with the strain—
Had the sword laid thee[2] with the mighty low,
  Pride might forbid e'en Friendship to complain:
But thus unlaurel'd to descend in vain,
  By all forgotten, save the lonely breast,
And mix unbleeding with the boasted slain,
  While Glory crowns so many a meaner crest!
What hadst thou done to sink so peacefully to rest?

XCII

Oh, known the earliest, and esteem'd the most!
  Dear to a heart where nought was left so dear!
Though to my hopeless days for ever lost,
  In dreams deny me not to see thee here!
And Morn in secret shall renew the tear
  Of Consciousness awaking to her woes,
And Fancy hover o'er thy bloodless bier,
  Till my frail frame return to whence it rose
And mourn'd and mourner lie united in repose[3].

---

1. *And thou.* Et toi.—John Wingfield, officier aux gardes, mourut de la fièvre à Coïmbre, en 1811. » Je l'avais connu dix ans, écrit Byron, la meilleure moitié de sa vie et la plus heureuse partie de la mienne. »

2. *Laid thee.* Réunissez *laid low*, couché à terre, abattu.

3. *In repose.* Ici Byron ajoutait

XCIII

Here is one fytte[1] of Harold's pilgrimage:
Ye who of him may further seek to know,
Shall find some tidings in a future page,
If he that rhymeth now may scribble moe[2].
Is this too much? stern Critic! say not so:
Patience! and ye shall hear what he beheld
In other lands, where he was doom'd to go:
Lands that contain the monuments of Eld[3],
Ere Greece and Grecian arts by barbarous hands were quelled.

---

dans une note en prose : « J'aurais dû peut-être consacrer quelques vers à la mémoire de Charles Caradit Mathews, agrégé du collège Downing, à Cambridge, mais il était trop au-dessus de mes louanges.

1. *Fytte*, archaïsme, un chant.
2. *Moe*, pour *more*.
3. *Eld*, l'antiquité, à rapprocher des mots plus connus, *old*, *elder*.

ARGUMENT ANALYTIQUE

DU CHANT DEUXIÈME

EN GRÈCE

Salut à Athéné, à Minerve, déesse de la pensée et de la sagesse, à son temple, le Parthénon. — Salut aux ruines illustres, et, à ce sujet, digression sur la mort, et sur la caducité des choses humaines. Y a-t-il une autre vie? Méditation sur les crânes vides qui ont été le séjour de la pensée. (Strophes I à X.)

La profanation des ruines. — Anathème contre ceux qui achètent et emportent les débris des monuments grecs. (Str. X à XV.)

En mer. — La traversée d'Espagne en Grèce. — Après les quinze premières strophes, qui forment une sorte d'exorde, et sont adressées directement au pays qui est l'objet même du chant IIe, Byron reprend l'histoire de son voyage et conduit Childe Harold à travers la Méditerranée. (Str. XVI à XVII.)

Le départ. — A bord. Un navire anglais. Éloge de la marine et de la discipline anglaises. Gibraltar. (Str. XVIII à XXIII.)

La Méditation et la Solitude — Les souvenirs d'affection. — Les solitaires du mont Athos. (Str. XXIII à XXVII.)

La beauté. — Celle des femmes ne vaut pas celle de la Nature. — Digression sur l'île de Calypso et de la rencontre que fait Byron de Mrs. Spencer Smith, qu'il appelle Florence. — Childe Harold est étranger à l'amour. (Str. XXVIII à XXXVII.)

En vue de la Grèce. — L'Albanie. — Le pays de Pénélope et de Sapho. — Souvenirs historiques et militaires. — Aspect sauvage du pays. — La croix et le croissant. (Str. XXXVIII à XLV.)

Voyage en Albanie. — Le couvent de Zitza. Le repos. — La grandeur de la nature. — Dodone. Où est-elle? (Str. XLVI à LIII.)

En Illyrie. — Visite à Tepalen et à la cour d'Ali-Pacha. — Le monde et le luxe musulmans. (Str. LIV à LXIV.)

Les Albanais. — Éloge de ces montagnards. — La danse et le chant de guerre des Palikares à Utrakey. (Str. LXV à LXXII.)

Un chant de guerre, composé par Byron, d'après les chants du pays. (Str. LXXII à LXXIII.)

La Grèce. — Misère et grandeur de ce pays. — Invective contre l'insouciance de la Grèce esclave. (Str. LXXIII à LXXVIII.)

Constantinople. — Une nuit sur les rives du Bosphore. (Str. LXXIX à LXXX.)

Retour aux Grecs et à la Grèce. — Nouvel appel à l'insurrection. — Magnificence de la contrée et de ses ruines de son histoire. — Souvenir de Marathon. — Respect que mérite ce pays. (Str. LXXXII à XCIII.)

Épilogue, ajouté par Byron au chant IIe. — Sa tristesse. Sa solitude morale. Ses affections perdues. (De la strophe XCIV à la fin.)

CANTO THE SECOND

Salut à Athéné, à Minerve, déesse de la pensée et de la sagesse, à son temple, le Parthénon. — Salut aux ruines illustres, et à ce sujet, digression sur la mort et sur la caducité des choses humaines. Y a-t-il une autre vie? Méditation sur les crânes vides, qui ont été le séjour de la pensée. (Str. I à X.)

I

Come, blue-eyed maid of heaven! — but thou, alas!
Didst never yet one mortal song inspire —
Goddess of Wisdom! here thy temple was,
And is, despite of war and wasting fire [1],
And years, that bade thy worship to expire:
But worse [2] than steel, and flame, and ages slow,
Is the dread sceptre and dominion dire
Of men who never felt the sacred glow
That thoughts of thee and thine on polish'd breasts bestow [3].

II

Ancient of days [4]! august Athena! where,
Where are thy men of might? thy grand in soul?

---

1. *Wasting fire.* Les Turcs ayant installé dans l'Acropole une poudrière, elle sauta à l'époque où les Vénitiens bombardèrent la ville, et une partie du temple fut détruite par le feu.

2. *But worse... is the sceptre... of men.* — Le joug des Turcs est pire que la faux du Temps.

3. *Polished breasts.* — Les âmes que l'art et la science ont en quelque sorte polies.

4. *Ancient of days!* — Expression biblique, appliquée par les protestants au Dieu unique et éternel. Byron l'applique à Athènes, à la métropole du polythéisme hellénique. On trouvera, dans les strophes suivantes, plusieurs allusions du même genre, dont la portée n'est pas

Gone—glimmering [1] through the dream of things that [were
First in the race that led to Glory's goal,
They won, and pass'd away—is this the whole?
A schoolboy's tale, the wonder of an hour!
The warrior's weapon and the sophist's stole
Are sought in vain, and o'er each mouldering tower,
Dim with the mist of years, gray flits [2] the shade of power.

III

Son of the morning [3], rise! approad you here:
Come—but molest not yon defenceless urn:
Look on this spot—a nation's sepulchre!
Abode of gods, whose shrines no longer burn.
Even gods must yield [4]— religions take their turn:
'Twas Jove's—tis Mahomet's—and other creeds
Will rise with other years, till man shall learn [5]
Vainly his incense soars, his victim bleeds;
Poor child of Doubt and Death, whose hope is built on reeds.

IV

Bound to the earth, he lifts his eye to heaven—
Is't not enough, unhappy thing! to know

douteuse, et qui révèlent l'intention hostile de tout ce passage. Byron attaque les « saints personnages » (strophe VIII) qui prêchent la supériorité de la religion chrétienne : « Toute religion a son heure », dit-il (strophe III). Il raille ceux qui croient à l'immortalité de l'âme et leurs « milliers d'homélies » (strophe IV). Ses sarcasmes étaient encore plus directs dans la rédaction primitive du poème : il a supprimé la strophe la plus violente.

1. *Glimmering*. Opposez *glimmer*, jeter une faible lueur, à *glow* (strophe I), qui indique la lumière éclatante et la flamme vive.
2. *Gray flits*, devient grise, pâle, et s'évanouit.
3. *Son of the morning*. — Fils de l'Orient, c'est-à-dire tout ce qui n'est pas grec, aussi bien le Juif que le Turc. C'est une expression employée dans la Bible et appliquée à Lucifer; le poète la détourne de son sens.
4. *Yield*, céder au temps.
5. *Learn vainly*, pour *learn that vainly*.

Thou art? Is this a boon[1] so kindly given,
That being, thou wouldst be again, and go,
Thou know'st not, reck'st not to what region, so[2]
On earth no more, but mingled with the skies?
Still wilt thou dream on future joy and woe?
Regard and weigh yon dust before it flies :
That little urn saith more than thousand homilies.

V

Or burst the vanish'd Hero's lofty mound[3];
Far on the solitary shore he sleeps :
He fell, and falling nations mourn'd around;
But now not one[4] of saddening thousands weeps,
Nor warlike worshipper his vigil keeps
Where demi-gods appear'd, as records tell.
Remove yon skull from out the scatter'd heaps :
Is that a temple where a God may dwell?
Why ev'n the worm at last disdains her shatter'd cell!

VI

Look on its broken arch[5], its ruin'd wall,
Its chambers desolate, and portals foul :
Yes, this was once Ambition's airy hall,
The dome of Thought, the palace of the Soul :

1. *A boon.* La vie est-elle donc un bien si généreusement accordé à l'homme?
2. *So,* pourvu que.
3. *Hero's lofty mound.* La tombe d'Ajax.
4. *Not one of...* Personne ne veille sur cette terre des demi-dieux, pas un de ces millions d'hommes qui sont supposés le regretter, pas une cipuse sentinelle!

5. *Broken arch,* la voûte brisée. Toute la strophe est dirigée contre ceux qui disent comme la Bible : « Vous êtes le temple du Dieu vivant. » Lord Byron s'écrie, en prenant un crâne : *Is that a temple?* On comparera ce passage à la page, très supérieure, de Shakespeare, sur la fragilité de la vie humaine (*Hamlet*, acte V, scène I).

Behold through each lack-lustre, eyeless hole,
The gay recess of Wisdom and of Wit
And Passion's host, that never brook'd control :
Can all saint, sage, or sophist ever writ,
People this lonely tower, this tenement refit?

VII

Well didst thou speak, Athena's wisest son!
" All that we know is, nothing can be known. "
Why should we shrink from what we cannot shun?
Each hath his pang, but feeble sufferers[1] groan
With brain-born dreams of evil all their own[2].
Pursue what Chance or Fate proclaimeth best;
Peace waits us on the shores of Acheron :
There no forced banquet claims the sated guest,
But Silence spreads the couch of ever welcome rest.

VIII

Yet if, as holiest men have deem'd; there be
A land of souls beyond that sable shore,
To shame[3] the doctrine of the Sadducee
And sophists, madly vain of dubious lore ;
How sweet it were in concert to adore
With those who made our mortal labours light !
To hear each voice we fear'd to hear no more !
Behold each mighty shade reveal'd to sight,
The Bactrian, Samian sage[4] and all who taught the right!

---

1. *Feeble sufferers.* Ceux qui n'ont pas la force de souffrir.
2. *All their own.* Ils se plaignent d'un mal qui est entièrement de leur fait.
3. *To shame,* pour confondre les saducéens. La secte juive des saducéens niait l'immortalité de l'âme.
4. *Bactrian, Samian.* — Le sage de la Bactriane est Zoroastre; le sage de Samos est Pythagore.

IX

There, thou[1]!—whose love and life together fled,
Have left me here to love and live in vain—
Twined with my heart, and can I deem thee dead
When busy Memory flashes on my brain?
Well—I will dream that we may meet again,
And woo the vision to my vacant breast:
If aught of young Remembrance then remain,
Be as it may Futurity's behest,
For me 't were bliss enough to know thy spirit blest!

X

Here let me sit upon this massy stone [2]
The marble column's yet unshaken base;
Here, son of Saturn! was thy fav'rite throne:
Mightiest of many such! Hence let me trace
The latent grandeur of thy dwelling-place.
It may not be[3], nor ev'n can Fancy's eye
Restore what Time hath labour'd to deface.
Ye these proud pillars claim no passing sigh[4];
Unmoved the Moslem sits, the light Greek carols by.

---

1. *There, thou!* — C'est ici que je devrais parler de toi. — Byron, admettant qu'il y a une autre vie, voudrait y retrouver une personne aimée, dont il garde le souvenir plein de jeunesse et qu'il ne nomme pas (voy. plus loin la strophe xcv).

2. *This massy stone.* — Il s'agit ici des ruines du temple de Jupiter Olympien, si célèbre, et dont tous les voyageurs ont parlé. Il fallut des siècles pour l'achever.

3. *It may not be.* — Il est impossible de décrire ce temple.

4. *Passing sigh*, la pitié du passant.

La profanation des ruines. — Anathème contre ceux qui achètent et qui emportent les débris des monuments grecs. (Str. x à xv).

XI

But who[1], of all the plunderers of yon fane
On high, where Pallas linger'd, loth to flee
The latest relic of her ancient reign ;
The last, the worst, dull spoiler, who was he ?
Blush, Caledonia ! such thy son could be !
England ! I joy no child he was of thine :
Thy free-born men should spare what once was free ;
Yet they could violate each saddening shrine,
And bear these altars o'er the long-reluctant[2] brine.

XII

But most the modern Pict's ignoble boast[3]
To rive what Goth, and Turk, and Time hath spared :
Cold as the crags upon his native coast,
His mind as barren and his heart as hard,
Is he whose head conceived, whose hand prepared,
Aught to displace Athena's poor remains :
Her sons too weak the sacred shrine to guard,
Yet felt[4] some portion of their mother's pains,
And never knew, till then, the weight of Despot's chains.

---

1. *But who... was ?* — Mais qui fut le plus grand pillard ? Byron attaque ici l'ambassadeur d'Angleterre en Turquie, l'Ecossais lord Elgin, qui, après avoir terminé son ambassade, entreprit un voyage d'antiquaire en Grèce, consacra six années à relever le dessin des monuments, dépensa 1 300 000 francs à acquérir des statues, des sculptures, des débris de toute sorte, et forma la collection connue sous le nom de marbres d'Elgin. Le poète condamne les collectionneurs de cette nature (voy. plus loin, strophes XXIX et XCIII).

2. *The long-reluctant brine.* — La mer brisa dans l'Archipel le vaisseau qui emportait les ruines des temples.

3. *But most ignoble boast.* — Mais c'est le grossier triomphe, sous-entendu *is*.

4. *Yet felt...* Byron lui-même a

CANTO THE SECOND.

XIII

What! shall it e'er be said by British tongue,
Albion was happy in Athena's tears?
Though in thy name the slaves her bosom wrung [1],
Tell not the deed to blushing Europe's ears;
The ocean queen, the free Britannia, bears
The last poor plunder from a bleeding land :
Yes, she, whose gen'rous aid her name endears,
Tore down those remnants with a harpy's hand,
Which envious Eld forbore, and tyrants left to stand.

XIV

Where was thine Ægis, Pallas! that appall'd [2]
Stern Alaric and Havoc on their way?
Where Peleus' son? whom Hell in vain inthralled,
His shade from Hades upon that dread day
Bursting to light in terrible array!
What! could not Pluto spare the chief once more,
To scare a second robber from his prey?
Idly he wander'd on the Stygian shore,
Nor now preserved the walls he loved to shield before.

XV

Cold is the heart, fair Greece! that looks on thee,
Nor feels as lovers o'er the dust they loved;
Dull is the eye that will not weep to see

---

rédigé une note pour expliquer ce vers. « M. Clarke, dit-il, a vu le *Disdar* essayer une larme en présence des mutilations subies par le Parthénon, et s'écrier : Assez! »

1. *Her bosom wrung.* — Ils ont déchiré le sein d'Athènes en fouillant le sol et en arrachant les antiquités.

2. *Appalled stern Alaric.* — Ton égide, qui a fait pâlir le rude Alaric et la Dévastation. Allusion à un passage de Zosime, qui rapporte qu'Alaric recula devant les images de Minerve et d'Achille.

Thy walls defaced, thy mouldering shrines removed
By British hands, which it had best behoved
To guard those relics ne'er to be restored.
Curst be the hour [1] when from their isle they roved,
And once again thy hapless bosom gored,
And snatch'd thy shrinking Gods to northern climes abhorr'd!

En mer. — La traversée d'Espagne en Grèce.—Après les quinze premières strophes, qui forment une sorte d'exorde, et sont adressées directement au pays qui est l'objet même du chant II°, Byron reprend l'histoire de son voyage et conduit Childe Harold à travers la Méditerranée. (Str. XVI à XVII.)

XVI

But where is Harold? shall I then forget
To urge the gloomy wanderer o'er the wave?
Little reck'd he of all that men regret;
No loved-one [2] now in feign'd lament could rave [3];
No friend the parting hand extended gave,
Ere the cold stranger pass'd to other climes :
Hard is his heart whom charms may not enslave;
But Harold felt not as in other times,
And left without a sigh the land of war and crimes.

---

1. *Curst be the hour!...* Maudite soit l'heure de ces brigandages! Byron voulait que les ruines restassent là où l'histoire les a placées et où elles rendent la nature pittoresque. Sa colère était telle contre lord Elgin, qui avait osé faire graver sur une des colonnes du temple de Minerve son nom et celui de lady Elgin, que lui-même, Byron, monta jusqu'au haut de la colonne, effaça le nom du mari et laissa l'autre. Mais il convient de rappeler ici que les musées et les collectionneurs ont sauvé bien des monuments, et qu'avant lord Elgin on avait vu le comte d'Arundel rapporter de Paros, en 1627, les fameux *marbres* qui contiennent toute la chronologie grecque.

2. *No loved-one.* — Il n'y eut, au départ de Childe Harold, ni bien-aimée, ni ami, qui serrassent la main de celui qui partait (*the parting*).

3. *Rave*, délirer. C'est l'ancien sens du mot français *rêver*.

CANTO THE SECOND.

XVII

He that has sail'd upon the dark blue sea
Has view'd at times, I ween, a full fair sight;
When the fresh breeze is fair as breeze may be,
The white sail set¹, the gallant frigate tight;
Masts, spires, and strand retiring to the right,
The glorious main expanding o'er the bow²,
The convoy³ spread like wild swans in their flight,
The dullest sailer wearing bravely now,
So gaily curl the waves before each dashing prow.

Le départ. — A bord. Un navire anglais. Éloge de la marine et de la discipline anglaises. Gibraltar. (Str. XVIII à XXII.)

XVIII

And oh, the little warlike world⁴ within!
The well-reeved guns, the netted canopy⁵,
The hoarse command, the busy humming din,
When, at a word, the tops are mann'd on high :
Hark, to the Boatswain's call, the cheering cry!
While through the seaman's hand the tackle glides ;
Or schoolboy Midshipman that, standing by,
Strains his shrill pipe⁶ as good or ill betides,
And well the docile crew that skilful urchin guides.

---

1. *Sail set*, la voile mise au vent.
2. *O'er the bow*, à l'avant du navire. Le mot *bow*, qui marque la courbe et l'inclinaison, désigne, en termes de marine, le bossoir.
3. *The convoy*, la flotte. On voit qu'il s'agit de plusieurs navires marchant de conserve, ce qui expliquera la strophe XX.

4. *Warlike world.* — Le vaisseau est, en petit, le monde de la guerre.
5. *Netted canopy.* — Un filet tendu protège le tillac contre les éclats qui pourraient y tomber.
6. *His shrill pipe*, sa voix grêle et aiguë. *Pipe*, indiquant toute espèce de conduit, veut dire ici *larynx, gosier. voix.*

XIX

White is the glassy deck, without a stain,
Where on the watch [1] the staid Lieutenant walks :
Look on that part which sacred doth remain
For the lone chieftain, who majestic stalks,
Silent and fear'd by all—not oft he talks,
With aught beneath him, if he would preserve
That strict restraint, which broken, ever balks
Conquest and fame : but Britons rarely swerve
From law [2], however stern, which tends their strength to nerve.

XX

Blow ! swiftly blow, thou keel-compelling gale !
Till the broad sun withdraws his lessening ray ;
Then must the pennant bearer [3] slacken sail,
That lagging barks may make their lazy way.
Ah ! grievance sore [4], and listless dull delay,
To waste on sluggish hulks the sweetest breeze !
What leagues are lost, before the dawn of day,
Thus loitering pensive on the willing seas,
The flapping sail haul'd down to halt for logs like these !

XXI

The moon is up ; by Heaven, a lovely eve !
Long streams of light o'er dancing waves expand ;

---

1. *On the watch,* de quart.
2. *Rarely swerve from law.* — Les Anglais respectent la loi. Byron, sur mer, redevient Anglais, et s'oublie jusqu'à louer l'Angleterre.
3. *Pennant-bearer,* le porte-pennon, c'est-à-dire le vaisseau qui porte le pavillon et dirige les autres.
4. *Ah! grievance sore!* mortel ennui! Byron se fâche d'être obligé d'attendre les navires mauvais marcheurs.

CANTO THE SECOND. 75

Now lads on shore may sigh, and maids believe[1]:
Such be our fate when we return to land !
Meantime some rude Arion's[2] restless hand
Wakes the brisk harmony that sailors love ;
A circle there of merry listeners stand,
Or[3] to some well-known measure featly move,
Thoughtless, as if on shore they still were free to rove.

XXII

Through Calpe's straits[4] survey the steepy shore ;
Europe and Afric on each other gaze !
Lands of the dark-eyed Maid[5] and dusky Moor
Alike beheld beneath pale Hecate's blaze :
How softly on the Spanish shore she plays[6],
Disclosing rock, and slope, and forest brown,
Distinct, though darkening with her waning phase ;
But Mauritania's giant-shadows frown,
From mountain-cliff to coast descending sombre down.

La Méditation et la Solitude. — Les souvenirs d'affection. — Les solitaires du mont Athos. (Str. XXIII à XXVII).

XXIII

'Tis night, when Meditation bids us feel
We once have loved, though love is at an end :

1. *Believe*, peuvent les croire.
2. *Meantime... Arion's.* — Cependant la main de quelque rude musicien... Tout le monde sait que la lyre d'Arion, le poète grec, charmait jusqu'aux dauphins.
3. *Stand or move... to...* — Ils font cercle, ou bien, dansent sur un rhythme bien connu.
4. *Calpe's straits*, le détroit de Calpe, aujourd'hui Gibraltar.
5. *Maid*, l'Espagnole.
6. *She plays.* — La lune se joue, éclairant le rivage tour à tour distinct ou obscur, le découvrant ou le laissant dans l'ombre.

The heart, lone mourner of its baffled zeal,
Though friendless now, will dream it had a friend.
Who with the weight of years would wish to bend [1],
When Youth itself survives young Love and Joy?
Alas! when mingling souls forget to blend [2],
Death hath but little left him to destroy!
Ah! happy years! once more who would not be a boy?

XXIV

Thus bending o'er the vessel's laving side,
To gaze on Dian's wave-reflected sphere [3],
The soul forgets her schemes of hope and pride,
And flies unconscious o'er each backward year.
None are so desolate but something dear,
Dearer than self, possesses [4] or possess'd
A thought, and claims the homage of a tear;
A flashing pang! of which the weary breast
Would still, albeit in vain, the heavy heart divest.

XXV

To sit on rocks, to muse o'er flood and fell [5],
To slowly trace the forest's shady scene,

---

1. *To bend... with*, se courber sous (le poids).
2. *Forget to blend.*—Quand deux âmes qui s'étaient unies oublient leur union.
3. *Dian's sphere*, le disque de la lune.
4. *Possesses.* — Il y a toujours quelqu'un qui possède une de nos pensées.
5. *To muse o'er flood and fell*, rêver sur les flots et sur les cimes. — Tout ce passage du poème est aussi sincère qu'il est beau. Nous savons, par lord Egerton Bridges, que Byron n'avait pas de plus grand plaisir que de contempler le ciel et les flots. A bord, il dormait dans son manteau sur les planches du tillac; et il vivait de rien, dînant d'une croûte de pain et d'un verre d'eau. De même dans les montagnes et les forêts, il était heureux de rêver, c'est-à-dire de jouir en artiste de la vue des choses. Dès l'enfance, en Écosse, il adorait la nature.

Where things that own not man's dominion dwell,
And mortal foot hath ne'er or rarely been;
To climb the trackless mountain all unseen,
With the wild flock that never needs a fold;
Alone o'er steeps and foaming falls to lean;
This is not solitude; tis but to hold
Converse with Nature's charms, and view her stores unroll'd.

XXVI

But midst the crowd, the hum, the shock of men,
To hear, to see, to feel, and to possess¹,
And roam along, the world's tired denizen,
With none who bless us, none whom we can bless;
Minions of splendour shrinking from distress!
None that, with kindred consciousness endued²,
If we were not, would seem to smile the less,
Of all that flatter'd, follow'd, sought, and sued;
This is to be alone; this, this his solitude!

XXVII

More blest the life of godly eremite,
Such as on lonely Athos³ may be seen,
Watching at eve upon the giant height,
Which looks o'er waves so blue, skies so serene,
That he who there at such an hour hath been ⁴

---

1. *To possess*, posséder la fortune.
2. *None that... endued...* — Le sens général est : Personne qui nous aime assez pour nous pleurer, si nous disparaissons.
3. *Lonely Athos.* — L'Athos solitaire (c'est-à-dire isolé du monde) renferme dix-neuf couvents, un peuple de solitaires.
4. *That he who hath been.* — Le voyageur venu là. Pour comprendre la suite de cette construction elliptique, rétablissez le sujet he. Il s'arrêtera, *he will linger, he will tear, he will sigh.*

Will wistful linger on that hallow'd spot;
Then slowly tear him from the'witching scene,
Sigh forth one wish that such had been his lot,
Then turn to hate a world he had almost forgot.

La beauté. — Celle des femmes ne vaut pas celle de la Nature. — Digression sur l'île de Calypso et sur la rencontre que fait Byron de Florence (Mrs. Spencer Smith). — Childe Harold est étranger à l'amour. (Str. XXVIII à XXXVII).

XXVIII

Pass we [1] the long, unvarying course, the track
Oft trod, that never leaves a trace behind;
Pass we the calm, the gale, the change, the tack,
And each well known caprice of wave and winds;
Pass we the joys and sorrows sailors find,
Coop'd in their winged sea-girt citadel;
The foul, the fair [2], the contrary, the kind,
As breezes rise and fall and billows swell,
Till on some jocund morn—lo, land! and all is well:

XXIX

But not in silence pass Calypso's isles [3],
The sister tenants of the middle deep;
There for the weary still a haven smiles,

---

1. *Pass we.* — Ne parlons pas de...
2. *The foul, the fair.* — Le beau ou le vilain temps. L'opposition est plus forte encore dans Shakspeare (*Macbeth*, 1, 1).
3. *Calypso's isles.* — On ne sait réellement pas où il faut placer le séjour de Calypso. Mais Byron admet que c'est l'île de Goza, composée de deux îles jumelles (*sister tenants*); le nom de Calypso sert de transition à ce qui suit.

Though the fair goddess long hath ceased to weep,
And o'er her cliffs a fruitless watch to keep
For him who dared prefer a mortal bride:
Here, too, his boy essay'd the dreadful leap
Stern Mentor urged from high to yonder tide;
While thus of both bereft, the nymph-queen doubly sigh'd.

XXX

Her reign is past, her gentle glories gone:
But trust not this; too easy youth[1], beware!
A mortal sovereign holds her dangerous throne,
And thou may'st find a new Calypso there.
Sweet Florence[2]! could another[3] ever share
This wayward, loveless heart, it would be thine;
But check'd by every tie, I may not dare
To cast a worthless offering at thy shrine,
Nor ask so dear a breast to feel one pang for mine.

XXXI

Thus Harold deem'd, as on that lady's eye
He look'd, and met its beam without a thought
Save admiration glancing harmless by:
Love kept aloof, albeit not far remote,
Who knew his votary often lost and caught,
But knew[4] him as his worshipper no more,

---

1. *Easy youth.* — O mon entraînable jeunesse! (cf. str. XXXII, *A youth so raw*). Il se parle à lui-même.

2. *Sweet Florence.* — Sous ce nom, Byron salue la belle Anglaise, Mrs. Spencer Smith, qui jouait alors un certain rôle politique et voyageait d'Orient en Occident avec une hardiesse égale à sa beauté.

3. *Could another.* — Si une autre femme pouvait.

4. *Who knew... but knew.* — Il le savait variable, mais cette fois il reconnut que... La même forme verbale sert à deux temps.

And ne'er again the boy his bosom sought :
Since now¹ he vainly urged him to adore,
Well deem'd the little God his ancient sway was o'er.

XXXII

Fair Florence found, in sooth with some amaze,
One who, 'twas said, still sigh'd to all he saw,
Withstand, unmoved, the lustre of her gaze,
Which others hail'd² with real or mimic awe,
Their hope, their doom, their punishment, their law,
All that gay Beauty from her bondsmen claims :
And much she marvell'd that a youth so raw
Nor felt, nor feign'd at least, the oft-told flames³,
Which, though sometimes, they frown, yet rarely anger dames.

XXXIII

Little knew she that seeming marble heart,
Now mask'd in silence or withheld by pride,
Was not unskilful in the spoiler's art⁴,
And spread its snares licentious far and wide ;
Nor from the base pursuit had turn'd⁵ aside,
As long as aught was worthy to pursue :
But Harold on such arts no more relied⁶ ;
And had he doted on those eyes so blue,
Yet never would he join the lover's whining crew.

---

1. *Now*, aujourd'hui, en cette rencontre.
2. *Others hailed... their hope.* — Les autres la saluaient comme leur espoir.
3. *The oft-told flames.* — Les déclarations de rigueur, celles qu'on leur répète toujours.
4. *Spoiler's art.* — L'art du séducteur.
5. *Nor had turned.* — Jadis il ne manquait pas de...
6. *No more relied.* — Il n'y songeait plus.

XXXIV

Not much he kens[1], I ween, of woman's breast,
Who thinks that wanton thing[2] is won by sighs;
What careth she for hearts when once possess'd
Do proper homage to thine idol's eyes;
But not too humbly, or she will despise
Thee and thy suit, though told in moving tropes:
Disguise ev'n tenderness, if thou art wise;
Brisk Confidence still best with woman copes:
Pique her and soothe in turn, soon Passion crowns thy hopes.

XXXV

'Tis an old lesson; Time approves it true,
And those who know it best, deplore it most;
When all is won that all desire to woo,
The paltry prize[3] is hardly worth the cost:
Youth wasted, minds degraded, honour lost,
These are thy fruits, successful Passion! these!
If, kindly cruel[4], early hope is crost[5],
Still to the last it rankles, a disease,
Not to be cured, when love itself forgets to please.

XXXVI

Away[6]! nor let me loiter in my song,
For we have many a mountain-path to tread,
And many a varied shore to sail along,

---

1. *He kens.* — Il connaît (cf. *to know*). Plus loin (strophe XXXVIII), *ken* signifie: la vue, la perspective.
2. *Wanton thing*, être capricieux. — *Wanton*, flotter, se jouer capricieusement.
3. *Paltry prize.* — La méprisable récompense.
4. *Kindly cruel.* — Cruauté qui est un bienfait.
5. *Crost*, traversé.
6. *Away!* — Assez sur ce sujet

By pensive Sadness, not by Fiction, led [1] —
Climes [2], fair withal as ever mortal head
Imagined in its little schemes of thought;
Or e'er in new Utopias were ared [3],
To teach man what he might be, or he ought;
If that corrupted thing could ever such be taught.

XXXVII

Dear Nature is the kindest mother still,
Though always changing in her aspect mild;
From her bare bosom let me take my fill [4],
Her never-wean'd, though not her favour'd child.
Oh! she is fairest in her features wild,
Where nothing polish'd dares pollute her path:
To me by day or night she ever smiled,
Though I have mark'd her when none other hath,
And sought her more and more, and loved her best in wrath [5].

En vue de la Grèce. — L'Albanie. — Le pays de Pénélope et de Sapho. — Souvenirs historiques et militaires. — Aspect sauvage du pays. — La croix et le croissant. (Str. XXXVIII à XLV.)

XXXVIII

Land of Albania! where Iskander [6] rose,
Theme of the young, and beacon of the wise,
And he his namesake, whose oft-baffled foes

---

1. *Not by Fiction led.* — Childe Harold n'est pas un roman.
2. *Climes...* — Les plus beaux climats d'ailleurs que...
3. *Ared*, à lire pour *a-read*.
4. *Take my fill*, me rassasier.
5. *In wrath*, quand elle est en courroux.
6. *Iskander*, Alexandre. Byron, qui rattache ingénieusement aux

Shrunk from his deeds of chivalrous emprize:
Land of Albania! let me bend mine eyes
On thee, thou rugged nurse of savage men!
The cross descends, thy minarets arise,
And the pale crescent sparkles in the glen,
Through many a cypress grove within each city's ken.

XXXIX

Childe Harold sail'd, and pass'd the barren spot [1],
Where sad Penelope o'erlook'd the wave;
And onward view'd the mount, not yet forgot,
The lover's refuge, and the Lesbian's grave [2]
Dark Sappho! could not verse immortal save
That breast imbued with such immortal fire?
Could she not live who life eternal gave?
If life eternal may await the lyre,
That only Heaven to which Earth's children may aspire.

XL

'T was on a Grecian autumn's gentle eve
Childe Harold hail'd Leucadia's cape afar;
A spot he long'd to see, nor cared to leave :
Oft did he mark the scenes of vanish'd war [3],
Actium, Lepanto, fatal Trafalgar;

montagnes de l'Épire *Alexandre le Grand* et *Scander-beg*, s'en excuse dans une note : « Je ne sais si j'ai eu raison de faire de Scanderbeg le compatriote d'Alexandre, qui était né à Pella, en Macédoine; mais j'ai suivi Gibbon, qui a donné le même titre à Pyrrhus, en parlant de ses exploits. »

1. *The barren spot.* — L'ile d'Ithaque.
2. *The Lesbian's grave.* — Le promontoire de Leucade, aujourd'hui Sainte-Maure.
3. *Vanish'd war.* — Les guerres du passé, qui mirent les nations aux prises à Actium, à Lépante, à Trafalgar.

Mark them unmoved, for he would not delight
(Born beneath some remote inglorious star)
In themes of bloody fray, or gallant fight,
But loathed the bravo's trade, and laughed at martial wight[1].

XLI

But when he saw the evening star above
Leucadia's far-projecting rock of woe[2],
And hail'd the last resort[3] of fruitless love,
He felt, or deem'd he felt, no common glow :
And as the stately vessel glided slow
Beneath the shadow of that ancient mount,
He watch'd the billows' melancoly flow,
And, sunk albeit in thought as he was wont,
More placid seem'd his eye, and smooth his pallid front.

XLII

Morn dawns; and with it stern Albania's hills[4],
Dark Suli's rocks[5], and Pindus' inland peak,
Robed half in mist, bedew'd with snowy rills,
Array'd in many a dun and purple streak,
Arise; and, as the clouds along them break,
Disclose the dwelling of the mountaineer :
Here roams the wolf, the eagle whets his beak,
Birds, beasts of prey, and wilder men appear,
And gathering storms around convulse[6] the closing year.

---

1. *Wight.* — Un être (cf. *Wicht, Bösewicht*, en allemand).
2. *Rock of woe.* — Le rocher du malheur, le rocher fatal.
3. *The last resort.* — Le dernier recours.
4. *Albania's hills.* — Le mot Albanie prend ici le sens général qu'il gardera dans toute la suite du chant. « L'Albanie, dit Byron, comprend une partie de la Macédoine, l'Illyrie, la Chaonie et l'Épire. »
5. *Suli's rocks*, les rochers de Souli, la petite république immortalisée par sa résistance à Ali-Pacha.
6. *Convulse.* — Ils apportent la tourmente aux derniers jours de l'année.

CANTO THE SECOND.

XLIII

Now Harold felt himself at length alone,
And bade to Christian tongues a long adieu;
Now he adventured on a shore unknown,
Which all admire, but many dread to wiew:
His breast was arm'd 'gainst fate, his wants were few;
Peril he sought not, but ne'er shrank to meet:
The scene was savage, but the scene was new;
This made the ceaseless toil of travel sweet,
Beat back [1] keen winter's blast, and welcomed summer's heat.

XLIV

Here the red cross, for still the cross is here,
Though sadly scoff'd at by the circumcised,
Forgets that pride to pamper'd priesthood dear;
Churchman and votary alike despised.
Foul Superstition! howsoe'er disguised,
Idol, saint, virgin, prophet, crescent, cross,
For whatsoever symbol throu ard prized,
Thou sacerdotal gain [2], but general loss!
Who from true worship's gold can separate thy dross?

XLV

Ambracia's gulf behold, where once was lost
A world for woman [3], lovely, harmless thing!

---

1. *Beat back.* — La nouveauté de la scène faisait oublier l'hiver (*mot à mot*, faisait la fatigue douce et l'hiver en fuite).
2. *Thou sacerdotal gain.* — Le prêtre y gagne, le monde y perd.
3. *For woman.* — Dans cette belle strophe, Byron résume toute l'histoire de ce rivage d'Actium, des lieux où Octave (le second César) battit Antoine et Cléopâtre, « être charmant, inoffensif », dit-il ironiquement. Le trophée du César était la ville de la victoire, Nicopolis, dont le poète visite les ruines à Prevesa Vecchia.

In yonder rippling bay, their naval host
Did many a Roman chief and Asian king
To doubtful conflict, certain slaughter bring :
Look where the second Cæsar's trophies rose :
Now, like the hands that rear'd them, withering :
Imperial anarchs, doubling human woes!
God! was thy globe ordained for such to win and lose [1]?

Voyage en Albanie. — Le couvent de Zitza. — Le repos. — La grandeur de la nature. — Dodone. Où est-elle? (Str. XLVI à LIII.)

XLVI

From the dark barriers of that rugged clime,
Ev'n to the centre of Illyria's vales,
Childe Harold pass'd o'er many a mount sublime,
Through lands scarce noticed in historic tales;
Yet in famed Attica such lovely dales
Are rarely seen; nor can fair Temple boast
A charm they know not; loved Parnassus fails [2],
Though classic ground and consecrated most,
To match some spots that lurk within this lowering coast.

XLVII

He pass'd bleak Pindus, Acherusia's lake,
And left the primal city [3] of the land,
And onwards did his further journey take

---

1. *Win and lose.* — Comparez le *won and lost*, de Shakespeare (*Macbeth*, 1, 4).
2. *Parnassus fails... to match.* — Le Parnasse n'arrive pas à égaler.
3. *The primal city.* — Janina, capitale du pachalik d'Albanie.

To greet Albania's chief[1], whose dread command
Is lawless law; for with a bloody hand
He sways a nation, turbulent and bold :
Yet here and there some daring mountain-band
Disdain his power, and from their rocky hold
Hurl their defiance far, nor yield, unless to gold.

XLVIII

Monastic Zitza[2]! from thy shady brow[3],
Thou small, but favour'd spot of holy ground !
Where'er we gaze, around, above, below,
What rainbow tints, what magic charms are found ?
Rock, river, forest, mountain, all abound,
And bluest skies that harmonise the whole :
Beneath, the distant torrent's rushing sound
Tells where the volumed cataract doth roll
Between those hanging rocks, that shock yet please the soul.

XLIX.

Amidst the grove that crowns yon tufted hill,
Which, were it not[4] for many a mountain nigh
Rising in lofty ranks, and loftier still,
Might well itself be deemed of dignity,
The convent's white walls glisten fair on high :

1. *Albania's chief.* — Ali-Pacha, né à Tchelen, en 1741, s'était emparé de l'Albanie et de presque toute la Grèce. Il avait fait alliance avec les Anglais. Le sultan Mahmoud le prit par ruse et le fit égorger en 1822.

2. *Zitza*, près de Janina. — « Il n'est point de plume ou de pinceau capable de rendre la beauté des sites qu'offrent les environs de Zitza et de Velvinachi, village placé sur la frontière de l'Épire et de l'Albanie proprement dite. » (Note de Byron.)

3. *Brow*, sommet. Le mot *brow* signifie sourcil, front, par extension, sommet.

4. *Were it not.* — Sans les montagnes voisines.

Here dwells the caloyer [1], nor rude is he,
Nor niggard of his cheer ; the passer by
Is welcome still ; nor heedless [2] will he flee
From hence, if he delight kind Nature's sheen to see.

L

Here in the sultriest season let him rest,
Fresh is the green beneath those aged trees ;
Here winds of gentlest wing will fan his breast,
From heaven itself he may inhale the breeze :
The plain is far beneath—oh ! let him seize
Pure pleasure while he can; the scorching ray
Here pierceth not, impregnate with disease :
Then let his [3] length the loitering pilgrim lay,
And gaze, untired, the morn, the noon, the eve away.

LI

Dusky and huge, enlarging on the sight,
Nature's volcanic amphitheatre,
Chimæra's alps [4] extend from left to right :
Beneath, a living valley seems to stir :
Flocks play, trees wave, streams flow, the mountain-fir
Nodding above ; behold black Acheron !
Once consecrated to the sepulchre.
Pluto ! if this be hell I look [5] upon,
Close shamed Elysium's gates, my shade shall seek for none.

---

1. *Caloyer.* — Les Grecs appellent le moine *caloyer*, c'est-à-dire le « bon vieillard » (de καλός et γέρων). Rabelais s'était surnommé lui-même « le caloyer des îles d'Hyères. »

2. *Nor heedless.* — Il ne les oubliera pas.

3. *Then let...* — On remarquera les allitérations de ce vers qui renferme *let, length, loitering, lay.*

4. *Chimæra's alps.* — Les monts de la Chimère sont l'ancienne chaîne des monts Acrocérauniens, laquelle court tout le long du rivage abrupt de l'Épire.

5. *I look*, sous-entendu *that* (I look).

LII

Ne city's[1] towers pollute the lovely view;
Unseen is Yanina, though not remote,
Veil'd by the screen of hills : here men are few,
Scanty the hamlet, rare the lonely cot :
But, peering down each precipice, the goat
Browseth; and, pensive[2] o'er his scatter'd flock,
The little shepherd in his white capote
Doth lean his boyish form along the rock,
Or in his cave awaits the tempest's short-lived shock.

LIII

Oh! where, Dodona[3]! is thine aged grove,
Prophetic fount, and oracle divine?
What valley echoed the response of Jove?
What trace remaineth of the Thunderer's shrine?
All, all forgotten — and shall man repine
That his frail bonds to fleeting life are broke[4]?
Cease, fool! the fate of gods may well be thine :
Wouldst thou survive the marble or the oak?
When nations, tongues, and worlds must sink beneath the stroke!

En Illyrie. — Visite à Tepalen et à la cour d'Ali-pacha. — Le monde et le luxe musulmans. (Str. LIV à LXIV.)

LIV

Epirus' bounds recede, and mountains fail;
Tired of up-gazing still, the wearied eye

---

1. *Ne city's,* pour *no city's.*
2. *Pensive* a ici le sens français, pensif.
3. *Dodona.* — Dodone, où Jupiter Tonnant rendait ses oracles, était au pied des monts Acrocérauniens. On ignorait, jusqu'à ces dernières années, la place exacte de Dodone. C'est pourquoi Byron écrit : *What trace remaineth...?* Un lieu si célèbre a été oublié?
4. *Broke,* pour *broken.*

Reposes gladly on as smooth a vale
As ever Spring yclad[1] in grassy dye:
Ev'n on a plain no humble beauties lie,
Where some bold river breaks[2] the long expanse,
And woods along the banks are waving high,
Whose shadows in the glassy waters dance,
Or with the moonbeam sleep in midnight's solemn trance.

LV

The sun had sunk behind vast Tomerit[3],
And Laos[4] wide and fierce came roaring by;
The shades of wonted night were gathering yet,
When, down the steep banks winding warily,
Childe Harold saw, like meteors in the sky,
The glittering minarets of Tepalen[5],
Whose walls o'erlook the stream; and drawing nigh,
He heard the busy hum of warrior-men
Swelling the breeze that sigh'd along the lengthening glen.

LVI

He pass'd the sacred Haram's[6] silent tower,
And underneath the wide o'erarching gate
Survey'd the dwelling of this chief of power,
Where all around proclaim'd his high estate.
Amidst no common pomp the despot sate,

---

1. *Yclad*, que le printemps ait jamais revêtu.

2. *Breaks*. — La rivière *en* rompt l'étendue.

3. *Tomerit*. — Le Tomarus (ou Tmarus) des anciens.

4. *Laos*. — L'Aos des anciens, le Laos d'aujourd'hui. Byron avoue qu'en regardant cette rivière comme la plus belle du Levant, il a peut-être été abusé, parce qu'elle était fort grosse à l'époque où il la vit.

5. *Tepalen*. — « En arrivant à Janina, nous fûmes invités à aller à Tepalani, lieu de naissance d'Ali-Pacha. Cette ville n'était qu'à une journée de Bérat, et le vizir y avait établi son quartier général. » (Note de Byron.)

6. *Haram*, le harem.

While busy preparation shook the court,
Slaves, eunuchs, soldiers, guests, and santons[1] wait;
Within, a palace, and without, a fort :
Here men of every clime[2] appear to make resort.

LVII

Richly caparison'd, a ready row
Of armed horse, and many a warlike store[3],
Circled the wide-extending court below;
Above, strange groups adorn'd the corridore;
And oft-times through the area's echoing door[4],
Some high-capp'd Tartar spurr'd his steed away :
The Turk, the Greek, the Albanian, and the Moor,
Here mingled in their many-hued array,
While the deep war-drum's sound announced the close of day.

LVIII

The wild Albanian[5] kirtled to his knee,
With shawl-girt head and ornamented gun,
And gold-embroider'd garments, fair to see;
The crimson-scarfed men of Macedon;
The Delhi with his cap of terror on,

---

1. *Santons*, derviches.
2. *Here men of every clime.* — Byron écrit quelque part : « Je n'oublierai jamais le singulier spectacle que j'eus en entrant à Tepalen. » Et il décrit la variété des costumes albanais, turcs et tartares. C'est cette description qu'il a mise en vers dans toutes les strophes qu'on va lire. Il est curieux de comparer ses vers et sa prose.

3. *Warlike store.* — Faisceau d'armes.
4. *Area's door.* — La voûte de la porte de la cour.
5. *The wild Albanian.* — « Les Arnautes ou Albanais me frappèrent par leur ressemblance avec les Highlanders de l'Écosse. » Byron compare leurs mœurs, leur costume, leur *khilt* ou jupon, aux usages des clans écossais.

And crooked glaive; the lively, supple Greek;
And swarthy Nubia's mutilated son;
The bearded Turk, that rarely deigns to speak,
Master of all around, too potent to be meek,

LIX

Are mixed conspicuous[1] : some recline in groups,
Scanning the motley scene that varies round;
There some grave Moslem to devotion stoops,
And some that smoke, and some that play, are found;
Here the Albanian proudly treads the ground;
Half whispering there the Greek is heard to prate;
Hark! from the mosque the nightly solemn sound[2],
The Muezzin's call doth shake the minaret,
"There is no god but God!—to prayer—lo! God is great!"

LX

Just at this season Ramazani's fast[3]
Through the long day its penance did maintain :
But when the lingering twilight hour was past,
Revel and feast assumed the rule[4] again :
Now all was bustle, and the menial train[5]
Prepared and spread the plenteous board within;
The vacant gallery now seem'd made in vain,
But from the chambers came the mingling din,
As page and slave anon were passing out and in.

---

1. *Are mixed conspicuous.* — Forment un brillant mélange.
2. *The nightly solemn sound.* — Le chant du soir, si solennel.
3. *Ramazani's fast.* — Le jeûne du Ramadan, qui dure (*penance maintains*) tout le long du jour.
4. *Assumed the rule.* — Reprit l'empire.
5. *Menial train.* — La suite des serviteurs, la *mesnie* du moyen âge français.

LXI

Here woman's voice is never heard: apart[1]
And scarce-permitted[2], guarded, veil'd, to move,
She yields to one her person and her heart,
Tamed[3] to her cage, nor feels a wish to rove:
For, not unhappy in her master's love,
And joyful in a mother's gentlest cares,
Blest cares! all other feelings far above!
Herself more sweetly rears the babe she bears,
Who never quits the breast[4], no meaner passion shares.

LXII

In marble-paved pavilion, where a spring
Of living water from the centre rose,
Whose bubbling did a genial freshness fling,
And soft voluptuous couches breathed repose[5]
Ali[6] reclined, a man of war and woes:
Yet in his lineaments ye cannot trace,
While Gentleness her milder radiance throws
Along that aged venerable face,
The deeds that lurk beneath, and stain him with disgrace[7].

LXIII

It is not that[8] yon hoary lengthening beard
Ill suits the passions which belong to youth;

---

1. *Apart.* — Vivant à part.
2. *Permitted.* — Réunissez *permitted to move.*
3. *Tamed,* accoutumées.
4. *Breast.* — Le sein, le cœur, qui n'a pas d'autre passion. Le complément *that* est sous-entendu. — Comparez cette strophe à la LIX du chant Ier, laquelle est moins bienveillante pour les femmes de l'Orient.

5. *Breathed repose.* — Respirait le repos.
6. *Ali.* — Au milieu de ce luxe est Ali-Pacha le féroce et doux vieillard. Byron dépeint le calme oriental de ce héros sanglant.
7. *Stain with disgrace,* le souillent et le déparent.
8. *It is not that.* — Non pas que... Je ne le blâme pas de...

Love conquers [1] age—so Hafiz [2] hath averr'd,
So sings the Teian, and he sings in sooth—
But crimes that scorn the tender voice of ruth,
Beseeming all men ill, but most the man
In years, have mark'd him with a tiger's tooth;
Blood follows blood, and, through their mortal span,
In bloodier acts conclude those who with blood began.

LXIV

'Mid many things most new to ear and eye
The pilgrim rested here his weary feet,
And gazed around on Moslem luxury,
Till quickly wearied with that spacious seat
Of Wealth and Wantonness, the choice retreat
Of sated Grandeur from the city's noise:
And were it humbler [3] it in sooth were sweet;
But Peace abhorreth artificial joys,
And Pleasure, leagued with Pomp, the zest of both destroys.

Les Albanais. — Éloge de ces montagnards. — La danse et le chant de guerre des Palikares à Utrakey. (Str. LXV à LXXII.)

LXV

Fierce are Albania's children, yet they lack
Not virtues, were [4] those virtues more mature.

---

1. *Conquers*, est plus fort que...
2. *Hafiz.* — Mohammed Hafiz, poète persan du quatorzième siècle, est resté célèbre par les odes anacréontiques qu'il composa. Aussi Byron le compare-t-il au vieillard de Téos (*Teian*), Anacréon.

3. *Were it humbler.* — Si le luxe était moins violent... Les trois derniers vers signifient que les plaisirs perdent leur saveur quand ils sont extrêmes et affectés.
4. *Were those...* Si ces vertus étaient...

CANTO THE SECOND.

Where is the foe that ever saw their back?
Who can so well the toil of war endure?
Their native fastnesses not more secure[1]
Than they in doubtful time of troublous need:
Their wrath how deadly! but their friendship sure,
When Gratitude or Valour bids them bleed,
Unshaken[2] rushing on where'er their chief may lead.

LXVI

Childe Harold saw them in their chieftain's tower
Thronging to war[3] in splendour and success;
And after view'd them, when, within their power
Himself awhile the victim of distress;
That saddening hour when bad men hotlier press,
But these did shelter him beneath their roof,
When less barbarians would have cheer'd him less,
And fellow-countrymen have stood[4] aloof—
In aught that tries the heart how few withstand the proof.

LXVII

It chanced[5] that adverse winds once drove his bark
Full on the coast of Suli's shaggy shore,
When all around was desolate and dark;
To land was perilous, to sojourn more;

---

1. *Not more secure.* — Ne donnent pas plus de sécurité.
2. *Unshaken*, intrépides.
3. *Thronging to war...* Assemblés pour la guerre.
4. *Have stood.* — Ils se seraient tenus à l'écart. Répétez *would* devant *have*, ce qui est régulier. « Ici, dit Byron, je fais allusion aux pillards de Cornouailles. » Walter Scott a raconté, dans le *Pirate*, comment les hommes du littoral pillaient les navires naufragés. C'était le *droit de bris*. Au contraire, en Albanie, Byron, forcé par le gros temps d'aborder sur une mauvaise côte, trouva asile et protection chez les rudes montagnards. Cet incident fera le sujet de la strophe suivante.
5. *It chanced.* — Au mois de novembre 1809, eut lieu ce demi-naufrage. Byron a raconté le désespoir de tous ses compagnons, qui pleuraient.

Yet for a while the mariners forbore [1]
Dubious to trust where treachery might lurk:
At length they ventured forth, though doubting sore [2]
That those who loathe alike the Frank and Turk
Might once again renew their ancient butcher-work.

LXVIII

Vain fear! the Suliotes stretch'd the welcome hand,
Led them o'er rocks and past the dangerous swamp,
Kinder than polish'd slaves though not so bland,
And piled the hearth, and wrung their garments damp,
And fill'd the bowl, and trimm'd the cheerful lamp,
And spread their fare; though homely, all they had [3]:
Such conduct bears Philanthropy's rare stamp:
To rest the weary and to soothe the sad,
Doth lesson happier men, and shames at least the bad.

LXIX

It came to pass, that when he did address
Himself to quit at length this mountain-land,
Combined marauders half-way barr'd egress,
And wasted far and near with glaive and brand;
And therefore did he take a trusty band
To travers Acarnania's forest [4] wide,
In war well season'd, and with labours tann'd,
Till he did greet white Achelous' tide,
And from his further bank Ætolia's wolds espied.

---

1. *Forbore.* — Ils hésitaient et s'*abstenaient* d'aborder.

2. *Doubting sore*, ayant ce pressentiment cruel.

3. *Though homely, all they had.* — Si peu que ce fût, c'était tout ce qu'ils avaient.

4. *Acarnania's forest.* — Byron et Hobhouse se risquèrent à aller à Missolonghi à travers les forêts de l'Acarnanie, alors infestées de brigands. Ils se fièrent à une escorte de cinquante Albanais, qui se montrèrent les plus fidèles des guides.

LXX

Where lone Utraikey[1] forms its circling cove,
And weary waves retire to gleam at rest,
How brown the foliage of the green hill's grove,
Nodding at midnight o'er the calm bay's breast,
As winds come lightly whispering from the west,
Kissing, not ruffling, the blue deep's serene :—
Here Harold was received a welcome guest;
Nor did he pass unmoved the gentle scene,
For many a joy could he from Night's soft presence glean.

LXXI

On the smooth shore the night-fires brightly blazed,
The feast was done, the red wine circling fast,
And he that unawares had there ygazed[2]
With gaping wonderment had stared aghast;
For ere night's midmost, stillest hour wast past,
The native revels of the troop began;
Each Palikar[3] his sabre from him cast,
And bounding hand in hand, man link'd to man,
Yelling their uncouth dirge, long daunced the kirtled clan.

Un chant de guerre, composé par Byron, d'après les chants du pays. (Str LXII.)

LXXII

Childe Harold at a little distance stood
And view'd, but not displeased, the revelrie,

---

1. *Utraikey.* Petit village maritime du golfe d'Arta, baie inconnue, immortalisée par le souvenir du poète. La strophe est merveilleuse, et le paysage nocturne sert de cadre à une scène qui peint un peuple.
2. *Ygazed*, archaïsme, pour *gazed*.
3. *Each Palikar.* Le mot πα-

Nor hated harmless mirth, however rude :
In sooth, it was no vulgar sight to see
Their barbarous, yet their not indecent, glee ;
And, as the flames along their faces gleamed,
Their gestures nimble, dark eyes flashing free
The long wild locks that to their girdles stream'd,
While thus in concert they this lay [1] half sang, hands-cream'd :

1

TAMBOURGI ! Tambourgi [2] ! thy 'larum afar
Gives hope to the valiant, and promise of war ;
All the sons of the mountains arise at the note,
Chimariot [3], Illyrian, and dark Suliote !

2

Oh ! who is more brave than a dark Suliote,
In his snowy camese [4] and his shaggy [5] capote ?
To the wolf and the vulture he leaves his wild flock,
And descends to the plain like the stream from the rock.

λιχαρι s'est appliqué à tous les soldats du pays. On croit qu'il signifiait *garçons*. Ce serait alors la même dérivation de sens que dans l'allemand *Knabe*, garçon, qui donne *Knecht, Landsknecht*.

1. *This lay*. Cette chanson. Byron, qui déjà, en Espagne, s'intéressait vivement aux chants populaires du passé, est tout à fait saisi par l'accent et la vivacité d'un chant national moderne. Il rapporte d'Albanie des chœurs (recueillis par un Grec d'Athènes) ; il en donne, dans ses notes, le texte et la traduction. Il fait mieux ; lui-même il en compose un, qu'il tire, dit-il, de plusieurs chants albanais. Il se trouve, sans le savoir, composer une sorte de prélude à cette guerre de l'indépendance grecque à laquelle il devait consacrer ses derniers jours (voy. strophe LXXIII).

2. *Tambourgi!* Le tambourgi est celui qui bat la caisse.

3. *Chimariot*, et, plus loin, *the sons of Chimari*. Les guerriers des monts Chimères (voy. str. LI).

4. *Camese*, la tunique blanche.

5. *Shaggy*, rugueux, à longs poils.

3

Shall the sons of Chimari, who never forgive
The fault of a friend, bid an enemy live?
Let [1] those guns so unerring such vengeances forego?
What mark is so fair as the breast of a foe?

4

Macedonia sends forth her invincible race;
For a time they abandon the cave and the chase:
But those scarfs of blood-red shall be redder, before
The sabre his sheathed and the battle is o'er.

5

Then the pirates of Parga [2] that dwell by the waves,
And teach the pale Franks [3] what it is to be slaves,
Shall leave on the beach the long galley and oar,
And track to his covert the captive on shore.

6

I ask not the pleasures that riches supply,
My sabre shall win what the feeble must buy;
Shall win the young bride with her long flowing hair,
And many a maid from her mother shall tear.

7

I love the fair face of the maid in her youth,
Her caresses shall lull me, her music shall sooth;

---

1. *Let.* Répétez *shall let*, laisseront-ils.
2. *Parga.* Les Klephtes de Parga étaient les plus célèbres de ces guerriers. Pirates, brigands et guerriers sont synonymes ici.
3. *The pale Franks.* Le poète parle le langage des populations musulmanes, qui confondent tous les chrétiens sous le nom de *Franks*, et tous ceux qui ne sont pas musulmans sous le nom de *giaours*.

Let her bring from the chamber her many-toned lyre,
And sing us a song on the fall of her sire.

8

Remember ¹ the moment when Previsa fell,
The shrieks of the conquer'd, the conquerors' yell;
The roofs that we fired, and the plunder we shared,
The wealthy we slaughter'd, the lovely we spared.

9

I talk not of mercy, I talk not of fear ;
He neither must know who would serve the Vizier :
Since the days of our prophet the Crescent ne'er saw
A chief ever glorious like Ali Pashaw.

10

Dark Muchtar ² his son to the Danube is sped, [dread;
Let the yellow-hair'd Giaours view his horsetail with
When his Delhis come dashing in blood o'er the banks,
How few shall escape from the Muscovite ranks !

11

Selictar³ ! unsheathe then our chiefs scimitar
Tambourgi ! thy' larum gives promise of war.

---

1. *Remember...* Rappelez-vous le beau pillage de Previsa! Ce petit port, qui est à l'entrée du golfe d'Arta, joue un rôle dans l'histoire. Il fut occupé tour à tour par les Turcs, les Vénitiens et les Français. En 1798, 600 soldats français le défendirent contre 11 000 assaillants. C'est alors qu'Ali-Pacha vint en faire le siège et qu'il s'en empara la même année. Le pillage et les meurtres qui eurent lieu font bondir de joie les palikares.

2. *Muchtar.* Ali-Pacha lance son fils contre les Russes aux cheveux jaunes (*yellow-haired*); ceux-ci redoutent le panache (*horse-tail*) du pacha et la cavalerie des « enfants perdus », les Delhis, dont le nom signifie, dit Byron, *forlorn hope*, enfants perdus.

3. *Selictar.* Nom du porte-glaive.

Ye mountains, that see us descend to the shore,
Shall view us as victors, or view us no more !

La Grèce. — Misère et grandeur de ce pays. — Invective contre l'insouciance de la Grèce esclave. (Str. LXXIII à LXXVIII.)

LXXIII

Fair Greece ! sad relic of departed worth [1] !
Immortal, though no more ; though fallen, great !
Who now shall lead thy scatter'd children forth,
And long accustom'd bondage uncreate ?
Not such thy sons who whilome did await,
The hopeless warriors of a willing doom [2]
In bleak Thermopylæ's sepulchral strait—
Oh ! who that gallant spirit shall resume,
Leap from Eurotas' banks, and call thee from the tomb ?

LXXIV

Spirit of freedom ! when on Phyle's [3] brow
Thou sat'st with Thrasybulus and his train,
Couldst thou forebode the dismal hour which now
Dims the green beauties of thine Attic plain ?
Not thirty tyrants now enforce the chain,
But every carle [4] can lord it o'er thy land ;

---

1. *Departed worth.* Une grandeur disparue.
2. *A willing doom.* Une mort volontaire.
3. *Phyle's brow.* Le sommet de Phylé. La colline et la ville de Thylé, qui dominent Athènes, furent le point sur lequel se retira Thrasybule, au moment de chasser les trente tyrans.
4. *Every carle.* Le premier rustre venu (*carl* ou *churl*) peut commander en maître là où la Grèce antique se faisait libre.

Nor rise thy sons, but idly rail in vain,
Trembling beneath the scourge of Turkish hand;
From birth till death enslaved; in word, in deed, unmann'd [1].

LXXV

In all save form [2] alone, how changed! and who
That marks the fire still sparkling in each eye,
Who but would deem their bosoms burn'd anew
With thy unquenched beam, lost Liberty!
And many dream withal the hour is nigh
That gives them back their fathers' heritage:
For foreign arms and aid they fondly sigh,
Nor solely dare encounter hostile rage,
Or tear their name defiled from Slavery's mournful page.

LXXVI

Hereditary bondsmen! know ye not
Who would be free themselves must strike the blow?
By their right arms [3] the conquest must be wrought?
Will Gaul or Muscovite redress ye? no!
True, they may lay your proud despoilers low,
But not for you will Freedom's altars flame.
Shades of the Helots! triumph o'er your foe!
Greece! change [4] thy lords, thy state is still the same;
Thy glorious day is o'er, but not thine years of shame.

---

1. *Unmanned.* Ce ne sont plus des hommes.
2. *In all save form....* Ils n'ont gardé que l'extérieur.
3. *By their right arms.* Le mot *right*, ici intraduisible, exprime le droit et le devoir, ce qui est dû et légitime.
4. *Change.* Tu peux changer en vain.

CANTO THE SECOND.

LXXVII

The city won for Allah from the Giaour [1],
The Giaour from Othman's race again may wrest;
And the Serai's impenetrable tower
Receive the fiery Frank, her former guest;
Or Wahab's rebel brood [2] who dared divest
The prophet's tomb of all its pious spoil,
May wind their path of blood along the West;
But ne'er will freedom seek this fated soil,
But slave succeed to slave through years of endless toil.

LXXVIII

Yet mark their mirth—ere lenten days [3] begin,
That penance which their holy rites prepare
To shrive from man his weight of mortal sin,
By daily abstinence and nightly prayer;
But ere his sackcloth garb [4] Repentance wear,
Some days of joyaunce are decreed to all,
To take of pleasaunce each his secret share,
In motley robe to dance at masking ball,
And join the mimic train of merry Carnival.

---

1. *The Giaour.* Le sens général de la strophe est que les autres nations peuvent reprendre l'empire de la terre, mais que la Grèce ne reprendra pas sa liberté.
2. *Wahab's brood.* Les Wahabites, qui venaient de s'emparer de la Mecque en 1801 et de Médine en 1808, voulaient que les hommes fussent égaux dans la mort et détruisaient les sépultures trop aristocratiques. Ils formaient une secte sévère et puissante, fondée par Mohammed ben Abd el Wahab.
3. *Lenten days*, le carême.
4. *Sackcloth garb.* Le cilice.

Constantinople. — Une nuit sur les rives du Bosphore.
(Str. LXXIX à LXXX.)

LXXIX

And whose[1] more rife with merriment than thine,
Oh Stamboul[2]! once the empress of their reign?
Though turbans now pollute Sophia's[3] shrine,
And Greece her very altars eyes in vain:
(Alas! her woes will still pervade my strain!)
Gay were her minstrels once, for free[4] her throng,
All felt the common joy they now must feign,
Nor oft I've seen such sight, nor heard such song,
As woo'd the eye, and thrill'd the Bosphorus along.

LXXX.

Loud was the lightsome tumult on the shore,
Oft Music changed, but never ceased her tone,
And timely echo'd back the measured oar,[5]
And rippling waters made a pleasant moan:
The Queen of tides on high consenting shone,
And when a transient breeze swept o'er the wave,
'T was, as if darting from her heavenly throne,
A brighter glance her form reflected gave,
Till[6] sparkling billows seem'd to light the banks they lave.

---

1. *And whose...* etc. Construction doublement elliptique. « Chez qui le carnaval règne-t-il avec plus d'empire et d'allégresse que chez les habitants de Constantinople? » *Whose (Carnaval is) more rife...*
2. *Stamboul,* Constantinople. —
3. *Sophia,* Sainte-Sophie, l'église devenue mosquée.
4. *For free.* Ellipse, pour *was free.*
5. *Measured oar.* La rame, frappant en cadence, fait écho à la musique du rivage.
6. *Till.* Jusqu'à ce point que....

LXXXI

Glanced many a light caique along the foam,
Danced on the shore the daughters of the land,
No thought had man or maid of rest or home,
While many a languid eye and thrilling hand
Exchanged the look few bosoms may withstand,
Or gently prest, returned the pressure still :
Oh Love! young Love! bound in thy rosy band[1],
Let sage or cynic prattle as he will,
These hours, and only these, redeem Life's years of ill!

Retour aux Grecs et à la Grèce. — Nouvel appel à l'insurrection. — Magnificence de la contrée, de ses ruines, de son histoire. — Souvenir de Marathon. — Respect que mérite ce pays. (Str. LXXXII à XCIII.)

LXXXII

But, midst the throng in merry masquerade,
Lurk there no hearts that throb with secret pain,
Even through the closest searment[2] half betray'd ?
To such the gentle murmurs of the main
Seen to re-echo all they mourn in vain ;
To such the gladness of the gamesome crowd
Is source of wayward thought and stern disdain :
How do they loathe the laugther idly loud,
And long to change the robe of revel for the shroud!

---

1. *Bound in thy band.* Couronné de ta couronne.
2. *Through the searment,* à travers cette robe qui le déguise. *Searment,* mieux écrit *cerement,* voulait dire l'enveloppe imperméable, la toile cirée qui servait de linceul. Ici le poète indique le costume impénétrable de l'homme masqué.

LXXXIII

This must he feel, the true-born son of Greece,
If Greece one true-born patriot still can boast :
Not such as prate of war, but skulk in peace,
The bondsman's peace, who sighs for all he lost,
Yet with smooth smile his tyrant can accost,
And wield the slavish sickle, not the sword :
Ah ! Greece ! they love thee least who owe thee most—
Their birth, their blood, and that sublime record
Of hero sires[1], who shame thy now degenerate horde !

LXXXIV

When riseth[2] Lacedemon's hardihood,
When Thebes Epaminondas rears again,
When Athens' children are with hearts endued,
When Grecian mothers shall give birth to men,
Then may'st thou be restored ; but not till then.
A thousand years scarce serve to form a state ;
An hour may lay it in the dust : and when
Can man its shatter'd splendour renovate,
Recall its virtues back, and vanquish Time and Fate ?

LXXXV

And yet how lovely in thine age of woe[3],
Land of lost gods and godlike men, art thou !
Thy vales of evergreen, thy hills of snow,
Proclaim thee Nature's varied favourite now :
Thy fanes, thy temples to thy surface bow,

---

1. *Hero sires*, des héros leurs aïeux. Plus haut dans le chant de guerre, la strophe VII nous offre le mot *sire* dans le sens de père.

2. *When riseth*. Le jour où se lèvera... Mettez le futur partout.

3. *In thine age of woe*. Dans ta vieillesse douloureuse.

Commingling slowly with heroic earth,
Broke by the share of every rustic plough :
So perish monuments of mortal birth,
So perish all in turn, save well-recorded Worth;

LXXXVI

Save[1] where some solitary column mourns
Above its prostrate brethren of the cave[2];
Save where Tritonia's airy shrine adorns
Colonna's cliff[3], and gleams along the wave;
Save o'er some warrior's half-forgotten grave,
Where the gray stones and unmolested grass
Ages, but not oblivion, feebly brave;
While strangers only not regardless pass,
Lingering like me, perchance, to gaze, and sigh "Alas!"

LXXXVII

Yet are thy skies as blue, thy crags as wild;
Sweet are thy groves, and verdant are thy fields,
Thine olive ripe as when Minerva smiled,
And still his honey'd wealth Hymettus yields;
There the blithe bee his fragrant fortress builds,
The freeborn wanderer of thy mountain-air;
Apollo still thy long, long summer gilds,
Still in his beam Mendeli's marbles[4] glare;
Art, Glory, Freedom fail, but Nature still is fair.

1. *Save...* Il ne reste rien excepté... C'est la suite de la strophe précédente.
2. *Brethren of the cave.* Une colonne reste, pleurant sur ses sœurs, les colonnes sorties de la même carrière, et maintenant gisantes sur le sol.
3. *Tritonia's... shrine — Colonna's cliff.* Excepté ces restes du temple de Pallas qui ornait le cap Sunium. Byron admira fort les seize colonnes restées debout sur le cap, qui a reçu pour cette raison le nom de cap Colonna.
4. *Mendeli's marbles.* Mendeli est le nom moderne du Pentélique. Dans les flancs du Pentélique était

LXXXVIII

Where'er we tread 'tis haunted[1], holy ground;
No earth of thine is lost in vulgar mould,
But one vast realm of wonder spreads around,
And all the Muse's tales seem truly told,
Till the sense aches with gazing to behold
The scenes[2] our earliest dreams have dwelt upon;
Each hill and dale, each deepening glen and wold[3]
Defies the power which crushed thy temples gone:
Age shakes Athena's tower, but spares gray Marathon.

LXXXIX

The sun, the soil, but not the slave, the same;
Unchanged in all except its foreign lord;
Preserves alike its bounds and boundless[4] fame
The Battle-field, where Persia's victim horde
First bow'd beneath the brunt of Hellas' sword,
As on the morn to distant Glory dear,
When Marathon became a magic word;
Which utter'd[5], to the hearer's eye appear
The camp, the host, the fight, the conquerors career,

XC

The flying Mede, his shaftless broken bow;
The fiery Greek, his red pursuing spear;

---

la carrière qui a fourni tout le marbre des monuments d'Athènes.

1. *Haunted.* Toute l'Europe a *visité* cette terre.

2. *The scenes.* Ajoutez *that.*

3. *Wold.* Ce mot saxon signifie plaine boisée et rappelle le *Wald* des Allemands comme le ὕλη des Grecs.

4. *Bounds* et *boundless.* Voici le champs et ses limites; sa réputation n'en a pas.

5. *Which uttered.* Une fois ce nom prononcé. Phrase absolue.

Mountains above, Earth's, Oceans plain below;
Death in the front, Destruction in the rear!
Such was the scene—what now remaineth here?
What sacred trophy marks the hallow'd ground,
Recording Freedom's smile and Asia's tear?
The rifled urn, the violated mound [1],
The dust thy courser's hoof, rude stranger! spurns around.

XCI

Yet to the remnants of thy splendour past
Shall pilgrims, pensive, but unwearied [2], throng;
Long shall the voyager, with th' Ionian blast [3],
Hail the bright clime of battle and of song;
Long shall thine annals and immortal tongue
Fill with thy fame the youth of many a shore;
Boast of the aged! lesson of the young!
Which sages venerate and bards adore,
As Pallas and the Muse unveil their awful lore.

XCII

The parted bosom [4] clings to wonted home,
If aught that's kindred cheer the welcome hearth
He that is lonely, hither let him roam,
And gaze complacent on congenial earth [5].

---

1. *Violated Mound*, la tombe violée. Byron raconte qu'on offrit de lui vendre pour 1600 piastres la plaine de Marathon, avec la cendre de Miltiade et les tombes fouillées par Fauvel, consul de France, lesquelles déjà du temps de Fauvel se trouvaient vides (*violated*).

2. *Pensive, but unwearied.* On a vu plus haut que le mot *pensive* a deux sens. Byron précise. Le pélerin n'est point fatigué de ce qu'il voit. Il est méditatif, et non pas abattu.

3. *Ionian blast.* Le vent qui pousse le voyageur vers l'Ionie.

4. *The parted bosom.* Le cœur loin de la patrie.

5. *Congenial earth.* La terre, le pays de votre esprit. Nous n'avons pas de mot qui réponde exactement

Greece is no lightsome land of social mirth :
But he whom Sadness sootheth may abide,
And scarce regret the region of his birth,
When wandering slow by Delphi's sacred side [1],
Or gazing o'er the plains where Greek and Persian died.

XCIII

Let such approach this consecrated land,
And pass in peace along the magic waste ;
But spare its relics—let no busy hand
Deface the scenes, already how defaced !
Not for such purpose were these altars placed :
Revere the remnants nations once revered :
So may our country's name be undisgraced,
So may'st thou [2] prosper where thy youth was rear'd,
By every honest joy of love and life endear'd !

Epilogue, ajouté par Byron au chant IIe. — Sa tristesse. Sa solitude morale. Ses affections perdues. (De la strophe XCIV à la fin.)

XCIV

For thee [3], who thus in too protracted song
Hast soothed thine idlesse [4] with inglorious lays,
Soon shall thy voice be lost amid the throng

à cette expression, si juste ici : le monde grec est celui dans lequel l'esprit de Byron retrouve ses sympathies et ses goûts.
1. *Side,* le penchant.
2. *So may'st thou.* Et puisses-tu, voyageur, si tu as respecté ce pays, trouver la joie dans le tien ! Ce vœu, mêlé de tristesse, était le dernier mot du poème dans la rédaction primitive.
3. *For thee.* Byron se parle à lui-même.
4. *Idlesse,* archaïsme.

CANTO THE SECOND.

Of louder minstrels in these later days:
To such¹ resign the strife for fading bays—
Ill may such contest now the spirit move
Which heeds nor keen reproach nor partial praise,
Since cold² each kinder heart that might approve,
And none are left to please when none are left to love.

XCV

Thou too³ art gone, thou loved and lovely one!
Whom youth and youth's affections bound to me;
Who did for me what none beside have done,
Nor shrank from one albeit unworthy thee,
What is my being? thou hast ceased to be!
Nor staid to welcome here thy wanderer home,
Who mourns o'er hours which we no more shall see—
Would they had never been, or were to come!
Would he had ne'er return'd to find fresh cause to roam!

XCVI

Oh! ever loving, lovely, and beloved!
How selfish Sorrow ponders⁴ on the past,
And clings to thoughts now better far removed!
But Time shall tear thy shadow from me last.
All thou couldst have of mine, stern Death! thou hast;
The parent, friend⁵, and now the more than friend:

---

1. *To such.* A ces gens-là..
2. *Since cold*, sous-entendu *is.*
3. *Thou too.* Toi aussi, tu es morte. Il s'agit ici d'une femme. Les uns veulent que ce soit Maria Chaworth; les autres rapportent cette strophe à la même personne dont il est question dans la strophe XIX. Comparez *young remembrance* (strophe IX) et ici *youth's affections*. Ce sont les mêmes termes.
4. *Ponders*, s'appesantit.
5. *The parent, friend.* La mère de Byron mourut en 1811, en Écosse pendant le voyage de son fils. Son ami, le jeune Eddlestone, mourut dans le même temps.

Ne'er yet for one thine arrows flew so fast,
And grief with grief continuing still to blend,
Hath snatch'd the little joy that life had yet to lend.

XCVII

Then must I plunge again into the crowd,
And follow all that Peace disdains to seek?
Where Revel calls, and Laughter, vainly loud,
False to the heart [1], distorts the hollow cheek,
To leave the flagging spirit doubly weak;
Still o'er the features, which perforce they cheer,
To feign the pleasure or conceal the pique?
Smiles from the channel of a future tear,
Or raise the writhing lip with ill-dissembled sneer.

XCVIII

What is the worst of woes that wait on age?
What stamps the wrinkle deeper on the brow [2]?
To view each loved one blotted from life's page,
And be alone on earth, as I am now.
Before the Chastener [3] humbly let me bow,
O'er hearts divided and o'er hopes destroyed:
Roll on, vain days! full reckless may ye flow,
Since time hath reft whate'er my soul enjoyed,
And with the ills of Eld mine earlier years alloyed.

---

1. *False to the heart.* Ce rire, qui se fait bruyant, ment au cœur et fait grimacer les joues qu'il creuse.

2. *On the brow.* Byron était nourri de la lecture de Shakspeare. Comparez à ce vers l'expression employée par le roi Lear quand il maudit sa fille : *Let it stamp wrinkles in her brow of youth.*

3. *The chastener,* celui qui châtie. Byron, au moment de la douleur, dément les sarcasmes du début, dictés par l'ironie.

ARGUMENT ANALYTIQUE

DU CHANT TROISIÈME

EN BELGIQUE — SUR LES BORDS DU RHIN EN SUISSE

A sa fille. — Byron quitte en 1816, pour la seconde et dernière fois, l'Angleterre, où il laisse sa fille Ada, sans l'avoir revue. — Il reprend son voyage et son poème dans un esprit nouveau. (Strophes I à VII.)

L'exil volontaire. — Sous le nom de Harold, Byron raconte ce qu'il vient de tenter : il a essayé de raviver son cœur par les voyages, puis de revenir en Angleterre. Le dégoût de la foule l'a ressaisi. Il s'exile de nouveau et va vers la mort, qui est la fin désirée. (Str. VIII à XVI.)

Waterloo. — Le champ de bataille. — Vanité des choses humaines. — Cette victoire est-elle la victoire de la liberté? — Le bal de Bruxelles et le canon de Waterloo. — La mort de Brunswick. — Le chant de guerre de Cameron et des Écossais. — La fin de Howard. — La douleur et la vie. (Str. XVII à XXXV.)

Bonaparte. — Son portrait, sa destinée, son caractère. — Condition supérieure et fatale de l'homme d'action, du conquérant, du poète. L'agitation est leur élément. (Str. XXXVI à XLV.)

Le Rhin. — Suite du voyage de Harold. — Les châteaux, les seigneurs brigands. — Les eaux du fleuve et le sang des batailles. — La nature et les hommes. (Str. XLVI à LI.)

A Coblentz. — Souvenir du pays, envoyé à sa sœur. — L'ode à une absente : *Pourquoi n'es-tu pas là?* (Str. LII à LV.)

Salut à la tombe de Marceau et à la forteresse d'Ehrenbreitstein. — Dernier adieu au Rhin et à ses bords admirables. (Str. LVI à LXI.)

La Suisse. Les Alpes. — Le champ de bataille de Morat. — La colonne solitaire. — Aventicum. — La tombe de Julia Alpinula. (Str. LXII à LXVII.)

Le Léman. — Opposition de la vie du monde et de la vie des lacs et des montagnes. — Grandeur de la nature dans laquelle le poète veut s'oublier. (Str. LXVIII à LXXV.)

Jean-Jacques Rousseau. — Son portrait. — L'amour idéal. — Pouvoir magique d'une âme éloquente. — Rousseau a soulevé la France. — Jugement de la Révolution. (Str. LXXVI à LXXXIV.)

Le soir et la nuit sur le lac Léman. — L'infini. — Le culte libre, sous le ciel. (Str. LXXXV à XCI.)

L'orage dans les montagnes. — Les convulsions de la nature et les déchirements du cœur de l'homme. — Les séparations. (Str. XCII à XCVIII.)

Clarens. — C'est le théâtre naturel de l'amour idéal, qui à son tour idéalise tout autour de lui. (Str. XCIX à CIV.)

Ferney et Voltaire; Lausanne et Gibbon. — Deux portraits littéraires. (Str. CV à CVIII.)

Epilogue. — L'auteur va reprendre ses voyages dans les Alpes. Il salue d'avance l'Italie. — Il envoie un dernier regard à sa patrie, au monde, à sa fille Ada. — Un jour tu m'aimeras! (Str. CIX à la fin.)

CANTO THE THIRD

> « Afin que cette vérité vous
> forçât de penser à autre chose.
> Il n'y a, en vérité, d'autre re-
> mède que celui-là, et le temps [1] »
>
> (Lettre du roi de Prusse à D'Alembert, 7 sept. 1776.)

A sa fille. — Byron quitte en 1816, pour la seconde et dernière fois, l'Angleterre, où il laisse sa fille Ada, sans l'avoir revue. — Il reprend son voyage et son poème dans un esprit nouveau. (Strophes I à VII.)

I

Is thy face like thy mother's, my fair child [1]!
Ada! sole daughter of my house and heart?
When last I saw thy young blue eyes they smiled,
And then we parted, — not as now we part,
But with a hope. —
          Awaking with a start,

---

* D'Alembert pleurait la mort de mademoiselle de Lespinasse. Le roi de Prusse lui conseille de se jeter dans un travail ardu, de chercher la solution d'un problème difficile, afin que l'étude de la « vérité » mathématique fasse diversion à la douleur morale.

1. *My fair child.* « Ressembles-tu à ta mère, mon bel enfant, Ada ? » s'écrie Byron. Il consacre à sa fille la première et la dernière strophe du IIIe chant; à elle encore se rapporte l'épigraphe citée plus haut. C'est le souvenir et l'accent des épreuves qu'il vient de subir. En effet il ignore quelle figure a sa fille depuis le jour où il l'a quittée. En janvier 1815, il s'est marié; en décembre 1815, il a une fille. « La petite est née le 10 décembre dernier, écrit-il quelque temps après. On l'a nommée *Augusta Ada*. Le second nom, très ancien dans la famille, n'avait plus été donné à une fille depuis le roi Jean. » Et ailleurs ; « C'est aussi le nom de la sœur de Charlemagne. » Ada avait cinq semaines, en janvier 1816, quand son père et sa mère se séparèrent pour toujours : Byron n'a donc vu qu'un instant le sourire de ses yeux bleus (*they smiled*).

The waters heave around me; and on high
The winds lift up their voices : I depart,
Whither I know not; but the hour's gone by[1],
When Albion's lessening shores could grieve or glad
  mine eye.

II

Once more upon the waters! yet once more!
And the waves bound beneath me as a steed
That knows his rider. Welcome to their roar!
Swift be their guidance, wheresoe'er it lead!
Though the strain'd mast should quiver as a reed,
And the rent canvas fluttering strew the gale,
Still must I on; for I am as a weed,
Flung from the rock, on Ocean's foam to sail
Where'er the surge may sweep, the tempest's breath
  prevail.

III

In my youth's summer I did sing of One,
The wandering outlaw of his own dark mind[2];
Again I seize the theme, then but begun,
And bear it with me, as the rushing wind
Bears the cloud onwards : in that Tale I find
The furrows of long thought, and dried-up tears,
Which, ebbing, leave a sterile track behind,
O'er which all heavily[3] the journeying years
Plod[4] the last sands of life, — where not a flower appears.

1. *Gone by*. L'heure est passée où je pouvais être ému de douleur ou de joie... Byron, à son premier départ, éprouvait et exprimait tour à tour des transports de gaîté et des accès de colère, comme le prouvent les variantes du premier chant. Cette heure est passée; le troisième chant ne ressemblera pas à ses aînés. Cela est vrai, malgré les vers tristes du Ier chant.

2. *Outlaw of his... mind*. Exilé de son cœur.

3. *All heavily*. Ici *all* a la valeur de notre superlatif *très*.

4. *Plod*, traverser péniblement.

IV

Since my young days of passion—joy, or pain,
Perchance my heart and harp¹ have lost a string,
And both may jar² : it may be, that in vain
I would essay as I have sung to sing.
Yet, though a dreary strain, to this I cling;
So that³ it wean me from the weary dream
Of selfish grief or gladness—so it fling
Forgetfulness around me—it shall seem
To me, though to none else, a not ungrateful theme.

V

He, who grown aged in this world of woe,
In deeds, not years, piercing the depths of life,
So that no wonder waits him; nor below⁴
Can love or sorrow, fame, ambition, strife,
Cut to his heart again with the keen knife
Of silent, sharp endurance : he can tell
Why thought seeks refuge in lone caves⁵, yet rife
With airy images, and shapes which dwell
Still unimpair'd, though old, in the soul's haunted cell.

VI

Tis to create, and in creating live
A being⁶ more intense than we endow
With form our fancy, gaining as we give
The life we image, even as I do now.

---

1. *Heart and harp.* Allitération.
2. *Jar.* Rendre des sons discordants.
3. *So that,* pourvu que.
4. *Nor below.* Construisez : *Nor love or sorrow can... cut to...* Les passions ne peuvent pas l'atteindre au cœur.
5. *In lone caves.* Il se réfugie dans l'âme comme dans une solitude peuplée d'images immortelles.
6. *Live a being.* Le sens général

What am I? Nothing: but not so art thou,
Soul of my thought! with whom I traverse earth.
Invisible but gazing, as I glow
Mixed with thy spirit, blended with thy birth,
And feeling still with thee in my crush'd feelings' dearth.

VII

Ye must I think less wildly:— I *have* thought
Too long and darkly, till my brain became,
In its own eddy boiling and o'erwrought.
A whirling gulf of phantasy and flame:
And thus, untaught in youth my heart to tame,
My springs of life were poisoned. 'Tis too late!
Yet am I changed[1]; though still enough the same
In strength to bear what time can not abate,
And feed on bitter fruits without accusing Fate.

L'exil volontaire. — Sous le nom de Harold, Byron raconte ce qu'il vient de tenter : il a essayé de raviver son cœur par les voyages, puis de revenir en Angleterre et de vivre de la vie de la strophe est celui-ci : Ces méditations font vivre le poète d'une vie nouvelle qu'il crée, qu'il reçoit lui-même en la donnant. Il n'a plus de sensibilité en face des choses, mais il sent en pensant, il a le feu de l'âme.

1. *Yet am I changed.* Dans tout ce passage, Byron explique le changement qui s'est fait en lui et qui se montre d'ailleurs dans son poème.

Hier il accusait le sort, il écrivait en désordre des strophes joyeusement ironiques ou des vers douloureux ; aujourd'hui il s'attache à la tristesse (*a dreary strain, to this I cling*, — str. IV). Il avoue que sa vie est perdue, parce qu'il n'a pas été élevé ; il est trop tard, dit-il. Maintenant il part avec le pressentiment et l'espoir de la mort. (Voy. la biographie.)

sociale. Le dégoût de la foule l'a ressaisi. Il s'exile de nouveau et va vers la mort, qui est la fin désirée (Str. VIII à XVI).

VIII

Something too much[1] of this:—but now 'tis past,
And the spell[2] closes with its silent seal.
Long absent HAROLD re-appears at last;
He of the breast[3] which fain no more would feel,
Wrung with the wounds which kill not, but ne'er heal;
Yet Time, who changes all, had alter'd him
In soul and aspect as in age: years steal
Fire from the mind as vigour from the limb;
And life's enchanted cup but sparkles near the brim.

IX

His had been quaff'd too quickly, and he found
The dregs were wormwood[4] but he fill'd again,
And from a purer fount, on holier ground,
And deem'd its spring perpetual; but in vain!
Still round him clung invisibly a chain
Which gall'd for ever, fettering though unseen,
And heavy though it clank'd not; worn with pain,
Which pined although it spoke not, and grew keen,
Entering with every step he took through many a scene.

1. *Something...* J'en ai un peu trop dit (sur moi-même et en mon propre nom). Revenons à Harold.
2. *The spell closes.* La fantasmagorie du passé va se clore dans le silence.
3. *He of the breast.* Celui qui à l'âme...
4. *Wormwood.* Au fond il trouva l'absinthe. Ce mot a perdu de sa force depuis que l'absinthe est une boisson. Encore au temps de Byron, il indiquait un breuvage amer et nauséabond, selon le sens primitif de l'ancien haut allemand, *Wermuode*, la mort aux vers, qui a donné *vermuth*, et par corruption, en anglais, *wormwood*.

X

Secure in guarded coldness, he had mix'd
Again in fancied safety with his kind[1],
And deem'd his spirit[2] now so firmly fix'd
And sheath'd with an invulnerable mind,
That, if no joy, no sorrow lurked behind;
And he, as one, might 'midst the many stand
Unheeded, searching through the crowd to find
Fit speculation[3]; such as in strange land
He found in wonder-works of God and Nature's hand.

XI

But who can view the ripen'd rose, nor seek
To wear it? who can curiously behold
The smoothness and the sheen of Beauty's cheek.
Nor feel the heart can never all grow old?
Who can contemplate Fame through clouds unfold
The star which rises o'er her steep, nor climb?
Harold, once more within the vortex, roll'd
On with the giddy circle, chasing Time[4],
Yet with a nobler aim than in his youth's fond prime[5].

XII

But soon he knew himself the most unfit
Of men to herd with Man[6], with whom he held

---

1. *With his kind.* Avec son espèce, avec les hommes.
2. *Spirit.* Son cœur lui semblait fixé et enveloppé par le scepticisme de son esprit.
3. *Speculation*, un sujet d'étude.
4. *Chasing Time*, donnant la chasse au temps (qui ne compte pas dans le feu des plaisirs).
5. *Fond prime.* Le printemps fou. C'est le sens premier du mot *fond* qui a signifié : 1° fou, 2° qui aime follement, 3° qui est amateur de...
6. *To herd with Man.* Vivre en troupeau avec les hommes.

Little in common; untaught to submit
His thoughts to others, though his soul was quell'd
In youth by his own thoughts; still uncompell'd,
He would not yield dominion of his mind
To spirits against whom his own rebell'd;
Proud though in desolation; which[1] could find
A life within itself, to breathe without mankind.

XIII

Where rose the mountains, there to him were friends
Where roll'd the ocean, thereon was his home;
Where a blue sky, and glowing clime, extends,
He had the passion and the power to roam;
The desert, forest, cavern, breaker's foam,
Were unto him[2] companionship; they spake
A mutual language, clearer than the tome
Of his land's tongue, which he would oft forsake
For Nature's pages glass'd by sunbeams on the lake.

XIV

Like the Chaldean, he could watch the stars,
Till he had peopled them with beings bright
As their own beams; and earth, and earth-born jars[3],
And human frailties, were forgotten quite:
Could he have kept his spirit to that flight
He had been happy; but this clay[4] will sink
Its spark immortal, envying it the light
To which it mounts, as if to break the link
That keeps us from yon heaven which woos us to its brink.

1. *Which*, lui qui pouvait... Il gardait l'orgueil dans le désespoir, pouvant..

2. *Unto him*. Pour lui, à ses yeux.

3. *Jars*, les querelles. Ce mot a ici le sens figuré. Dans la strophe IV, il avait son sens primitif.

4. *This clay*. Cette argile dont nous sommes faits.

XV

But in Man's dwellings he became a thing
Restless and worn, and stern and wearisome,
Droop'd as a wild-born falcon with clipt wing,
To whom the boundless air alone were home:
Then came his fit again, which to o'ercome,
As eagerly the barr'd-up bird will beat
His breast and beak¹ against his wiry dome
Till the blood tinge his plumage, so the heat
Of his impeded soul would through his bosom eat.

XVI

Self-exiled Harold wanders forth again,
With nought of hope left, but with less of gloom;
The very knowledge that he lived in vain,
That all was over on this side the tomb,
Had made Despair a smilingness assume,   [wreck²
Which, though 't were wild, — as on the plunder'd
When mariners would madly meet their doom³
With draughts intemperate on the sinking deck, —
Did yet inspire a cheer, which he forebore to check.⁴

---

1. *Breast and beak*, allitération.
2. *Plundered wreck*, le vaisseau désemparé.
3. *Meet their doom*. Tenir tête au destin, lutter contre lui.

4. *To check*. Toute cette strophe, dans laquelle Byron déclare que sa vie est finie et perdue, résume les strophes précédentes et justifie ce qui a été dit dans la *Notice*.

Waterloo. — Le champ de bataille. — Vanité des choses humaines. — Cette victoire est-elle la victoire de la liberté ? — Le bal de Bruxelles et le canon de Waterloo. — La mort de Brunswick. — Le chant de guerre de Cameron et des Écossais. — La fin de Howard. — La douleur et la vie. (Str. XVII à XXXV.)

XVII

Stop ! — for thy tread is on an Empire's dust !
An Earthquake's spoil is sepulchred below !
Is the spot[1] mark'd with no colossal bust ?
Nor column trophied for triumphal show ?
None ; but the moral's truth tells simpler so,
As the ground was before, thus let it be ; —
How that red rain hath made the harvest grow !
And is this all the world has gain'd by thee,
Thou first and last of fields ! king-making[2] Victory ?

XVIII

And Harold stands upon this place of skulls,
The grave of France, the deadly Waterloo !
How in an hour the power which gave annuls
Its gifts, transferring fame as fleeting too !
In " pride of place[3] " here last the eagle flew,
Then tore with bloody talon[4] the rent plain,

---

1. *Is the spot.* N'y a-t-il pas ici de statue ou de trophée... ? Rien.

2. *King-making.* Waterloo faiseur de rois ! Waterloo a fait la Restauration. C'est la victoire des rois, et non pas celle de la liberté, dit Byron, qui va développer cette thèse, et qui annonce son opinion dans l'épithète rapide qu'il jetto là pour traduire d'un mot sa pensée.

3. *In pride of place.* L'aigle prit son vol le plus haut, le plus fier. Expression archaïque que Byron emprunte à la langue de la fauconnerie, et qui d'ailleurs est renouvelée de Shakspeare : *A falcon tow'ring in his pride of place* (*Macbeth*, II, 4).

4. *With talon*, avec ses serres. Byron avait écrit d'abord *with*

Pierced by the shaft of banded nations through;
Ambition's life and labours all were vain;
He wears the shatter'd links of the world's broken chain.

XIX

Fit retribution[1]! Gaul may champ the bit[2]
And foam in fetters; — but is Earth more free?
Did nations combat to make *One* submit;
Or league to teach all kings true sovereignty?
What! shall reviving Thraldom again be
The patch'd-up idol of enlighten'd days?
Shall we, who struck the Lion down, shall we
Pay the Wolf homage? proffering lowly gaze
And servile knees to thrones? No; *prove* before ye praise!

XX

If not, o'er one fallen despot boast no more!
In vain fair cheeks[2] were furrow'd with hot tears
For Europe's flowers long rooted up before
The trampler of her vineyards; in vain years
Of death, depopulation, bondage, fears,
Have all been borne, and broken by the accord
Of roused-up millions; all that most endears
Glory, is when the myrtle wreathes a sword
Such as Harmodius[4] drew on Athen's tyrant lord.

bloody beak. Un peintre illustra les vers de Byron et corrigea sans le dire, l'image du poète : il dessina l'aigle attaquant la terre avec ses serres. Byron comprit et modifia de bonne grâce le vers primitif.

1. *Fit retribution... but...* Juste retour, mais... Ici Byron développe sa pensée. En dépit des félicitations que l'Angleterre s'adresse à elle-même, il dit : Sommes-nous plus libres pour cela? Attendez le résultat, l'épreuve, avant de louer. *Prove, before ye praise.*

2. *Champ the bit.* Ronger son frein.

3. *Fair cheeks.* De beaux visages de femmes.

4. *Harmodius.* Byron copie ici le premier vers du chant célèbre d'Harmodius et d'Aristogiton : *With myrtle,* etc.

XXI

There was a sound of revelry¹ by night,
And Belgium's capital had gather'd then
Her Beauty and her Chivalry, and bright
The lamps shone o'er fair women and brave men;
A thousand hearts beat happily; and when
Music arose with its voluptuous swell,
Soft eyes look'd love² to eyes which spake again,
And all went merry as a marriage bell;
But hush! hark! a deep sound strikes like a rising knell!

XXII

Did ye not hear it? — No; 't was but the wind,
Or the car rattling o'er the stony street;
On with³ the dance! let joy be unconfined;
No sleep till morn, when Youth and Pleasure meet
To chase the glowing Hours with flying feet —
But hark! — that heavy sound breaks in once more
As if the clouds its echo would repeat;
And nearer, clearer, deadlier than before!
Arm! Arm! it is — it is — the cannon's opening⁴ roar!

XXIII

Within a window'd niche of that high hall
Sate Brunswick's⁵ fated chieftain; he did hear

---

1 *Revelry.* Il y avait, dit-on, un grand bal à Bruxelles, quand tout à coup le bruit de l'orchestre fut couvert par le bruit du canon. C'était Bonaparte qui entrait en Belgique. De cette coïncidence Byron a fait une scène dramatique : il va décrire le bal, l'alarme et la bataille.

2. *Looked love.* Les yeux exprimaient l'amour, et d'autres yeux leur répondaient. Ce trait prépare la strophe XXIV sur « le dernier regard ».

3. *On with.* Continuons la danse.

4. *Opening.* Le rugissement du canon qui ouvre l'action.

5. *Brunswick.* Le chef (marqué

That sound the first amidst the festival,
And caught its tone with Death's prophetic ear;
And when they smiled because he deem'd it near,
His heart more truly knew that peal too well
Which stretch'd his father on a bloody bier,
And roused the vengeance[1] blood alone could quell;
He rush'd into the field, and, foremost fighting, fell.

XXIV

Ah! then and there was hurrying[2] to and fro,
And gathering tears, and tremblings of distress,
And cheeks all pale, which but an hour ago
Blush'd at the praise of their own loveliness;
And there were sudden partings, such as press
The life from out[3] young hearts, and choking sighs
Which ne'er might[4] be repeated; who could guess
If ever more should meet those mutual eyes,
Since upon night so sweet such awful morn could rise!

XXV

And there was mounting[5] in hot haste: the steed,
The mustering[6] squadron, and the clattering car,
Went pouring forward with impetuous speed,
And swiftly forming in the ranks of war;
And the deep thunder peal on peal afar;
And near, the beat of the alarming drum

---

par le destin) de la famille de Brunswick. En effet, le duc de Brunswick allait être tué à Quatre-Bras, lorsqu'il espérait venger son père, tué à Iéna. La fatalité frappait cette famille.

1. *The vengeance.* Ajoutez *that (blood alone).*

2. *There was hurrying.* Construisez : *hurrying, and tears gathering, and tremblings.*
3. *Press... out*, qui arrachent.
4. *Which ne'er might...,* qui pourraient être les derniers.
5. *Mounting.* On monte à cheval.
6. *Mustering,* l'escadron qui se

Roused up the soldier ere the morning star;
While throng'd the citizens with terror dumb,
Or whispering, with white lips—"The foe! They come!
 they come!"

XXVI

And wild and high the "Cameron's gathering[1]" rose!
The war note of Lochiel, which Albyn's hills
Have heard, and heard, too have her Saxon foes :—
How in the noon of night that pibroch thrills,
Savage and shrill! But with the breath which fills
Their mountain-pipe, so fill the mountaineers
With the fierce native daring which instils
The stirring memory of a thousand years,
And Evan's, Donald's fame rings in each clansman's ears.

XXVII

And Ardennes[2] waves above them her green leaves,
Dewy with nature's tear-drops, as they pass,
Grieving, if aught inanimate e'er grieves,
Over the unreturning brave,—alas!
Ere evening to be trodden like the grass

---

rassemble. La revue militaire au moyen âge s'appelait la *monstre*.

1. *Cameron's gathering.* On entend tout à coup « l'appel de Cameron », c'est-à-dire le chant de guerre des Écossais, celui de Sir Evan Cameron, qui jadis a si bien combattu pour les Stuarts, celui maintenant de son descendant, *Donald Cameron de Lochiel*, qui vient se faire tuer à Waterloo. Dans cette strophe, *Albyn* veut dire l'Écossea et le Saxon c'est l'Anglais.

2. *Ardennes.* C'est-à-dire le bois de Soignies. « J'ai adopté, dit Byron, le nom qui s'associe à des souvenirs nobles plutôt que celui qui ne rappelle que des scènes de carnage. » En effet, la forêt d'Ardennes était le théâtre légendaire des contes héroïques du moyen âge. C'est là que nous transporte Shakspeare dans la pièce intitulée : *As you like it.*

Which now beneath them, but above shall grow
In its next verdure, when this fiery mass
Of living valour, rolling on the foe
And burning with high hope, shall moulder cold and low.

XXVIII

Last noon beheld them full of lusty life,
Last eve in Beauty's circle proudly gay,
The midnight brought the signal-sound of strife,
The morn the marshalling in arms,—the day
Battle's magnificently stern array!
The thunder-clouds close o'er it, which when rent [1]
The earth is covered thick with other clay,
Which her own clay shall cover, heap'd and pent,
Rider and horse,—friend, foe, in one red burial bent [2]!

XXIX

Their praise is hymned by loftier harps than mine;
Yet one I would select [3] from that proud throng,
Partly because they blend me with his line,
And partly that I did his sire some wrong,
And partly that bright names will hallow song;
And his was of the bravest, and when shower'd
The death-bolts deadliest the thinned files along,
Even where the thickest of war's tempest lower'd,
They reach'd no nobler breast than thine, young, gallant Howard!

---

1. *Which when rent.* Quand ces nuages de fumée sont déchirés, la terre est couverte (de morts, de l'argile dont nous sommes faits).
2. *Blent,* pour *blended.*
3. *One I would select.* Allusion au major Howard, tué à Waterloo. Il était fils du tuteur de Byron, avec lequel le poète eut des démêlés et qu'il attaqua dans ses vers. Le poète se fit montrer la place où était tombé le major. « La charrue y a passé, dit-il, et le grain y germe. Mais deux arbres épargnés marquent encore cette place. » — Voyez la strophe suivante.

CANTO THE THIRD.

XXX

There have been tears and breaking hearts for thee,
And mine were nothing, had I such[1] to give;
But when I stood beneath the fresh green tree,
Which living waves where thou didst cease to live,
And saw around me the wide field revive
With fruits and fertile promise, and the Spring
Come forth her work of gladness to contrive[2]
With all her reckless birds upon the wing[3],
I turn'd from all she brought to those she could not bring[4].

XXXI

I turned to thee, to thousands, of whom each
And one as all a ghastly gap did make
In his own kind and kindred, whom to teach
Forgetfulness were mercy for their sake[5]:
The Archangel's trump, not Glory's, must awake
Those whom they thirst for; though the sound of Fame
May for a moment soothe, it cannot slake
The fever of vain longing, and the name
So honour'd but assumes a stronger, bitterer claim[6].

---

1. *Had I such* ... Si je pouvais pleurer.
2. *To contrive.* Pour accomplir son œuvre de joie.
3. *Upon the wing*, apportant sur son aile.
4. *Bring.* La plaine de Waterloo, dit lord Byron, semble le théâtre prédestiné de quelque grande action. Est-ce un pur effet de l'imagination? J'ai examiné attentivement les champs de bataille de Platée, de Troie, de Mantinée, de Leuctres, de Chéronée, de Marathon. Le territoire du Mont-Saint-Jean et d'Hougoumont, si l'on y eût défendu une meilleure cause, si le temps y eût mis cette auréole indéfinissable, mais saisissante, que le cours des âges donne aux lieux célèbres, le disputerait en intérêt à tous les autres, Marathon excepté.
5. *Were mercy for their sake*, serait une charité, un bienfait pour eux.
6. *A claim*, un droit aux regrets.

XXXII

They mourn[1], but smile at length; and, smiling, mourn:
The tree will wither long before it fall;
The hull drives on, though mast and sail be torn;
The roof-tree sinks, but moulders on the hall
In massy hoariness; the ruin'd wall
Stands when its wind-worn battlements are gone;
The bars survive the captive they enthral;
They day drags through, though storms keep out the sun
And thus the heart will break, yet brokenly live on:

XXXIII

Even as a broken mirror[2], which the glass
In every fragment multiplies, and makes
A thousand images of one that was,
The same, and still[3] the more, the more it breaks;
And thus the heart will do which not forsakes,
Living in shatter'd guise; and still, and cold,
And bloodless, with its sleepless sorrow aches,
Yet withers on till all without[4] is old,
Showing no visible sign, for such things are untold.

XXXIV

There is a very life[5] in our despair,
Vitality of poison,—a quick root

---

1. *They mourn.* On pleure. Ici le sens est général. Le poète passe à des réflexions philosophiques, qui vont remplir trois strophes.

2. *Broken mirror.* En brisant le miroir, on multiplie le miroir et l'image. Vieille comparaison, devenue proverbiale.

2. *Still*, toujours, plus bas *still*, muet.

3. *All without*, tout ce qui est son enveloppe extérieure. Le sens premier de *without* est la dehors, opposé au sens de *within*, le dedans.

1. *Life... Vitality... quick.* Il y

Which feeds these deadly branches; for it were
As nothing did we die; but Life will suit [1]
Itself to Sorrow's most detested fruit,
Like to the apples on the Dead Sea's shore,
All ashes [2] to the taste. Did man compute
Existence by enjoyment, and count o'er
Such hours 'gainst years of life,—say, would he name threescore?

XXXV

The Psalmist [3] numbered out the years of man:
They are enough; and if thy tale [4] be *true*,
Thou, who didst grudge him even that fleeting span,
More than enough, thou fatal Waterloo!
Millions of tongues record thee, and anew
Their children's lips shall echo them, and say—
"Here, where the sword united nations drew,
Our countrymen were warring on that day!"
And this is much, and all which will not pass away.

a une *vie* dans le désespoir, une force *vitale* dans le poison, une racine *vivace* sous l'arbre mort.

1. *Suit itself*, s'associe.
2. *Ashes*. Byron ici a mis en note qu'il empruntait à Tacite (*Hist.* V, 7) le *velut in cinerem vanescunt.*
3. *The psalmist.* Cette fois Byron indique lui-même l'une des allusions qu'il a faites à la Bible : « *The days of our life are threescore years and ten,* » dit le psalmiste.
4. *If thy tale...* Si ton compte est vrai. Le mot *tale* est pris dans le sens étymologique : *Zahl* (allemand), *tale* (anglais), signifient nombre, compte. De là *to tell*, raconter, dire, faire le dénombrement des faits. De même en français nous avons dit *compter* puis *raconter;* mais on a voulu distinguer par l'orthographe deux mots que l'on croyait différents, et l'on a écrit *conter*. Chaque siècle apporte de ces petites erreurs imposées par le pédantisme et la fausse érudition.

Bonaparte. — Son portrait, sa destinée, son caractère. — Condition supérieure et fatale de l'homme d'action, du conquérant du poète. L'agitation est leur élément. (Str. XXXVI à XLV.)

XXXVI

There sunk the greatest, nor the worst of men [1],
Whose spirit, antithetically mixt [2],
One moment of the mightiest, and again
On little objects with like firmness fixt;
Extreme in all things! hadst thou been betwixt;
Thy throne had still been thine, or never been;
For daring made thy rise as fall : thou seek'st.
Even now to re-assume the imperial miën [3],
And shake again the world, the Thunderer [4] of the scene!

XXXVII

Conqueror and captive of the earth art thou!
She trembles at thee still, and thy wild name [5]
Was ne'er more bruited in men's minds than now
That thou art nothing, save the jest of Fame,

---

1. *Nor the worst of men.* Pour l'Europe entière, Napoléon était le dernier des hommes, depuis sa chute. Des milliers d'écrits le traînaient dans la boue. *The whole host of hatred stood hard by*; une armée des haines l'enveloppait, dit Byron (voy. ci-dessous la strophe XXXIX). Le poète leur répondit par les vers qu'on lit ici.

2. *Antithecally mixt...* Son esprit offrait ce mélange et cette antithèse, qu'il se portait et sur les plus grandes choses et sur les moindres détails. La construction de cette phrase n'est pas très grammaticale, mais le sens en est très net.

3. *Mien*, la figure et le rôle d'un empereur.

4. *The Thunderer*, le Jupiter Tonnant.

5. *Wild name.* Ton nom terrible. C'est un des emplois les plus hardis de ce mot *wild* qui est si familier à Byron, à Shakspeare et à toute l'Angleterre. *Wild*, sauvage, farouche, indompté, s'applique en effet à toutes les manifestations de l'indépendance.

Who woo'd thee once, thy vassal, and became
The flatterer of thy fierceness[1], till thou wert
A god unto thyself; nor less the same[2]
To the astounded kingdoms all inert,
Who deem'd thee for a time whate'er thou didst assert.

XXXVIII

Oh, more or less than man — in high or low,
Battling with nations, flying from the field;
Now making monarchs' necks thy footstool, now
More than thy meanest soldier taught to yield;
An empire thou couldst crush, command, rebuild,
But govern not thy pettiest passion, nor,
However deeply in men's spirits skill'd[3],
Look through thine own, nor curb the lust of war,
Nor learn that tempted Fate will leave the loftiest star.

XXXIX

Yet well thy soul hath brook'd the turning tide
With that untaught innate philosophy,
Which, be it wisdom, coldness, or deep pride,
Is gall and wormwood to an enemy.
When the whole host of hatred stood hard by,
To watch and mock thee shrinking[4], thou hast smiled
With a sedate and all-enduring eye; —
When Fortune fled her spoil'd and favourite child,
He stood unbow'd beneath the ills upon him piled.

1. *Fierceness*, ton orgueil.
2. *The same*... Tu fus un dieu pour toi et un dieu pour eux.
3. *Skilled*. Habile à juger, connaisseur en hommes.

4. *To watch... thee shrinking*... Pour épier ta chute. On ne peut pas rendre *to shrink*, qui signifie en même temps reculer et s'amoindrir.

XL.

Sager than in thy fortunes; for in them
Ambition steel'd thee on too far to show
That just habitual scorn[1], which could contemn
Men and their thoughts; 't was wise to feel, not so
To wear it ever on thy lip and brow,
And spurn[2] the instruments thou wert to use
Till they were turn'd unto thine overthrow;
'Tis but a worthless world to win or lose;
So hath it proved to thee, and all such lot who choose.

XLI

If, like a tower upon a headlong rock,
Thou hadst been made to stand or fall alone,
Such scorn of man had help'd to brave the shock :
But men's thoughts[3] were the steps which paved thy
Their admiration thy best weapon shone[4];   [throne,
The part of Philip's son was thine, not then
(Unless aside thy purple had been thrown)
Like stern Diogenes to mock at men;
For sceptred cynics[5] earth were far too wide a den.

XLII

But quiet[6] to quick bosoms is a hell,
And *there* hath been thy bane; there is a fire

---

1. *That just habitual scorn* Ce mépris, qui est une habitude et qui est juste.
2. *Spurn*, frapper du pied, puis *repousser*.
3. *Men's thoughts*, l'opinion.
4. *Their admiration... shone*. Le rayonnement de leur admiration fit ton arme la plus sûre.
5. *Sceptred cynics*. On ne peut pas avoir le rôle de roi et le rôle de cynique. En France, nous dirions les cyniques couronnés.
6. *Quiet*, le repos.

And motion of the soul which will not dwell
In its own narrow being [1], but aspire
Beyond the fitting medium [2] of desire;
And, but once kindled, quenchless evermore,
Preys upon high adventure, nor can tire
Of aught but rest; a fever at the core,
Fatal to him who bears, to all who ever bore.

XLIII

This makes the madmen who have made men mad [3]
By their contagion; Conquerors and Kings,
Founders of sects and systems, to whom add
Sophists, Bards [4], Statesmen, all unquiet things
Which stir too strongly the soul's secret springs,
And are themselves the fools to those they fool [5];
Envied, yet how unenviable! what stings
Are theirs! One breast laid open were a school
Which would unteach mankind the lust to shine or rule:

XLIV

Their breath [6] is agitation, and their life
A storm whereon they ride, to sink at last,
And yet so nursed and bigoted to strife,
That should their days, surviving perils past,
Melt to calm twilight, they feel overcast
With sorrow and supineness, and so die;

---

1. *In its narrow being...* Dans les étroites limites de son être.
2. *Fitting medium*, le milieu raisonnable.
3. *Madmen... made men mad.* Autre exemple, et très étrange, de l'allitération.
4. *Bards*, les poètes. On a deviné déjà que Byron assimile la destinée de Napoléon à la sienne propre, par un secret retour sur lui-même.
5. *They fool.* Ceux qu'ils ont affolés les regardent à leur tour comme des fous.
6. *Their breath*, leur souffle, leur existence.

Even as a flame unfed, which runs to waste [4]
With its own flickering, or a sword laid by
Which eats into itself, and rusts ingloriously.

XLV

He who ascends to mountain-tops, shall find
The loftiest peaks most wrapt in clouds and snow;
He who surpasses or subdues mankind,
Must look down on the hate of those below [2].
Though high *above* [3] the sun of glory glow,
And far *beneath* the earth and ocean spread,
Round him are icy rocks, and loudly blow
Contending tempests on his naked head,
And thus reward the toils which to those summits led.

Le Rhin. — Suite du voyage de Harold. — Les châteaux, les seigneurs brigands. — Les eaux du fleuve et le sang des batailles. — La nature et les hommes. (Str. XLVI à LI.)

XLVI

Away with these [4]! true Wisdom's world will be
Within its own creation [5], or in thine,
Maternal Nature! for who teems like thee,

---

1. *Runs to waste*, se précipite vers sa fin.
2. *Those below*. Ceux qui sont en bas, les petits, les inférieurs.
3. *Above*. La gloire est au-dessus d'eux, la terre au-dessous : ils vivent dans la région intermédiaire, celle des tempêtes.

4. *These*. Fuyons ces ambitieux.
5. *Creation*. Le bonheur est dans ce monde de la pensée qu'on se crée à soi-même, et que Byron a déjà décrit plus haut (voy. strophe VI), ou dans le monde de la nature.

Thus on the banks of thy majestic Rhine?
There Harold gazes on a work divine,
A blending of all beauties; streams and dells,
Fruit, foliage, crag, wood, cornfield, mountain, vine,
And chiefless castles breathing stern farewells[1]
From gray but leafy walls, where Ruin greenly dwells.

XLVII

And there they stand, as stands a lofty mind,
Worn, but unstooping to the baser crowd[2],
All tenantless, save to the crannying[3] wind,
Or holding dark communion with the cloud.
There was a day when they were young and proud;
Banners on high, and battles passed below;
But they who fought are in a bloody shroud,
And those which waved[4] are shredless dust ere now,
And the bleak battlements shall bear no future blow.

XLVIII

Beneath these battlements, within those walls,
Power dwelt amidst her passions; in proud state
Each robber chief[5] upheld his armed halls,

---

1. *Castles breathing farewells:* Ces rudes châteaux, qu'on aperçoit longtemps, semblent vous dire adieu de loin.
2. *The baser crowd.* Ils ne veulent pas s'incliner devant la foule d'en bas. Prosper Mérimée, en parlant de Jacquemont, avoue que les esprits élevés exaspèrent les gens médiocres en leur laissant voir qu'ils les estiment peu.
3. *Crannying.* Le vent qui rend visite aux brèches et aux fentes de ces vieux remparts.
4. *Waved.* Les drapeaux flottants ne sont pas même des lambeaux : (*shredless*) : c'est de la poussière.
5. *Robber chief*, chef de brigands. — Il s'agit des seigneurs qui détroussaient les passants et qui de combat en combat, pouvaient devenir rois. Dans cette strophe, Byron fait allusion, il le dit lui-même, à la Ballade sur Johnny

Doing his evil will, nor less elate
Than mightier heroes of a longer date.
What want these outlaws conquerors should have
But History's purchased page¹ to call them great?
A wider space, an ornamented grave?
Their hopes were not less warm, their souls were full
    as brave.

XLIX

In their baronial feuds and single² fields,
What deeds of prowess unrecorded died!
And Love, which lent a blazon³ to their shields,
With emblems well devised by amorous pride,
Through all the mail of iron hearts would glide;
But still their flame was fierceness, and drew on
Keen contest and destruction near allied,
And many a tower for some fair mischief⁴ won,
Saw the discoloured Rhine beneath its ruin run.

L

But Thou, exulting and abounding river!
Making thy waves a blessing as they flow
Through banks whose beauty would endure for ever
Could man but⁵ leave thy bright creation so,
Nor its fair promise from the surface mow

Armstrong. Ce lord venant se soumettre à Jacques V, avait un si grand air que le roi s'écria : « Que manque-t-il à ce brigand de ce qui fait un roi ? Rien que l'épée royale et la couronne. » — « Le premier qui fut roi, dit Voltaire, fut un soldat heureux. »

1. *Purchased page,* une histoire vénale.

2. *Single,* à part, petit, c'est-à-dire inconnu du monde.

3. *Lent a blazon.* Leur blason portait les couleurs de leurs dames.

4. *Fair mischief.* Combat de beauté (pour la beauté).

5. *Could man.* Réunissez *would endure, could man...* Ta beauté serait impérissable, si l'homme te laissait tel que tu as été créé.

With the sharp scythe of conflict, — then to see
Thy walley of sweet waters, were to know
Earth paved[1] like Heaven; and to seem[2] such to me,
Even now what wants thy stream? — that it should Lethe be.

LI

A thousand battles have assail'd thy banks,
But these and half their fame have pass'd away,
And Slaughter heap'd on high his weltering ranks[3];
Their very graves are gone, and what are they?
Thy tide wash'd down the blood of yesterday,
And all was stainless, and on thy clear stream
Glass'd, with its dancing light, the sunny ray;
But o'er the blacken'd memory's blighting[4] dream
Thy waves would vainly roll, all sweeping as they seem.

A Coblentz. — Souvenir du pays, envoyé à sa sœur. — L'ode à une absente : *Pourquoi n'es-tu pas ici ?* (Str. LII à LV.)

LII

Thus Harold inly said, and pass'd along,
Yet not insensible[5] to all which here
Awoke the jocund birds to early song

1. *Paved like*, comme les parvis du ciel.
2. *To seem.* Pour me paraître.
3. *Ranks.* A amoncelé les rangs de cadavres.
4. *Blighting*, qui flétrit, qui assombrit.
5. *Yet not insensible.* Pourtant Harold n'était pas insensible... Byron (qui veut ici faire entrer dans son poème quelques-uns de ses vers d'amour), explique par une strophe de transition que les sceptiques ne sont pas toujours sceptiques. Ce passage est un peu artificiel, nécessairement.

In glens which might have made even exile dear:
Though on his brow were graven lines austere,
And tranquil sternness¹, which had ta'en the place
Of feelings fierier far but less severe,
Joy was not always absent from his face,
But o'er it in such scenes would steal² with transient trace.

LIII

Nor was all love shut from him, though his days
Of passion had consumed themselves to dust.
It is in vain that we would coldly gaze
On such as smile upon us; the heart must
Leap kindly back to kindness, though disgust
Hath weaned it from all worldlings : thus he felt,
For there was soft remembrance, and sweet trust
In one fond breast³ to which his own would melt,
And in its tenderer hour on that his bosom dwelt⁴.

LIV

And he had learn'd to love, — I know not why,
For this in such as him seems strange of mood, —
The helpless looks⁵ of blooming infancy,
Even in its earliest nurture; what subdued,
To change like this, a mind so far imbued

---

1. *Tranquil sternness*, une tranquille rigidité. Byron essaye d'être calme.
2. *Would steal*. Elle passait fugitive.
3. *One fond breast*, un cœur affectueux. Byron pense, sur les bords du Rhin, à sa sœur absente, à Augusta, à laquelle il envoie des fleurs et des vers.
4. *Dwelt*, reposait.
5. *The helpless looks*, les regards innocents. Il s'agit probablement ici de sa fille Ada, dont il rappelait plus haut les yeux bleus et souriants.

With scorn of man, it little boots to know;
But thus it was; and though in solitude
Small power the nipp'd affections [1] have to grow,
In him this glow'd when all beside had ceased to glow.

LV

And there was one soft breast [2], as hath been said,
Which unto his was bound by stronger ties
Than the church links withal; and, though unwed,
That love was pure, and, far above disguise,
Had stood the test [3] of mortal enmities
Still undivided, and cemented more
By peril, dreaded most in female eyes [4];
But this was firm, and from a foreign shore
Well to that heart might his these absent greetings pour!

1

The castled crag of Drachenfels [5]
Frowns o'er [6] the wide and winding Rhine,
Whose breast of waters [7] broadly swells
Between the banks which bear the vine,
And hills [8] all rich with blossom'd trees,

---

1. *Nipped affections.* Les affections qui ont été frappées d'un coup mortel. *Nip* appartient à une grande famille de mots qui signifient *frapper* d'un coup de bec, *saisir, happer,* puis *couper, pincer, détruire.*

2. *One soft breast.* Il s'agit encore de sa sœur, dont il vient de parler (*as hath been said*).

3. *The test,* l'épreuve.

4. *In female eyes,* redouté des femmes.

5. *Drachenfels.* Le château du Dragon, situé sur le plus haut pic des Sept montagnes, et d'où Byron contemple le cours du Rhin.

6. *Frowns o'er.* Domine, sourcilleux, le cours du Rhin.

7. *Breast of waters.* Il gonfle ses eaux et son sein.

8. *And hills...* Construisez : des collines, des champs, des villes parsèment le paysage (*have strewed*), expression qu'on trouvera à la page suivante.

And fields which promise corn and wine,
And scatter'd cities crowning these,
Whose far white walls along them shine,
Have strew'd a scene, — which I should see
With double joy, wert *thou* with me.

2

And peasant girls, with deep blue eyes,
And hands which offer early flowers,
Walk smiling o'er this paradise;
Above, the frequent feudal towers
Through green leaves lift their walls of gray [1];
And many a rock which steeply lowers,
And noble arch in proud decay,
Look o'er this vale of vintage-bowers,
— But one thing want these banks of Rhine, —
Thy gentle hand to clasp in mine!

3

I send the lilies given to me;
Though long before thy hand they touch,
I know that they must wither'd be,
— But yet reject them not as such [2];
For I have cherish'd them as dear,
Because [3] they yet may meet thine eye,
And guide thy soul to mine even here,
When thou behold'st [4] them drooping nigh,
And know'st them gather'd by the Rhine,
And offer'd from my heart to thine!

---

1. *Walls of gray*, leurs murailles grises. Cette locution, *of gray*, qui équivaut absolument à un adjectif, est fréquente dans tout le poème.

2. *As such*, comme flétries,
parce que les fleurs sont flétries.

3. *As dear because*. Si je les aime, c'est que... Mot à mot : *chères en tant que...*

4. *Behold'st...* Quand tu regarderas.

4

The river nobly foams and flows,
The charm¹ of this enchanted ground,
And all its thousand turns disclose
Some fresher beauty varying round :
The haughtiest breast its wish might bound
Through life to dwell delighted here;
Nor could on earth a spot be found
To nature and to me so dear,
Could² thy dear eyes in following mine
Still sweeten more these banks of Rhine!

Salut à la tombe de Marceau et à la forteresse d'Ehrenbreitstein. — Dernier adieu au Rhin et à ses bords admirables. (Str. LVI à LXI.)

LVI

By Coblentz, on a rise of gentle ground,
There is a small and simple pyramid,
Crowning the summit of the verdant mound;
Beneath its base are heroes' ashes hid,
Our enemy's — but let not that forbid
Honour to Marceau³! o'er whose early tomb
Tears, big tears, gush'd from the rough soldier's lid,
Lamenting and yet envying such a doom,
Falling for France, whose rights he battled to resume.

---

1. *The charm...* Le fleuve (qui est) le charme. Apposition.
2. *Could thy... eyes...* Si tes regards pouvaient... C'est la forme hypothétique et optative, comme plus haut : *Wert thou...!* et (strophe L) : *Could man...!*

3. *Honour to Marceau!* Marceau, né à Chartres, en 1769, mort à Altenkirchen en 1796, fut adoré des Français, admiré des ennemis, pleuré par tous. C'est Byron qui s'exprime ainsi, et il exprime le sentiment général.

LVII

Brief, brave, and glorious was his young career, —
His mourners were two hosts, his friends and foes;
And fitly may the stranger lingering here
Pray for his gallant spirit's bright repose;
For he was Freedom's champion, one of those,
The few in number[1], who had not o'erstept
The charter to chastise[2] which she bestows
On such as wield her weapons; he had kept
The whiteness of his soul, and thus men o'er him wept.

LVIII

Here Ehrenbreitstein[3] with her shatter'd wall
Black with the miner's blast[4], upon her height
Yet shows of what she was[5], when shell[6] and ball
Rebounding idly on her strength did light:
A tower of victory! from whence the flight
Of baffled foes was watch'd along the plain:
But Peace destroy'd what War could never blight,
And laid those proud roofs bare to Summer's rain —
On which the iron shower for years had pour'd in vain.

---

1. *The few in number.* C'est le petit nombre.
2. *The charter to chastise.* Ceux qui ne vont pas au delà du droit d'employer la force, droit que la Liberté prête à ceux qui portent les armes de la Liberté (*her weapons*).
3. *Ehrenbreitstein.* — La forteresse d'Ehrenbreitstein (mot à mot: la grande pierre de l'honneur), située en face de Coblentz, sur l'autre rive du Rhin.
4. *Blast.* L'explosion de la mine. La forteresse fut démantelée par les Français, qui la firent sauter.
5. *Of what she was*, ce qu'elle valait, de quelle valeur elle était.
6. *Shell*, la bombe. Proprement *shell* veut dire *coque*. Les Allemands avaient appelé *Haubitze*, la coiffe (*die Haube*) ou coque dans laquelle on enferme la poudre. Nous en avons fait *obus*. Les Anglais ont dit *hobit, howitzer-shell*, puis *shell* tout seul, les langues tendant oujours à abréger.

LIX

Adieu to thee, fair Rhine! How long delighted
The stranger fain would linger on his way!
Thine is a scene alike where[1] souls united
Or lonely Contemplation thus might stray;
And could the ceaseless vultures[2] cease to prey
On self-condemning bosoms, it were here,
Where Nature, nor too sombre nor too gay,
Wild but not rude, awful yet not austere,
Is to the mellow Earth as Autumn to the year.

LX

Adieu to thee again! a vain adieu[3]!
There can be no farewell to scene like thine;
The mind is colour'd by thy every hue;
And if reluctantly the eyes resign
Their cherish'd gaze upon thee, lovely Rhine!
'Tis with the thankful glance of parting praise[4];
More mighty spots may rise more glaring shine,
But none unite in one attaching maze
The brilliant, fair, and soft,—the glories of old days.

LXI

The negligently grand[5], the fruitful bloom
Of coming ripeness, the white city's sheen,
The rolling stream, the precipice's gloom,

---

1. *Alike where.* Où pourraient également se trouver, soit l'union des âmes, soit la solitude.
2. *Could...* Si les vautours pouvaient... (les pensées déchirantes).
3. *A vain adieu!* Non, on ne te dit pas adieu.
4. *Parting praise.* L'admiration qu'on exprime en partant.
5. *The negligently grand,* la grandeur sans apprêts.

The forest's growth, and Gothic walls between,
The wild rocks shaped, as they had¹ turrets been,
In mockery of man's art; and these withal²
A race of faces happy as the scene,
Whose fertile bounties³ here extend to all,
Still springing o'er thy banks, though Empires near them fall.

La Suisse. Les Alpes. — Le chant de bataille de Morat. — La colonne solitaire. — Aventicum. — La tombe de Julia Alpinula. (Str. LXII à LXVII.)

LXII

But these recede⁴. Above me are the Alps,
The palaces of Nature, whose vast walls
Have pinnacled in clouds their snowy scalps,
And throned Eternity⁵ in icy halls
Of cold sublimity, where forms⁶ and falls
The avalanche — the thunderbolt of snow!
All that expands the spirit, yet appals⁷,
Gather around these summits, as to show
How Earth may pierce to Heaven, yet leave vain man below.

LXIII

But ere these matchless heights I dare to scan,
There is a spot should not be pass'd in vain,—

---

1. *As they had*, pour *as if they had.*
2. *These withal*, outre cela.
3. *Bounties*, libéralités.
4. *But these recede.* Mais ces tableaux disparaissent à l'horizon.
5. *Throned Eternity.* Font un trône à l'éternité.
6. *Forms*, se forme (sens neutre).
7. *Yet appals.* Tout en l'épouvantant.

Morat[1]! the proud, the patriot field! where man
May gaze on ghastly trophies of the slain.
Nor blush for those who conquer'd on that plain;
Here Burgundy bequeath'd his tombless host,
A bony heap, through ages to remain,
Themselves their monument[2];— the Stygian coast
Unsepulchred they roam'd, and shriek'd each wandering ghost.

LXIV

While Waterloo[3] with Cannæ's carnage vies,
Morat and Marathon twin names shall stand;
They were true Glory's stainless victories,
Won by the unambitious heart and hand
Of a proud, brotherly, and civic band,
All unbought champions in no princely cause
Of vice-entailed Corruption[4]; they no land
Doom'd to bewail the blasphemy of laws
Making kings' rights divine, by some Draconic clause.

LXV

By a lone wall a lonelier column rears
A gray and grief-worn aspect[5] of old days;

---

1. *Morat!* Byron visita la pyramide élevée par les Suisses en souvenir de leur victoire, pyramide d'ossements bourguignons. Elle diminuait de jour en jour, chacun en prenant un morceau, les Bourguignons pour détruire ce souvenir, les postillons pour vendre les os blanchis à des industriels qui en faisaient des manches de couteau.

2. *Themselves their monument.* Leurs cadavres mêmes sont leur monument funèbre.

3. *Waterloo.* Byron revient sur la comparaison des champs de bataille (voy. strophe XXX et la note). A Morat on a combattu pour la liberté.

4. *Vice-entailed corruption.* La cause du mal, fils du vice. Le vice le transmet légalement et l'impose aux hommes, au moyen des traités et de leurs clauses draconiennes. *Entail,* transmettre, substituer.

5. *Grief-worn aspect,* l'aspect triste et usé de la douleur. Cette colonne semble une personne pétrifiée.

'Tis the last remnant of the wreck of years.
And looks as with the wild-bewilder'd gaze
Of one to stone converted by amaze,
Yet still with consciousness; and there it stands
Making a marvel[1] that it not decays,
When the coeval pride of human hands,
Levell'd Aventicum[2], hath strew'd her subject lands.

LXVI

And there — oh! sweet and sacred be the name! —
Julia[3] — the daughter, the devoted — gave
Her youth to Heaven; her heart, beneath a claim[4]
Nearest to Heaven's, broke o'er a father's grave.
Justice is sworn[5] 'gainst tears, and hers would crave[6]
The life she lived in; but the judge was just,
And then she died on him she could not save.
Their tomb was simple, and without a bust,
And held within their urn one mind[7], one heart, one dust.

LXVII

But these are deeds which should not[8] pass away,
And names that must not wither, though the earth

---

1. *Making a marvel that...* Elle accomplit ce tour de force de ne pas tomber.
2. *Aventicum*, Avenches, près de Morat. C'était jadis la capitale de l'Helvétie romaine.
3. *Julia.* Byron recueille et voue à l'immortalité le nom de Julia Alpinula, jeune prêtresse d'Aventicum qui se dévoua pour sauver son père condamné à mort par Aulus Cæcina. Ce trait lui semble trop oublié.
4. *Beneath a claim.* Sous l'influence de l'amour le plus sacré, l'amour filial; mot à mot : sous un droit.
5. *Is sworn,* est engagée par serment à résister aux larmes.
6. *Crave the life,* sauver par ses prières la vie dont la sienne dépendait.
7. *One mind,* un seul et même esprit.
8. *Should not,* ne devraient pas.

Forgets her empires with a just decay,
The enslavers and the enslaved, their death and birth;
The high, the mountain-majesty of worth [1]
Should be, and shall, survivor of its woe,
And from its immortality look forth
In the sun's face, like yonder Alpine snow,
Imperishably pure beyond all things below.

Le Léman. — Opposition de la vie du monde et de la vie des lacs et des montagnes. — Grandeur de la nature, dans laquelle le poète veut s'oublier. (Str. LXVIII à LXXV.)

LXVIII

Lake Leman woos me with its crystal face,
The mirror where the stars and mountains view
The stillness of their aspect in each trace [2].
Its clear depth yields of their far height and hue:
There is too much of man [3] here, to look through
With a fit mind the might which I behold;
But soon in me shall Loneliness renew
Thoughts hid, but not less cherish'd than of old,
Ere mingling with the herd had penn'd [4] me in their fold.

---

1. *Worth.* Le bien, la vertu, le vrai mérite.

2. *In each trace,* dans chaque image (qui les *retrace*).

3. *There is too much of man.* Le lac Léman présente, en effet, sur ses bords, tantôt la vie des cités populeuses, tantôt celle des solitudes alpestres. D'un côté il s'enfonce entre les dernières pentes des montagnes et conduit à la route du Simplon; de l'autre il baigne les quais de Genève. De là deux aspects : la nature et la foule des hommes.

4. *Penned,* enfermé. Le participe passé de *pen* est *penned,* comme ici, ou *pent,* comme dans la strophe XXVIII.

LXIX

To fly from, need not be to hate, mankind:
All are not fit with them to stir and toil,
Nor is it discontent to keep the mind
Deep in its fountain, lest it overboil
In the hot throng [1] where we become the spoil
Of our infection, till too late and long
We may deplore and struggle with the coil,
In wretched interchange of wrong for wrong
Midst a contentious world, striving where none are strong.

LXX

There, in a moment, we may plunge our years [2]
In fatal penitence, and in the blight
Of our own soul turn all ou blood to tears,
And colour things to come with hues of Night;
The race of life becomes a hopeless flight
To those that walk in darkness: on the sea,
The boldest steer but where [3] their ports invite;
But there are wanderers o'er Eternity
Whose bark drives on and on, and anchor'd ne'er shall be.

LXXI

Is it not better, then, to be alone.
And love Earth only for its earthly sake [4]?
By the blue rushing of the arrowy Rhone,

---

1. *In the throng*, dans la foule. Le sens général est : nos vices se développent dans le tumulte et l'ardeur des villes; et le jour où nous n'estimons plus le monde et ce genre de vie, nous commençons à lutter de malice avec les hommes dans des querelles mesquines.

2. *Our years*. Notre vie entière peut être vouée aux regrets.

3. *Steer but where*. Ils gouvernent sur un point déterminé.

4. *For its earthly sake*. Aimer la terre pour l'amour d'elle.

Or the pure bosom of its nursing lake,
Which feeds it as a mother who doth make
A fair but froward infant her own care,
Kissing its cries away as these awake;—
Is it not better thus our lives to wear,
Than join the crushing crowd, doomed to inflict or bear?

LXXII

I live not in myself, but I become
Portion of that around me; and to me
High mountains are a feeling [1], but the hum
Of human cities torture : I can see
Nothing to loathe in nature, save to be
A link reluctant in a fleshly chain,
Class'd among creatures, when the soul can flee,
And with the sky, the peak, the heaving plain
Of ocean, or the stars, mingle, and not in vain.

LXXIII

And thus I am absorb'd, and this is life;
I look upon the peopled desert [2] past,
As on a place of agony and strife,
Where, for some sin, to sorrow I was cast [3],
To act and suffer, but remount at last
With a fresh pinion, which I feel to spring,
Though young, yet waxing vigorous as the blast
Which it would cope with, on delighted wing,
Spurning the clay-cold bonds which round our being cling.

---

1. *Are a feeling.* Les hautes montagnes sont pour moi une émotion, les cités humaines une torture.

2. *Peopled desert.* Les villes, désert populeux que j'ai traversé.

3. *I was cast.* Je fus jeté là pour souffrir.

LXXIV

And when, at length, the mind shall be all free
From what it hates in this degraded form,
Reft of its carnal life, save what [1] shall be
Existent happier in the fly and worm,—
When elements to elements conform,
And dust is as it should be, shall I not
Feel all I see, less dazzling, but more warm?
The bodiless thought? the Spirit [2] of each spot?
Of which, even now, I share at times the immortal lot?

LXXV

Are not the mountains, waves, and skies, a part
Of me an of my soul, as I of them?
Is not the love of these deep in my heart
With a pure passion? Should I not contemn
All objects, if compared with these? and stem [3]
A tide of suffering, rather than forego
Such feelings for the hard and worldly phlegm [4]
Of those whose eyes are only turn'd below,
Gazing upon the ground, with thoughts which dare not glow?

---

1. *Save what*. Lorsqu'il n'en restera que ce qui doit revivre dans le papillon, et d'une vie plus heureuse.

2. *The Spirit*, le génie de chaque lieu. Comparez les strophes sur l'Albanie et la Grèce.

3. *Stem a tide*, supporter un flot de douleurs. *Stem*, tenir ferme contre.

4. *Phlegm*, l'indifférence glaciale. Notre mot *phlegme* dit moins que l'expression anglaise.

Jean-Jacques Rousseau. — Son portrait. — L'amour idéal. — Pouvoir magique d'une âme éloquente. — Rousseau a soulevé la France. — Jugement sur la Révolution. (Str. LXXVI à LXXXIV).

LXXVI

But this is not my theme; and I return
To that which is immediate [1], and require
Those who find contemplation in the urn,
To look on One, whose dust was once all fire,
A native of the land where I respire
The clear air for a while—a passing guest,
Where he became a being,—whose desire
Was to be glorious; 't was a foolish quest,
The which to gain and heep, he sacrificed all rest.

LXXVII

Here the self-torturing sophist [2], wild Rousseau,
The apostle of affliction, he who threw
Enchantement over passion, and from woe
Wrung overwhelming eloquence, first drew
The breath which made him wretched; yet he knew
How to make madness beautiful, and cast
O'er erring deeds and thoughts, a heavenly hue
Of words, like sunbeams, dazzling as they past
The eyes, which o'er them shed tears feelingly and fast.

---

1. *Which is immediate.* Au sujet qui est là devant moi.
2. *The self-torturing sophist*, le sophiste qui se tortura lui-même, Rousseau, le farouche. Ici le jugement de Byron est d'autant plus curieux, qu'il est lui-même un des enfants intellectuels de Rousseau, comme aussi Alfred de Musset et Georges Sand.

LXXVIII

His love was passion's essence :—as a tree
On fire by lightning [1], with ethereal flame
Kindled he was, and blasted; for to be
Thus, and enamour'd, were in him the same.
But his was not the love of living dame,
Nor of the dead who rise upon our dreams,
But of ideal beauty, which became [2]
In him existence, and o'erflowing teems
Along his burning page, distemper'd though it seems.

LXXIX

This breathed itself to life [3] in Julie, *this*
Invested her with all that's wild and sweet;
This hallow'd, too, the memorable kiss
Which every morn [4] his fever'd lip would greet,
From hers, who but with friendship his would meet;
But to that gentle touch, through brain and breast
Flash'd the thrill'd spirit's love-devouring heat;
In that absorbing sigh perchance more blest
Than vulgar minds may be with all they seek possest.

LXXX

His life was one long war with self-sought foes,
Or friends by him self-banish'd; for his mind

---

1. *On fire by lightning.* Embrasé par la foudre qui le frappe.
2. *Which became... existence.* — Sens général : Chez lui l'amour, qui n'a pour objet aucune personne réelle, mais seulement l'idéal et le beau, devient la vie et déborde. Étrange amour ! dit le vulgaire.
3. *This breathed to life.* Il a donné le souffle et la vie à la *Julie* de la *Nouvelle Héloïse*.
4. *Every morn.* Chaque matin

Had grown Suspicion's sanctuary, and chose,
For its own cruel sacrifice, the kind¹,
'Gainst whom he raged with fury strange and blind.
But he was phrensied, — wherefore, who may know?
Since cause might be which skill² could never find;
But he was phrensied by disease or woe,
To that worst pitch of all, which wears a reasoning show.

LXXXI

For then he was inspired, and from him came,
As from the Pythian's mystic cave of yore,
Those oracles which set the world in flame,
Nor ceased to burn till kingdoms were no more:
Did he not this for France? which lay before
Bow'd to the inborn tyranny of years³?
Broken and trembling to the yoke she bore,
Till by the voice of him and his compeers⁴
Roused up to too much⁵ wrath, which follows o'ergrown fears?

LXXXII

They made themselves a fearful monument!
The wreck⁶ of old opinions — things which grew,
Breathed from the birth of time : the veil they rent,
And what behind it lay, all earth shall view.
But good with ill they also overthrew,

Rousseau échangeait avec Mme d'Houdetot un salut d'amitié. Allusion au passage des *Confessions* dans lequel Rousseau a raconté ce détail.

1. *The kind*, les bons, les cœurs bienveillants pour lui.
2. *Which skill*, de cette espèce que la pénétration de la science ne découvre pas.

3. *Of years*, depuis des siècles. Cf. *of yore*.
4. *Compeers*, ses disciples.
5. *Too much*. On est passé de l'excès de la crainte à l'excès de la colère.
6. *The wreck*. Ce monument fut le monceau de débris fait de la ruine des préjugés.

Leaving but ruins, wherewith to rebuild [1]
Upon the some foundation, and renew
Dungeons and thrones, which the same hour refill'd,
As heretofore, because ambition was self-will'd.

LXXXIII

But this will not endure, nor be endured!
Mankind have felt their strength, and made it felt.
They might have used [2] it better, but, allured
By their new vigour, sternly have they dealt
On one another; pity ceased to melt
With her once natural charities. — But they,
Who in oppression's darkness caved had dwelt,
They were not eagles, nourish'd with the day [3];
What marvel then, at times, if they mistook their prey?

LXXXIV

What deep wounds ever closed without a scar?
The heart's [4] bleed longest, and but heal to [5] wear
That which disfigures it; and they who war
With their own hopes, and have been vanquish'd, bear
Silence, but not submission : in his lair
Fix'd Passion [6] holds his breath, until the hour

---

1. *Wherewith to rebuild*, avec lesquelles, dans lesquelles (ruines) on trouva de quoi reconstruire...
2. *They might have used.* Comparez ce jugement de Byron sur la Révolution française à celui que Gœthe a exprimé dans son poème d'*Hermann et Dorothée*.
3. *With the day*. Nourris de jour, de lumière, accoutumés à l'éclat du soleil. Ils n'avaient pas été élevés comme les aigles.
4. *The heart's*. Celles du cœur, les blessures morales.
5. *But heal to.* Elles ne guérissent que pour nous laisser une cicatrice, qui nous défigure.
6. *Passion*, ressentiment. Ce mot avait le sens français de *passion* dans la strophe LXXVI.1.

CANTO THE THIRD.

Which shall atone for years; none need despair:
It came, it cometh, and will come, — the power
To punish or forgive — in *one*[1] we shall be slower.

Le soir et la nuit sur le lac Léman. — L'infini. — Le culte libre, sous le ciel. (Str. LXXXV à XCI.)

LXXXV

Clear, placid Leman! thy contrasted lake[2],
With the wild world I dwelt in, is a thing
Which warns[3] me, with its stillness, to forsake
Earth's troubled waters for a purer spring.
This quiet sail[4] is as a noiseless wing
To waft me from distraction[5]; once I loved
Torn ocean's roar, but thy soft murmuring
Sounds sweet as if a Sister's voice reproved,
That I with stern delights should e'er have been so moved.

LXXXVI

It is the hush of night, and all between
Thy margin and the mountains, dusk, yet clear,
Mellow'd and mingling, yet distinctly seen,

---

1. *In one.* Dans le châtiment, il y a deux pouvoirs; *l'un*, celui de punir; l'autre, celui de pardonner. Nous serons moins prompts à employer le premier (*in one*).
2. *Contrasted lake.* La paix du lac, qui fait contraste avec...
3. *Warns... with,* m'avertit par...
4. *This sail,* cette petite voile.

Le bonheur du poète, quand il habitait la villa de Diodati, à Coligny, était de descendre la côte rapide, de s'embarquer sur le lac et de se laisser vivre ainsi.

5. *Distraction.* Le monde. C'est le mot du moyen âge en parlant de l'étourdissement de la vie mondaine, qui nous enlève à nous-même et ne nous permet pas de penser.

Save darken'd Jura, whose capt heights[1] appear
Precipitously steep; and drawing near[2],
There breathes a living fragrance from the shore,
Of flowers yet fresh with childhood; on the ear,
Drops the light drip of the suspended oar,
Or chirps the grasshopper one good-night carol more:

LXXXVII

He is an evening reveller[3], who makes
His life an infancy, and sings his fill;
At intervals, some bird from out the brakes
Starts into voice[4] a moment, then is still.
There seems a floating whisper on the hill,
But that is fancy, for the starlight dews
All silently their tears of love instil,
Weeping themselves away, till they infuse
Deep into Nature's breast the spirit of her hues.

LXXXVIII

Ye stars! which are the poetry of heaven!
If in your bright leaves[5] we would read the fate
Of men and empires, — 't is to be forgiven,
That in our aspirations to be great,
Our destinies o'erleap their mortal state,

---

1. *Whose capt heights*, les cimes encapuchonnées. Dans le langage populaire des pays de montagnes, on dit qu'une montagne *a son bonnet;* par exemple à Salins : « Poupey a mis son bonnet », quand le sommet est *coiffé* de nuages, *capped* (ici *capt*).

2. *Drawing near*, en m'approchant du lac.

3. *Reveller*. L'animal est de ceux qui fêtent le soir.

4. *Starts into voice*, se met à chanter.

5. *In your leaves*, dans vos pages.

And claim a kindred¹ with you; for ye are
A beauty and a mystery, and create
In us such love and reverence from afar,
That fortune, fame, power, life, have named themselves a star.

LXXXIX

All heaven and earth are still — though not in sleep,
But breathless, as we grow when feeling most;
And silent, as we stand in thoughts too deep : —
All heaven and earth are still : From the high host
Of stars, to the lull'd² lake and mountain-coast,
All is concenter'd in a life intense,
Where not a beam, nor air, nor leaf is lost,
But hath a part of being, and a sense
Of that which is of all Creator³ and defence.

XC

Then stirs the feeling infinite, so felt
In solitude, where we are *least* alone;
A truth⁴, which through our being then doth melt,
And purifies from self : it is a tone,
The soul and source of music, which makes known
Eternal harmony, and sheds a charm

---

1. *Claim a kindred.* Nos destinées veulent s'unir aux vôtres.

2. *Lulled.* Le lac qui se berce et s'endort.

3. *That which is ˜... Creator.* Ce qui est le créateur. Expression volontairement équivoque. Byron ne dit pas comme Shelley, qui, voyageant avec lui, écrit sur l'album du couvent de Chamouny « Shelley, ἄθεος. » Il ne dit pas comme Wordsworth, qui oppose à l'agitation de l'homme la providence du créateur. Il parle de Ce qui a créé.

4. *A truth.* Le sens de l'infini est une vérité supérieure, qui nous dégage de notre moi, de notre égoïsme (*self*).

Like to the fabled Cytherea's zone,
Binding all things with beauty; — 't would disarm
The spectre Death, had he substantial[1] power to harm.

XCI

Not vainly did the early Persian make
His altar the high places[2], and the peak
Of earth-o'ergazing mountains, and thus take
A fit and unwall'd temple, there to seek
The Spirit, in whose honour shrines are weak,
Uprear'd of human hands. Come, and compare
Columns and idol-dwellings, Goth or Greek,
With Nature's realms of worship, earth and air,
Nor fix on fond abodes to circumscribe thy pray'r!

L'orage dans les montagnes. — Les convulsions de la nature et les déchirements du cœur de l'homme. — Séparations. (Str. XCII à XCIX.)

XCII

The sky is changed[3]! — and such a change! Oh night,
And storm, and darkness, ye are wondrous strong,

---

1. *Substantial*, une forme corporelle. Si cette puissance du mal avait un corps, si c'était une puissance personnifiée.

2. *High places.* Les hauteurs. Ici Byron, s'annotant lui-même, a décrit en prose l'impression esthétique, oratoire, et religieuse que produisent sur l'homme les montagnes ou le plein air. Il rappelle le Sermon sur la montagne, de Jésus-Christ (*the divine Founder of Christianity*), les harangues antiques sur le Forum et dans l'Agora, la popularité récente des méthodistes qui parlent sur les places, et les cérémonies *coram populo* des musulmans; — le tout pour l'opposer aux pratiques intérieures des temples ou églises de nos cités.

3. *The sky is changed.* « J'ai fait allusion ici à un orage qui eut lieu

Yet lovely in your strength, as is the light
Of a dark eye in woman! Far along,
From peak to peak, the rattling crags among
Leaps the live thunder! Not from one lone cloud,
But every mountain now hath found a tongue,
And Jura answers, through her misty shroud,
Back to the joyous Alps, who call to her aloud!

XCIII

And this is in the night: — Most glorious night!
Thou wert not sent for slumber[1]! let me be
A sharer in thy fierce and far delight, —
A portion of the tempest and of thee!
How the lit lake[2] shines, a phosphoric sea,
And the big rain comes dancing to the earth!
And now again 't is black, — and now, the glee
Of the loud hills shakes with its mountain-mirth,
As if they did rejoice o'er a young earthquake's birth.

XCIV

Now[3], where the swift Rhone[4] cleaves his way between
Heights which appear as lovers who have parted
In hate, whose mining depths so intervene,

le 13 juin 1816, à minuit, au milieu des monts Acrocérauniens. J'ai été témoin de plusieurs autres, plus terribles que celui-ci; mais aucun ne fut plus beau. » (Byron.)

1. *Not... for slumber.* Cette nuit n'est pas une de ces nuits qui sont faites pour dormir.

2. *Lit lake.* Le lac éclairé et embrasé.

3. *Now...* A ce moment. Mais Byron ne donne qu'à la strophe suivante la phrase qui doit venir logiquement après ce *now.* Aussi le répète-t-il.

4. *The Rhone.* Le Rhône en Suisse est étroitement encaissé dans les rochers qu'il a séparés pour se frayer un passage. Byron compare cette séparation, qui se creuse toujours, à celle qui s'est faite entre lui et lady Byron.

That they can meet no more, though broken-hearted;
Though in their souls, which thus each other thwarted,
Love was the very root of the fond rage
Which blighted their life's bloom, and then departed: —
Itself expired, but leaving them an age
Of years all winters, — war within themselves to wage.

XCV

Now, where the quick Rhone thus hath cleft his way,
The mightiest of the storms hath ta'en his stand:
For here, not one, but many, make their play,
And fling their thunder-bolts from hand to hand,
Flashing and cast around: of all the band
The brightest through these parted hills hath fork'd
His lightnings,—as if he did understand,
That in such gaps as desolation work'd,
There the hot shaft[1] should blast whatever therein lurk'd.

XCVI

Sky, mountains, river, winds, lake, lightnings! ye!
With night, and clouds, and thunder, and a soul
To make these felt and feeling, well may be
Things that have made me watchful; the far roll
Of your departing voices, is the knoll
Of what in me is sleepless,—if I rest.[2]
But where of ye, O tempests! is the goal?
Are ye like those within the human breast?
Or do ye find, at length, like eagles, some high nest?

---

1. *The hot shaft*, le trait de feu, la foudre, qui va chercher là et détruire ce qui peut rester encore de caché.

2. *If I rest.* Si jamais je repose. Il y a quelque chose en moi qui ne dort pas, une douleur, un deuil, dont le glas ne cesse point.

XCVII

Could I embody¹ and unbosom now
That which is most within me,—could I wreak
My thoughts upon expression, and thus throw
Soul, heart, mind, passions, feelings, strong or weak,
All that I would have sought, and all I seek,
Bear, know, feel, and yet² breathe—into *one* word,
And that one word were Lightning, I would speak;
But as it is, I live and die unheard,
With a most voiceless thought, sheathing it as a sword.

XCVIII

The morn is up again, the dewy morn,
With breath all incense, and with cheek all bloom,
Laughing the clouds away³ with playful scorn,
And living as if earth contain'd no tomb,—
And glowing into⁴ day: we may resume
The march of our existence: and thus I,
Still on thy shores, fair Leman! may find room
And food for meditation, nor pass by
Much, that may give us pause, if ponder'd fittingly.

---

1. *Embody*, incarner. Si je pouvais rassembler en un seul corps, en un seul mot, tout ce que j'éprouve, en faire un éclair, et le lancer comme la foudre, oh ! alors je par'erais! mais...

2. *And yet...* Je souffre, et pourtant je ne meurs pas.

3. *Laughing away*, écartant avec un sourire.

4. *Glowing into...* Sa lumière devient celle du jour.

Clarens. — C'est le théâtre naturel de l'amour idéal, qui à son tour idéalise tout autour de lui. (Str. XCIX à CIV.)

XCIX

Clarens! sweet Clarens, birthplace of deep Love!
Thine air is the young breath of passionate thought;
Thy trees take root in Love; the snows above
The very Glaciers have his colours caught,
And sun-set into rose-hues sees them wrought [1]
By rays which sleep there lovingly : the rocks,
The permanent crags, tell here of Love, who sought
In them a refuge from the worldly shocks,
Which stir [2] and sting the soul with hope that woos then mocks.

C

Clarens [3]! by heavenly feet thy paths are trod,—
Undying Love's, who here ascends a throne
To which the steps are mountains; where the god
Is a pervading life and light,—so shown
Not on those summits solely, nor alone
In the still cave and forest; o'er the flower
His eye is sparkling, and his breath hath blown,
His soft and summer breath, whose tender power
Passes the strength of storms in their most desolate hour.

---

1. *Wrought into...* Il les voit se teindre en rose.

2. *Which stir...* Ce vers rapide, fait de monosyllabes et d'allitérations, est une phrase imitative.

3. *Clarens!* Clarens est la scène choisie par Jean-Jacques Rousseau pour servir de théâtre aux romanesques aventures de la *Nouvelle Héloïse*. L'immense succès de ce livre éloquent fit de Clarens une sorte d'Eden connu de toute l'Europe. « En juillet 1816, dit Byron, j'ai fait un voyage autour du lac de Genève ; j'ai visité avec la plus grande attention et le plus vif intérêt tous les lieux célèbres dans la *Nouvelle Héloïse.* » C'est ce qui explique les strophes C, CI, CII, CIII et CIV, et le dithyrambe du poète en l'honneur de ce royaume de l'amour.

CI

All things are here of *him*[1]; from the black pines,
Which are his shade on high, and the loud roar
Of torrents, where he listeneth, to the vines
Which slope his green path downward to the shore,
Where the bow'd[2] waters meet him, and adore,
Kissing his feet with murmurs; and the wood,
The covert of old trees, with trunks all hoar,
But light leaves, young as joy, stands where it stood,
Offering to him, and his[3], a populous solitude.

CII

A populous solitude of bees and birds,
And fairy-form'd and many-colour'd things,
Who worship him with notes more sweet than words,
And innocently open their glad wings,
Fearless and full of life: the gush of springs,
And fall of lofty fountains, and the bend
Of stirring branches, and the bud which brings
The swiftest thought of beauty, here extend,
Mingling, and made by Love, unto one mighty end.

CIII

He who hath loved not, here would learn that lore,
And make his heart a spirit; he who knows
That tender mystery, will love the more;
For this is Love's recess, where[4] vain men's woes,

---

1. *Of him.* Tout vient de lui.
2. *Bowed,* prosternées.
3. *To him and his,* à lui et aux siens.

4. *Where...* Construction serrée. C'est là que les misères humaines ont forcé l'amour à se réfugier, loin d'elles.

And the world's waste, have driven him far from those
For 'tis his nature to advance or die;
He stands not still, but or decays, or grows
Into a boundless blessing, which may vie
With the immortal lights, in its eternity!

CIV

'T was not for fiction[1] chose Rousseau this spot,
Peopling it with affections; but he found
It was the scene wich Passion must allot
To the mind's purified beings; 't was the ground
Where early Love his Psyche's zone unbound,
And hallow'd it with loveliness: 'tis lone,
And wonderful, and deep, and hath a sound,
And sense, and sight of sweetness; here the Rhone
Hath spread himself a couch, the Alps have rear'd a throne

Ferney et Voltaire, Lausanne et l'historien Gibbon. — Deux portraits littéraires. (Str. CV à CVIII.)

CV

Lausanne! and Ferney[2]! ye have been the abodes
Of names which unto you bequeath'd a name;

---

1. *'Twas not for fiction.* Byron explique lui-même sa pensée. « Il m'a paru que Rousseau n'avait pas exagéré les beautés de Clarens. »
2. *Lausanne! Ferney!* A Lausanne, Gibbon préparait son grand travail sur la *Décadence romaine*, œuvre pleine de science et de hardiesse froide, publiée de 1776 à 1788. — A Ferney, habita Voltaire qui personnifiait la guerre à la religion. Byron les compare aux Titans attaquant le ciel. Le poète est encore du dix-huitième siècle.

Mortals, who sought and found, by dangerous roads,
A path to perpetuity of fame:
The were gigantic minds, and their steep aim
Was, Titan-like, on daring doubts to pile
Thoughts which should call down thunder, and the flame
Of Heaven again assail'd, if Heaven the while
On man and man's research could deign do more than smile.

CVI

The one [1] was fire and fickleness, a child
Most mutable in wishes, but in mind
A wit as various,—gay, grave, sage, or wild,—
Historian, bard, philosopher, combined;
He multiplied himself among mankind,
The Proteus of their talents : but his own [2]
Breathed most in ridicule,— which, as the wind,
Blew where it listed, laying all things prone,—
Now to o'erthrow a fool, and now to shake a throne.

CVII

The other [3], deep and slow, exhausting thought,
And hiving [4] wisdom with each studious year,
In meditation dwelt, with learning wrought,
And shaped his weapon with an edge severe,
Sapping a solemn creed with solemn sneer;
The lord of irony,— that master-spell,
Which stung his foes to wrath, which grew from fear,
And doom'd him to the zealot's ready Hell,
Which answers to all doubts so eloquently well.

---

1. *The one.* Voltaire.
2. *His own.* Le sien vivait de...
3. *The other.* Gibbon.
4. *Hiving.* Rapportant dans sa ruche les résultats de ses recherches.

CVIII

Yet, peace be with their ashes, — for by them,
If merited, the penalty is paid;
It is not ours to judge, — far less condemn;
The hour must come when such things shall be made
Known unto all, or hope and dread allay'd
By slumber, on one pillow, in the dust,
Which, thus[1] much we are sure, must lie decay'd;
And when it shall revive, as is our trust,
'T will be to be forgiven, or suffer what is just.

Épilogue. — L'auteur va reprendre ses voyages dans les Alpes. Il salue d'avance l'Italie. — Il envoie un dernier regard à sa patrie, au monde, et à sa fille Ada. (Str. CIX à la fin.)

CIX

But let me quit man's works, again to read
His Maker's[2], spread around me, and suspend
This page, which from my reveries I feed,
Until it seems prolonging without end.
The clouds above me to the white Alps tend,
And I must pierce them, and survey whate'er
May be permitted, as my steps I bend
To their most great and growing region, where
The earth to her embrace compels the powers of air.

---

1. *Thus...* Voilà ce qui est certain.
2. *His Maker's.* Ici Byron nomme directement le Créateur. Mais la strophe se termine par un vers de panthéiste.

CX

Italia[1]! too, Italia! looking on thee,
Full flashes on the soul the light of ages,
Since the fierce Carthaginian almost won thee,
To the last halo of the chiefs and sages
Who glorify thy consecrated pages;
Thou wert the throne and grave of empires; still,
The fount at which the panting mind assuages
Her thirst of knowledge, quaffing there her fill,
Flows from the eternal source of Rome's imperial hill.

CXI

Thus far have I proceeded in a theme
Renew'd with no kind auspices: — to feel
We are not what we have been, and to deem
We are not what we should be, and to steel
The heart against itself; and to conceal,
With a proud caution, love, or hate, or aught, —
Passion or feeling, purpose, grief, or zeal, —
Which is the tyrant spirit of our thought,
Is a stern task of soul: — No matter, — it is taught[2].

CXII

And for these words[3], thus woven into song,
It may be that they are a harmless wile, —
The colouring of the scenes which fleet along,

---

1. *Italia!* Ce mot annonce le quatrième chant.
2. *It is taught.* Je le sais maintenant; j'y suis fait.
3. *These words.* Mes paroles, devenues des chants, ont servi à tromper ma douleur. *Woven* rappelle qu'il mettait sa prose en vers

Which I would seize, in passing, to beguile
My breast, or that of others, for a while.
Fame is the thirst of youth, but I am not
So young as to regard men's frown or smile,
As loss or guerdon of a glorious lot;
I stood and stand alone, — remember'd or forgot.

CXIII

I have not loved the world, nor the world me [1];
I have not flatter'd its rank breath, nor bow'd
To its idolatries a patient knee,
Nor coin'd my cheek to smiles, nor cried aloud
In worship of an echo; in the crowd
They could not deem me one of such; I stood
Among them, but not of them; in a shroud
Of thoughts which were not their thoughts, and still could
Had I not filed my mind, which thus itself subdued.

CXIV

I have not loved the world, nor the world me, —
But let us part fair foes; I do believe [2],
Though I have found them not, that there may be
Words which are things, hopes which will not deceive,
And virtues which are merciful, nor weave
Snares for the failing; I would also deem

---

1. *Nor the world me.* Le monde ne m'a point aimé. Byron fait allusion aux calomnies dont on le poursuivait. « Si ces accusations sont vraies, disait-il, je ne suis pas digne de revoir l'Angleterre. Si elles ne sont pas vraies, l'Angleterre n'est pas digne de me revoir. »

2. *I do believe.* C'est un *credo* ironique. Eh bien! oui, je crois qu'il y a des âmes dévouées et indulgentes; je crois qu'il y en a deux, ou peut-être une, quelque part dans le monde.

O'er others' griefs that some sincerely grieve;
That two, or one, are almost what they seem,
That goodness is no name, and happiness no dream.

CXV

My daughter! with thy name this song begun;
My daughter! with thy name thus much shall end;
I see thee not, I hear thee not, but none
Can be so wrapt in thee[1]; thou art the friend
To whom the shadows of far years extend:
Albeit my brow thou never should'st behold,
My voice shall with thy future visions blend,
And reach into thy heart, when mine is cold,
A token and a tone, even from thy father's mould.

CXVI

To aid thy mind's development, to watch
Thy dawn of little joys, to sit and see
Almost thy very growth, to view thee catch
Knowledge of objects, — wonders yet to thee!
To hold thee lightly on a gentle knee,
And print on thy soft cheek a parent's kiss, —
This, it should seem, was not reserved for me;
Yet this was in my nature: as it is,
I know not what is there, yet something like to this.

---

1. *So wrapt in thee.* Expression usuelle en Angleterre pour dire que l'on vit tout entier dans une pensée, une affection. Le sens général de la strophe est : Personne ne t'aime comme moi. De mon passé déjà lointain, l'ombre se projette vers toi, et dans l'avenir l'écho de ma voix arrivera jusqu'à toi comme un accent (*a tone*) et un gage (*a token*) d'amour. Cette prédiction se réalisa.

CXVII

Yet, though dull Hate[1] as duty should be taught,
I know that thou wilt love me; though my name
Should be shut from thee, as a spell still fraught
With desolation, and a broken claim:
Though the grave closed between us,—'t were the same,
I know that thou wilt love me; though to drain
My blood from out thy being were an aim,
And an attainment,— all would be in vain,—
Still thou would'st love me, still that more than life retain.

CXVIII

The child of love, though born in bitterness,
And nurtured in convulsion. Of thy sire
These were the elements, and thine no less.
As yet such are around thee, but thy fire
Shall be more temper'd, and thy hope far higher.
Sweet be thy cradled slumbers! O'er the sea
And from the mountains where I now respire,
Fain would I waft such blessing upon thee,
As, with a sigh, I deem thou might'st have been to me!

---

1. *Dull hate.* On t'enseigne la haine de ton père. Ce mot explique la fin comme le début du IIIe chant. Byron n'a pas pu voir sa fille; il ne la verra pas. Il sait que la mère est implacable. Il adresse à l'enfant, pour qu'elle les lise plus tard, ces vers d'outre-tombe et lui dit: « Je sais qu'un jour tu m'aimeras! » Ce jour vint fort tard, mais il vint : Ada, en mourant, demanda à être ensevelie auprès de son père.

TO

JOHN HOBHOUSE, ESQ., A.M., F.R.S.[1]

ETC. ETC. ETC.

« Visto ho Toscana, Lombardia, Romagna,
Quel monte che divide, e quel che serra
Italia, e un mare e l'altro, che la bagna. »
(ARIOSTO, *Satira III.*)

Venice, January 2, 1818.

MY DEAR HOBHOUSE,

AFTER an interval of eight years between the composition of the first and last cantos of Childe Harold, the conclusion of the poem is about to be submitted to the public. In parting with so old a friend, it is not extraordinary that I should recur to one still older and better,—to one who has beheld the birth and death of the other, and to whom I am far more indebted for the social advantages of an enlightened friendship, than—though not ungrateful—I can, or could be, to Childe Harold, for any public favour reflected through the poem on the poet, to one whom I have known long, and accompanied far, whom I have found wakeful over my sickness and kind in my sorrow, glad in my prosperity and firm in my adversity, true in counsel and trusty in peril,—to a friend often tried and never found wanting;— to yourself.

In so doing, I recur from fiction to truth; and in dedicating to you in its complete, or at least concluded state, a poetical work which is the longest, the most thoughtful and comprehensive of my compositions, I wish to do honour to myself by the record of many years' intimacy with a man of learning, of

---

1. John Hobhouse, Esquire, Artium magister, Fellow Royal Society (maître ès arts, membre de la Société royale de Londres).

talent, of steadiness, and of honour. It is not for minds like ours to give or to receive flattery; yet the praises of sincerity have ever been permitted to the voice of friendship; and it is not for you, nor even for others, but to relieve a heart which has not elsewhere, or lately, been so much accustomed to the encounter of good-will as to withstand the shock firmly that I thus attempt to commemorate your good qualities, or rather the advantages which I have derived from their exertion. Even the recurrence of the date of this letter, the anniversary of the most unfortunate day of my past existence[1], but which cannot poison my future while I retain the resource of your friendship, and of my own faculties, will henceforth have a more agreeable recollection for both, inasmuch as it will remind us of this my attempt to thank you for an indefatigable regard, such as few men have experienced, and no one could experience without thinking better of his species and of himself.

It has been our fortune to traverse together, at various periods, the countries of chivalry, history, and fable—Spain, Greece, Asia Minor, and Italy; and what Athens and Constantinople were to us a few years ago, Venice and Rome have been more recently. The poem also, or the pilgrim, or both, have accompanied me from first to last; and perhaps it may be a pardonable vanity which induces me to reflect with complacency on a composition which in some degree connects me with the spot where it was produced, and the objects it would fain describe; and however unworthy it may be deemed of those magical and memorable abodes, however short it may fall of our distant conceptions and immediate impressions, yet as a mark of respect for what is venerable, and of feeling for what is glorious, it has been to me a source of pleasure in the production, and I part with it with a kind of regret, which I hardly suspected that events could have left me for imaginary objects.

With regard to the conduct of the last canto, there will be found less of the pilgrim than in any of the preceding, and that little slightly, if at all, separated from the author speaking in his own person. The fact is, that I had become weary of drawing a line which every one seemed determined not to perceive : like the Chinese in Goldsmith's " Citizen of the World ", whom nobody

---

1. *The most unfortunate day.* Le jour de son mariage, selon lui.

would believe to be a Chinese, it was in vain that I asserted, and imagined that I had drawn, a distinction between the author and the pilgrim; and the very anxiety to preserve this difference, and disappointment at finding it unavailing, so far crushed my efforts in the composition, that I determined to abandon it altogether—and have done so. The opinions which have been, or may be, formed on that subject, are *now* a matter of indifference: the work is to depend on itself, and not on the writer; and the author, who has no resources in his own mind beyond the reputation, transient or permanent, which is to arise from his literary efforts, deserves the fate of authors.

In the course of the following canto it was my intention, either in the text or in the notes, to have touched upon the present state of Italian literature, and perhaps of manners. But the text, within the limits I proposed, I soon found hardly sufficient for the labyrinth of external objects, and the consequent reflections; and for the whole of the notes, excepting a few of the shortest, I am indebted to yourself, and these were necessarily limited to the elucidation of the text.

It is also a delicate, and no very grateful task, to dissert upon the literature and manners of a nation so dissimilar; and requires an attention and impartiality which would induce us,—though perhaps no inattentive observers, nor ignorant of the language or customs of the people amongst whom we have recently abode—to distrust, or at least defer our judgment, and more narrowly examine our information. The state of literary, as well as political party, appears to run, or to *have* run, so high, that for a stranger to steer impartially between them is next to impossible. It may be enough, then, at least for my purpose, to quote from their own beautiful language—" Mi pare che in un paese tutto
« poetico, che vanta la lingua la più nobile ed insieme la più
« dolce, tutte tutte le vie diverse si possono tentare, e che sinche
« la patria di Alfieri e di Monti non ha perduto l'antico valore,
« in tutte essa dovrebbe essere la prima." Italy has great names still—Canova, Monti, Ugo Foscolo, Pindemonte, Visconti, Morelli, Cicognara, Albrizzi, Mezzophanti, Mai, Mustoxidi, Aglietti, and Vaca, will secure to the present generation an honourable place in most of the departments of Art, Science, and Belles Lettres; and in some the very highest—Europe—the World—has but one Canova.

It has been somewhere said by Alfieri, that "La pianta uomo « nasce più robusta in Italia che in qualunque altra terra—e che gli « stessi atroci delitti che vi si commettono ne sono una prova." Without subscribing to the latter part of his proposition, a dangerous doctrine, the truth of which may be disputed on better grounds, namely, that the Italians are in no respect more ferocious than their neighbours, that man must be wilfully blind, or ignorantly heedless, who is not struck whit the extraordinary capacity of this people, of, if such a word be admissible, their *capabilities*, the facility or their acquisitions, the rapidity of their conceptions, the fire of their genius, their sense of beauty, and, amidst all the disadvantages of repeated revolutions, the desolation of battles, and the despair of ages, their still unquenched "longing after immortality",—the immortality of independence. And when we ourselves, in riding round the walls of Rome, heard the simple lament of the labourers' chorus, "Roma! Roma! Roma! Roma non è più come era prima,", it was difficult not to contrast this melancholy dirge with the bacchanal roar of the songs of exultation still yelled from the London taverns, over the carnage of Mont St. Jean, and the betrayal of Genoa, of Italy, of France, and of the world, by men whose conduct you yourself have exposed in a work worthy of the better days of our history. For me,—

> "Non movero mai corda
> Ove la turba di sue ciance assorda"

What Italy has gained by the late transfer of nations, it were useless for Englishmen to inquire, till it becomes ascertained that England has acquired something more than a permanent army and a suspended Habeas Corpus; it is enough for them to look at home. For what they have done abroad, and especially in the South, "Verily the *will have* their reward", and at no very distant period.

Wishing you, my dear Hobhouse, a safe and agreeable return to that country whose real welfare can be dearer to none than to yourself, I dedicate to you this poem in its completed state; and repeat once more how truly I am ever

Your obliged
And affectionate friend,
BYRON.

ARGUMENT ANALYTIQUE.

DU CHANT QUATRIÈME

EN ITALIE

Venise. — Gloire passée de la reine de l'Adriatique. Sa beauté présente. Elle est immortalisée par la littérature. (Str. I à IV.)

Le culte du beau et de l'idéal est une seconde vie à laquelle nous conduisent l'espérance dans la jeunesse, et la déception dans l'âge mûr. (Str. V à VI.)

Digression. — Byron a connu rêves et réalités. Il est prêt à tous les changements. Il est cosmopolite. Mais s'il a quitté son pays, il l'aime et en est fier. (Str. VII à X.)

Décadence de Venise, si grande jadis. — Au nom de la poésie du moins, Byron proteste contre la servitude de Venise, qu'il a toujours aimée. (Str. XI à XIX.)

La douleur. — Le poète qui évoque ces souvenirs peut en évoquer d'autres qui lui sont personnels. — La douleur, tour à tour vaincue et renaissante, est toujours en nous. (Str. XX à XXIV.)

L'Italie. — Salut à cette terre de la puissance et de la beauté. — Un coucher de soleil aux bords de la Brenta. (Str. XXV à XXIX.)

Arqua et Pétrarque. — Solitude poétique. Elle convient à la misanthropie et à la tristesse. (Str. XXX à XXXIV.)

Ferrare et le Tasse. — Le duc et le poète. — Malédiction contre l'aristocratie, contre la critique, contre la poésie française. — Grandeur de la poésie italienne. — Dante. — Boccace. (Str. XXXV à XLI.)

Les ruines de l'Italie. — Jadis les Romains contemplaient avec tristesse les grandes ruines des villes grecques. Aujourd'hui on médite sur les ruines de l'Italie, pays de la beauté et de la douleur. — Souvenirs de Filicaja, du Pogge et de Sulpicius. (Str. XLII à XLVII.)

Florence. — La vallée de l'Arno. La Toscane. — La Vénus de Médicis. — Santa-Croce. — Les cendres des poètes toscans exilées. (Str. XLVIII à LX.)

De Florence à Rome. — Le lac de Pérouse, la bataille de Trasimène et le Sanguinetto. — Le temple de Clitumnus. — Le Velino et la cataracte de Terni. — Les Apennins et le Soracte. — Boutade contre Horace. (Str. LXI à LXXVII.)

Rome, la Niobé des nations. — Patrie des ruines et des cœurs ruinés. — Génies qui la ressuscitent. — Coup d'œil jeté sur l'histoire du génie politique romain et sur celle de la Liberté. — Sylla, César, Pompée. Leurs successeurs modernes : Cromwell, Bonaparte. Au-dessus d'eux Washington. (Str. LXXVIII à XCVIII.)

La tombe de Cécilia Metella. — Qui était-elle ? — Méditation sur le néant et l'orgueil de l'humanité. (Str. XCIX à CVI.)

Nouvelle promenade parmi les ruines et les souvenirs de Rome. — Tout change et se mêle. — Le Palatin, la colonne Trajane, la roche Tarpéienne. — Le Forum. — Cicéron. — Rienzi. — Les drames de la liberté ou de l'anarchie. (Str. CVII à CXIV.)

Égérie. — Numa. — L'amour, illusion sublime que l'homme se forge à lui-même, et qui n'est qu'un mirage. (Str. CXV à CXXVII.)

Le Colisée. — Le Temps l'a marqué de sa main. Le Temps embellit la mort. Il amène la Justice. C'est lui et Némésis qui vengeront Byron calomnié. (Str. CXXVIII à CXXXVIII.)

Le Gladiateur mourant. — Suite et fin de la description du Colisée. (Str. CXXXIX à CXLV.)

Le Panthéon. — Sanctuaire commun de l'art, du génie et de la piété. (Str. CXLVI et CXLVII.)

Saint-Nicolas in carcere. — La jeune Romaine. — Le lait de la vie. — Le môle d'Adrien. (Str. CXLVIII à CLII.)

Saint-Pierre. — Œuvre colossale ; effet toujours grandissant. — Education des sens par l'art. (Str. CLIII à CLIX.)

Le Vatican. — Le groupe du *Laocoon.* — *L'Apollon du Belvédère.* (Str. CLX à CLXIII.)

Fin du poème. — Byron abandonne Childe Harold et fait rentrer ce fantôme dans le néant où tout doit rentrer. — La mort. — Bonheur de ne pas recommencer la vie. — Chant de deuil sur une jeune princesse et une jeune mère. (Str. CLXIV à CLXXII.)

Byron achève son voyage, en saluant le lac de Némi, l'Albano, le Latium ; puis il s'arrête et, embrassant du regard les pays qu'il a parcourus, il contemple, au milieu de la terre pleine de ruines, l'Océan immortel. (Str. CLXXIII à la fin.)

CANTO THE FOURTH

Venise. — Gloire passée de la reine de l'Adriatique. Sa beauté présente. Elle est immortalisée par la littérature. (Str. 1 à iv.)

I

I stood in Venice, on the Bridge of Sighs;
A palace and a prison on each hand[1]:
I saw from out the wave her structures rise
As from the stroke of the enchanter's wand:
A thousand years their cloudy wings expand
Around me, and a dying Glory smiles
O'er the far times, when many a subject land
Look'd to the winged Lion's marble piles[2],
Where Venice sate in state, throned on her hundred isles.

II

She looks a sea Cybele, fresh from ocean,
Rising with her tiara of proud towers[3]
At airy distance[4], with majestic motion,
A ruler of the waters and their powers:
And such she was; — her daughters had their dowers
From spoils of nations, and the exhaustless East
Pour'd in her lap all gems in sparkling showers.
In purple was she robed, and of her feast
Monarchs partook, and deem'd their dignity increased.

---

1. *On each hand.* L'un à droite, l'autre à gauche.
2. *Piles.* Les monuments.
3. *Towers.* Comparez à ce vers la phrase de Sabellicus : « Quo fit ut qui superne urbem contempletur, turritam telluris imaginem medio Oceano figuratam se putet inspicere. »
4. *At airy distance.* La perspective et les lointains sont bien plus diaphanes dans les pays du Midi et de l'Orient que dans la patrie de lord Byron.

III

In Venice Tasso's echoes are no more,
And silent rows the songless gondolier;
Her palaces are crumbling to the shore,
And music meets not always now the ear :
Those days are gone — but Beauty still is here.
States fall, arts fade — but Nature doth not die,
Nor yet forget how Venice once was dear,
The pleasant place of all festivity,
The revel of the earth, the masque[1] of Italy!

IV

But unto us[2] she hath a spell beyond
Her name in story, and her long array
Of mighty shadows, whose dim forms despond
Above the dogeless city's vanished sway :
Ours is a trophy which will not decay
With the Rialto; Shylock and the Moor,
And Pierre, can not be swept or worn away —

---

1. *The masque.* Le carnaval de l'Italie. Le sens du mot *masque* s'est étendu; il a signifié : masque, costume d'acteur, pièce de théâtre, puis déguisement de carnaval, et carnaval.

2. *But unto us...* Mais pour nous Venise est immortalisée par ce cortège (*array*) de figures vénitiennes dont le roman et le drame ont fait des créations littéraires. Byron, dans cette strophe et dans la XVIIIe, fait allusion aux personnages d'*Othello*, le More de Venise, et de *Shylock*, le Juif de Venise, tels que les présente Shakspeare; puis à Pierre Jaffier, qui apparaît dans la *Venise sauvée*, d'Otway. Plus loin, il rappelle que Schiller, dans la *Conjuration de Fiesque*, et Anne Radcliffe, dans les *Mystères d'Udolphe*, ont pris Venise pour théâtre des aventures qu'ils retraçaient.

The keystones[1] of the arch! though all were o'er
For us repeopled were the solitary shore.

Le culte du beau et de l'idéal est une seconde vie à laquelle nous conduisent l'espérance dans la jeunesse et la déception dans l'âge mûr. (Str. v à vi.)

V

The beings of the mind are not of clay;
Essentially immortal, they create
And multiply in us a brighter ray
And more beloved existence : that which[2] Fate
Prohibits to dull life, in this our state
Of mortal bondage, by these spirits supplied,
First exiles, then replaces what we hate;
Watering the heart whose early flowers have died,
And with a fresher growth replenishing the void.

VI

Such is the refuge of our youth and age,
The first from Hope, the last from Vacancy[3];
And this worn feeling[4] peoples many a page,
And, may be, that which grows beneath mine eye :
Yet there are things whose strong reality

---

1. *The keystones.* Ces personnages sont la clef de voûte de l'édifice.
2. *That which...* Sens général : cette existence supérieure, que le sort nous refuse et que les créations intellectuelles nous donnent, permet d'abord d'échapper à des réalités odieuses, ensuite de les remplacer par de grandes images.
3. *From Vacancy.* Par le sentiment du vide.
4. *Worn feeling.* Les blessures de mon âme.

Outshines our fairy-land; in shape and hues
More beautiful than our fantastic sky,
And the strange constellations which the Muse
O'er her wild universe is skilful to diffuse:

Digression. — Byron a connu rêves et réalités. Il est prêt à tous les changements. Il est cosmopolite. Mais, s'il a quitté son pays, il l'aime et en est fier. (Str. VII à X.)

VII

I saw or dream'd of such, — but let them go, —
They came like truth, and disappear'd like dreams;
And whatsoe'er they were — are now but so [1] :
I could replace them if I would; still teems
My mind with many a form which aptly seems
Such as I sought for, and at moments found;
Let these too go — for waking Reason deems
Such over-weening phantasies unsound,
And other voices speak, and other sights surround.

VIII

I've taught me other tongues, and in strange eyes
Have made me not a stranger; to the mind
Which is itself, no changes bring surprise;
Nor is it harsh to make, nor hard to find
A country with — ay, or without mankind;
Yet was I born where men are proud to be, —
Not without cause; and should I leave [2] behind

---

1. *Are now but so.* Ne sont plus que cela, des rêves.

2. *Should I leave.* Quand il serait vrai que j'ai abandonné l'An-

The inviolate island of the sage and free,
And seek me out a home by a remoter sea,

IX

Perhaps I loved it well; and should I lay
My ashes in a soil which is not mine,
My spirit shall resume it — if we may
Unbodied choose a sanctuary. I twine
My hopes of being remember'd in my line
With my land's language : if too fond and far
These aspirations in their scope incline, —
If my fame should be, as my fortunes[1] are,
Of hasty growth and blight, and dull Oblivion bar

X

My name from out the temple where the dead
Are honour'd by the nations — let it be —
And light the laurels on a loftier head!
And be the Spartan's epitaph on me —
"Sparta hath many a worthier[2] son than he."
Meantime I seek no sympathies, nor need;
The thorns which I have reap'd are of the tree
I planted; they have torn me, and I bleed :
I should have known what fruit would spring from such
  a seed.

---

gleterre, eh bien! qui sait si je ne l'ai pas bien aimée?
1. *As my fortunes*, comme ma destinée.
2. *Many a worthier.* On louait Brasidas, général lacédémonien, devant sa mère. « Sparte, répondit-elle, a perdu plus d'un fils qui lui est supérieur. » Souvenir classique que Byron ne dédaigne pas.

Décadence de Venise, si grande jadis. — Au nom de la poésie du moins, Byron proteste contre la servitude de Venise, qu'il a toujours aimée. (Str. XI à XIX.)

XI

The spouseless Adriatic[1] mourns her lord;
And, annual marriage now no more renew'd,
The Bucentaur lies rotten unrestored,
Neglected garment of her widowhood!
St. Mark yet sees his lion where he stood
Stand, but in mockery of his wither'd power,
Over the proud Place where an Emperor sued,
And monarchs gazed and envied in the hour
When Venice was a queen with an unequall'd dower.

XII

The Suabian sued[2], and now the Austrian reigns —
An Emperor tramples where an Emperor knelt;
Kingdoms are shrunk to provinces, and chains
Clank over sceptred cities; nations melt
From power's high pinnacle, when they have felt

---

1. *The spouseless Adriatic.* Nous ne sommes plus au temps où le doge épousait l'Adriatique. Pour comprendre les strophes XI, XII et XIII, il faut se rappeler l'histoire de Venise au douzième siècle. Elle est puissante, elle se met du côté du pape Alexandre III contre Frédéric Barberousse, empereur de la maison de Souabe. Celui-ci est vaincu et vient en 1177 à Venise, s'humilier devant le pape (*he sued*). Alexandre III, en récompense, donne à Venise la propriété de l'Adriatique, il remet au doge l'anneau nuptial que celui-ci jette à l'Adriatique du haut du navire le *Bucentaure*, pour marquer qu'il est le seigneur et l'époux de la mer. Cette cérémonie symbolique ne se fait plus, dit Byron.

2. *The Suabian.* Le Souabe Barberousse. Byron réclame l'expulsion des Autrichiens.

The sunshine for a while, and downward go
Like lauwine loosen'd from the mountain's belt;
Oh for one hour of blind old Dandolo [1] !
Th' octogenarian chief, Byzantium's conquering foe.

XIII

Before St. Mark still glow his steeds of brass,
Their gilded collars glittering in the sun;
But is not Doria's menace come to pass [2] ?
Are they not *bridled?* — Venice, lost and won,
Her thirteen hundred years of freedom done,
Sinks, like a sea-weed, into whence she rose!
Better be whelm'd beneath the waves, and shun,
Even in destruction's depth, her foreign foes,
From whom submission wrings an infamous repose.

XIV

In youth she was all glory, — a new Tyre;
Her very by-word [3] sprung from victory,

---

1. *Oh! for one hour of... Dandolo.* Qui ressuscitera pour une heure le vieux Dandolo ? — Henrico Dandolo, élu doge à quatre-vingt-deux ans, était à la quatrième croisade (1202), attaquait l'empire grec (dont un des chefs, Manuel Comnène, lui avait fait crever les yeux), entrait dans Constantinople et donnait à Venise, avec des possessions nouvelles, des œuvres d'art, parmi lesquelles les célèbres chevaux de bronze de Saint-Marc.

2. *But is come to pass...?* Pierre Doria jurait de brider le lion de Saint-Marc. Il n'y a pas réussi lui-même, mais sa prophétie s'est enfin réalisée. Elle *a passé*.

3. *Her by-word.* Son surnom vulgaire. Byron rappelle cette étymologie, d'après laquelle Venise, plantant le lion de Saint-Marc sur tous les rivages, le Vénitien serait le planteur de lions, *pianta-leone.* C'est un jeu de mots populaire dans lequel on confondait volontiers le nom de saint Pantaléon, patron de Venise, avec cette forme nouvelle et fabriquée : *pianta-leone*, que lord

The "Planter of the Lion", which through fire
And blood she bore o'er subject earth and sea;
Though making many slaves, herself still free,
And Europe's bulwark 'gainst the Ottomite;
Witness Troy's rival[1], Candia! Vouch it, ye
Immortal waves that saw Lepanto's[2] fight!
For ye are names no time nor tyranny can blight.

XV

Statues of glass — all shiver'd — the long file
Of her dead Doges are declined to dust;
But where they dwelt, the vast and sumptuous pile
Bespeaks the pageant of their splendid trust[3];
Their sceptre broken, and their sword in rust,
Have yielded to the stranger: empty halls,
Thin[4] streets, and foreign aspects[5], such as must
Too oft remind her who and what enthrals,
Have flung a desolate cloud o'er Venice' lovely walls.

XVI

When Athens' armies fell at Syracuse,
And fetter'd thousands bore the yoke of war,
Redemption rose up in the Attic Muse[6],

Byron cite comme l'expression de l'orgueil national, et non comme une étymologie scientifique. On sait que, depuis, le mot *Pantalon* a désigné le personnage ridicule du vieux Vénitien qui, dans les farces italiennes, joue le rôle d'un vieux frileux : ayant froid aux jambes, il a allongé ses hauts-de-chausses et il en a fait un *pantalon*.

1. *Troy's rival.* Candie subit un siège de vingt-cinq ans.
2. *Lepanto.* Venise fut, avec l'Espagne, le rempart de l'Europe à la bataille de Lépante (1571).
3. *Trust*, leur splendeur.
4. *Thin*, mince et vide.
5. *Foreign aspects.* Les figures étrangères (des Autrichiens).
6. *The Attic Muse.* Jadis le souvenir d'Euripide, sauva des

Her voice their only ransom from afar :
See! as they chant the tragic hymn, the car
Of the o'ermaster'd victor stops, the reins
Fall from his hands, his idle scimitar
Starts from its belt — he rends his captive's chains,
And bids him thank the bard for freedom and his strains.

XVII

Thus, Venice, if no stronger claim were thine,
Were all thy proud historic deeds forgot,
Thy choral memory of the Bard divine,
Thy love of Tasso[1], should have cut the knot
Which ties thee to thy tyrants; and thy lot
Is shameful to the nations, most of all,
Albion! to thee : the Ocean queen should not
Abandon Ocean's children; in the fall
Of Venice think of thine, despite thy watery wall.

XVIII

I loved her from my boyhood; she to me
Was as a fairy city of the heart,
Rising like water-columns from the sea,
Of joy the sojourn, and of wealth the mart;
And Otway[2], Radcliffe, Schiller, Shakspeare's art,
Had stamp'd her image in me, and even so,
Although I found her thus, we did not part[3];
Perchance even dearer in her day of woe,
Than when she was a boast, a marvel, and a show.

captifs, quelques vers de ce poète ayant touché le vainqueur. (Voy. Plutarque, *Vie de Nicias*.)

1. *Tasso*. La ville poétique où le gondolier chante les vers du Tasse, peut être défendue par les poètes.

2. *Otway*. Voy. la note à la strophe IV, pour ces allusions que Byron répète.

3. *We did not part*. Nous ne nous séparons pas. Je ne veux pas l'abandonner.

XIX

I can repeople with the past — and of
The present there is still for eye and thought,
And meditation chasten'd down[1], enough;
And more, it may be, than I hoped or sought;
And of the happiest moments which were wrought
Within the web of my existence, some
From thee, fair Venice! have their colours caught:
There are some feelings Time can not benumb,
Nor Torture shake, or mine would now be cold and dumb.

La douleur. — Le poète qui évoque ces souvenirs peut en évoquer d'autres qui lui sont personnels. — La douleur, tour à tour vaincue et renaissante, est toujours en nous. (Str. XX à XXIV.)

XX

But from their nature will the tannen[2] grow
Loftiest on loftiest and least shelter'd rocks,
Rooted in barrenness, where nought below
Of soil supports them 'gainst the Alpine shocks
Of eddying storms; yet springs the trunk, and mocks
The howling tempest, till its height and frame
Are worthy of the mountains from whose blocks
Of bleak, gray granite into life it came,
And grew a giant tree; — the mind may grow the same.

---

1. *Chastened down.* La méditation mélancolique qui suit les épreuves de la vie.

2. *The tannen.* Les sapins des Alpes, appelés *tannen*, ne croissent que sur des parties tout à fait rocheuses où ils trouvent à peine de la terre pour nourrir leurs racines. Et pourtant ils dépassent en hauteur les autres arbres (observation de Byron). Le mot *tanne* est allemand.

XXI

Existence may be borne, and the deep root
Of life and sufferance make its firm abode
In bare and desolated bosoms[1]; mute
The camel labours with the heaviest load,
And the wolf dies in silence, — not bestow'd
In vain should such example be; if they,
Things of ignoble or of savage mood,
Endure and shrink not, we of nobler clay
May temper it to[2] bear, — it is but for a day.

XXII

All suffering doth destroy, or is destroy'd,
Even by the sufferer; and, in each event,
Ends : Some, with hope replenish'd and rebuoy'd,
Return to whence they came — with like intent,
And weave their web again; some, bow'd and bent,
Wax gray and ghastly, withering ere their time,
And perish with the reed on which they leant;
Some seek devotion, toil, war, good or crime;
According as their souls were form'd to sink or climb[3].

XXIII

But ever and anon of griefs subdued[4]
There comes a token like a scorpion's sting,
Scarce seen, but with fresh bitterness imbued;
And slight withal may be the things which bring

---

1. *Bosoms.* Des cœurs, des êtres.
2. *Temper it to...* L'habituer à...
3. *Climb*, monter. Sens premier : s'attacher à, puis grimper, monter.

4. *Subdued.* Insistez, en traduisant, sur ce mot, qui sert de transition aux deux strophes. « Même vaincue, la douleur se réveille. »

Back on the heart the weight which it would fling
Aside for ever : it may be a sound —
A tone of music — summer's eve — or spring —
A flower — the wind — the ocean — which shall wound,
Striking the electric chain wherewith we are darkly
    bound;

XXIV

And how and why we know not, nor can trace
Home[1] to its cloud this lightning of the mind,
But feel the shock renew'd, nor can efface
The blight and blackening which it leaves behind,
Which out of things familiar, undesign'd,
When least we deem of such, calls up to view
The spectres whom no exorcism can bind[2] —
The cold[3], the changed, perchance the dead — anew,
The mourn'd, the lov'd, the lost — too many ! — yet how
    few !

L'Italie. — Salut à cette terre de la puissance et de la beauté. — Un coucher de soleil aux bords de la Brenta. (Str. XXV à XXIX.)

XXV

But my soul wanders; I demand it back[4]
To meditate amongst decay, and stand
A ruin amidst ruins; there to track
Fall'n states and buried greatness, o'er a land
Which *was* the mightiest in its old command,

---

1. *Home.* Chez lui, à son point de départ.
2. *Bind.* Lier, enchaîner et assujettir.
3. *The cold.* Les cœurs froids, ou ceux qui changent.
4. *I demand it back.* Je la rappelle.

And *is* the loveliest, and must ever be
The master-mould of Nature's heavenly hand;
Wherein were cast the heroic and the free,
The beautiful, the brave, the lords of earth and sea.

XXVI

The commonwealth of kings, the men of Rome!
And even since, and now, fair Italy!
Thou art the garden of the world, the home
Of all¹ Art yields, and Nature can decree;
Even in thy desert, what is like to thee?
Thy very weeds are beautiful, thy waste
More rich than other climes' fertility;
Thy wreck² a glory, and thy ruin graced
With an immaculate charm which cannot be defaced.

XXVII

The moon is up³, and yet it is not night;
Sunset divides⁴ the sky with her; a sea
Of glory streams along the Alpine height
Of blue Friuli's mountains; Heaven is free
From clouds, but of all colours seems to be, —
Melted to⁵ one vast Iris of the West, —

---

1. *All*, tout (ce que).
2. *Thy wreck a glory*. Tes débris sont un genre de gloire.
3. *Is up*. La description de ce pays, vu au clair de lune, remplit ici trois strophes qui sont aussi vraies qu'elles paraissent exagérées. Nous avons vu la Brenta dans les mêmes conditions. « On pourra croire, dit ici Byron lui-même, dans une note, si l'on n'a jamais vu le ciel d'Italie ou le ciel d'Orient, que cette peinture est sortie de mon imagination ou exagérée. Je ne donne pourtant ici que la description exacte d'une soirée du mois d'août. »
4. *Divides*, partage.
5. *Melted to*. Des couleurs se fondant en arc-en-ciel.

Where the Day joins the past Eternity;
While, on the other hand, meek Dian's crest
Floats through the azure air — an island of the blest!

XXVIII

A single star is at her side, and reigns
With her o'er half the lovely heaven; but still
Yon sunny sea heaves brightly, and remains
Roll'd[1] o'er the peak of the far Rhætian hill,
As Day and Night contending were, until
Nature reclaim'd her order : gently flows
The deep-dyed Brenta, — where their hues instil
The odorous purple of a new-born rose,
Which streams upon her stream, and glassed within it glows,

XXIX

Fill'd with[2] the face of heaven, which, from afar,
Comes down upon the waters; all its hues,
From the rich sunset to the rising star,
Their magical variety diffuse :
And now[3] they change; a paler shadow strews
Its mantle o'er the mountains; parting day
Dies like the dolphin, whom each pang[4] imbues
With a new colour as it gasps away,
The last still loveliest, till—'tis gone—and all is gray.

---

1. *Rolled.* Les flots de soleil roulant sur les cimes.
2. *Filled with.* La surface de la Brenta couverte par l'image des cieux, qui s'y réflète.

1. *And now.* Voici maintenant que...
4. *Each pang.* Chaque tressaillement du dauphin (de la daurade) qui meurt.

Arqua et Pétrarque. — Solitude poétique. Elle convient à la misanthropie et à la tristesse. (Str. XXX à XXXIV.)

XXX

There is a tomb in Arqua[1];—rear'd in air,
Pillared in their sarcophagus, repose
The bones of Laura's lover[2] : here repair
Many familiar with his well-sung woes,
The pilgrims of his genius. He arose
To raise a language, and his land reclaim
From the dull yoke of her barbaric foes :
Watering the tree which bears his lady's name
With his melodious tears, he gave himself to fame.

XXXI

They keep his dust in Arqua, where he died;
The mountain-village where his latter days
Went down the vale of years; and 'tis their pride[3] —
An honest pride—and let it be their praise,
To offer to the passing stranger's gaze
His mansion and his sepulchre; both plain
And venerably simple, such as raise
A feeling more accordant with his strain
Than if a pyramid form'd his monumental fane.

---

1. *In Arqua.* Le village d'Arqua, à douze milles de Padoue, garde encore la tombe de Pétrarque et la villa qu'il habita sur la fin de sa vie. La tombe en forme de sarcophage, est élevée sur quatre piliers.

2. *Laura's lover*, et plus bas *his lady's name.* Il chanta *Laure* et versa des pleurs sur le *laurier*.

3. *'Tis their pride.* La comtesse de Blessington, dans ses *Souvenirs d'Italie*, écrit à ce sujet : « On a conservé le fauteuil dans lequel mourut Pétrarque; il est de chêne, d'une forme bizarre et grossièrement sculpté. On montre aussi aux voyageurs le squelette de son chat favori. »

XXXII

And the soft quiet hamlet where he dwelt
Is one of that complexion [1] which seems made
For those who their mortality have felt,
And sought a refuge from their hopes decay'd
In the deep umbrage of a green hill's shade,
Which shows [2] a distant prospect far away
Of busy cities, now in vain display'd,
For they can lure no further; and the ray
Of a bright sun can make sufficient holiday,

XXXIII

Developing the mountains, leaves, and flowers,
And shining in the brawling brook, where-by,
Clear [3] as its current, glide the sauntering hours
With a calm languor, which, though to the eye
Idlesse it seem, hath its morality.
If from society we learn to live,
'Tis solitude should teach us how to die;
It hath no flatterers; vanity can give
No hollow aid [4]; alone—man with his God must strive:

XXXIV

Or, it may be, with demons [5], who impair
The strength of better thoughts, and seek their prey
In melancholy bosoms, such as were

---

1. *Complexion*, de ce caractère.
2. *Which shows*. De cette colline on voit..
3. *Clear*. Les heures limpides.
4. *Hollow aid*. Une assistance vide et vaine.

5. *With demons.* « Nous combattons vraisemblablement avec les démons, tout autant qu'avec nos pensées les meilleures. Satan choisit un désert pour y tenter Notre Seigneur. » (Note de Byron).

Of moody texture¹ from their earliest day,
And loved to dwell in darkness and dismay,
Deeming themselves predestined to a doom
Which is not of the pangs² that pass away;
Making the sun like blood, the earth a tomb,
The tomb a hell, and hell itself a murkier gloom.

Ferrare et le Tasse. — Le duc et le poète. — Malédiction contre l'aristocratie, contre la critique, contre la poésie française. — Grandeur de la poésie italienne. — Dante. — Boccace. (Str. XXXV à XLI.)

XXXV

Ferrara³! in thy wide and grass-grown streets,
Whose symmetry was not for solitude,
There seems as 't were a curse upon the seats
Of former sovereigns, and the antique brood
Of Este⁴ which for many an age made good
Its strength within thy walls, and was of yore
Patron or tyrant, as the changing mood
Of petty power impell'd, of those who wore
The wreath which Dante's brow alone had worn before.

---

1. *Of moody texture.* D'une nature triste.
2. *Of the pangs.* De douleurs passagères.
3. *Ferrara.* A propos de Ferrare et du Tasse, Byron écrit cinq strophes violentes contre les ducs de Ferrare, contre les critiques, Boileau et la littérature française. On y retrouve le ton et le style exagérés du jeune Byron à ses débuts lorsqu'il lançait l'anathème contre ceux qui osent juger ou combattre un écrivain.
4. *The brood of Este.* La maison d'Este. Elle a beaucoup fait pour les lettres et la Renaissance. Mais Byron, ne partant que du Tasse persécuté, est très sévère pour Alphonse II, qui a frappé *un poète*.

XXXVI

And Tasso is their glory and their shame.
Hark to his strain! and then survey his cell[1]!
And see how dearly earned Torquato's fame,
And where Alfonso bade his poet dwell :
The miserable despot could not quell
The insulted mind he sought to quench, and blend[2]
With the surrounding maniacs, in the hell
Where he had plunged it. Glory without end
Scattered the clouds away, and on that name attend.

XXXVII

The tears and praises of all time; while thine
Would rot its oblivion[3]—in the sink
Of worthless dust, which from thy boasted line
Is shaken into nothing—but the link
Thou formest in his fortunes bids us think
Of thy poor malice, naming thee with scorn;
Alfonso! how thy ducal pageants shrink
From thee! if in another station born,
Scarce fit to be[4] the slave of him thou madest to mourn :

XXXVIII.

Thou! form'd to eat, and be despised, and die,
Even as the beasts that perish, save that thou

---

1. *His cell.* La cellule du prisonnier. D'après une légende aujourd'hui très contestée, le poète Torquato Tasso, ayant conçu une violente passion pour Léonore, sœur d'Alphonse II, duc de Ferrare, celui-ci le fit enfermer pendant dix ans (1576-1586) dans une maison de fous.

2. *And blend.* Construisez : *he sought to blend.*

3. *Its oblivion,* dans son oubli. Ne traduisez pas par « l'oubli ». *Its* a un sens méprisant.

4. *Fit to be.* Sous-entendez *thou,* toi fait pour...

Hadst a more splendid trough and wider sty:
He! with a glory round his furrow'd brow,
Which[1] emanated then, and dazzles now,
In face of all his foes, the Cruscan quire[2],
And Boileau[3], whose rash envy could allow
No strain which shamed his country's creaking lyre
That whetstone of the teeth—monotony in wire[4]!

XXXIX

Peace to Torquato's injured shade! 't was his
In life and death to be the mark where Wrong
Aim'd with her poisoned arrows,—but to miss[5].
Oh, victor unsurpassed in modern song!
Each year brings forth its millions[6]; but how long
The tide of generations shall roll on,
And not the whole combined and countless throng
Compose a mind like thine? though all in one
Condensed their scatter'd rays, they would not form a sun.

XL

Great as thou art, yet[7] parallel'd by those,
Thy countrymen, before thee born to shine,
The Bards of Hell and Chivalry[8] : first rose

---

1. *Which*, gloire qui a rayonné.
2. *Cruscan quire.* Le chœur des critiques, l'Académie de la Crusca qui a pris pour objet l'analyse de la *Jérusalem délivrée.*
3. *Boileau.* Allusion aux vers célèbres de Boileau contre « le sot de qualité » qui préfère à l'or de Virgile le clinquant du Tasse.
4. *Monotony in wire!* Leur lyre a des cordes de laiton, très criardes
5. *To miss.* Le vise pour le manquer.
6. *Its millions*, ses millions d'hommes.
7. *Yet.* Après *yet* sous-entendez, *thou art.*
8. *The bards of Hell.* Dante le Toscan; *and chivalry,* Boccace, le Walter Scott de l'Italie.

The Tuscan father's comedy divine;
Then, not unequal to the Florentine,
The southern Scott, the minstrel who call'd forth
A new creation with his magic line,
And, like the Ariosto of the North,
Sang ladye-love and war, romance and knightly worth.

XLI

The lightning rent from Ariosto's bust
The iron crown of laurel's mimick'd leaves [1];
Nor was the ominous element unjust,
For the true laurel-wreath which Glory weaves
Is of the tree [2] no bolt of thunder cleaves,
And the false semblance but disgraced his brow;
Yet still, if fondly Superstition grieves,
Know, that the lightning sanctifies below
Whate'er it strikes; — yon head is doubly sacred [3] now.

Les ruines de l'Italie. — Jadis les Romains contemplaient avec tristesse les grandes ruines des villes grecques. Aujourd'hui on médite sur les ruines de l'Italie, pays de la beauté et de la douleur. — Souvenirs de Filicaja, du Pogge et de Sulpicius. (Str. XLII à XLVII.)

XLII

Italia! oh Italia [4]! thou who hast
The fatal gift of beauty, which became

---

1. *Mimick'd leaves*. Allusion à la couronne de laurier « artificiel » que portait le buste de l'Arioste : il paraît que la foudre l'avait ébréché.

2. *The tree (that)...*

3. *Sacred*. La foudre rendait sacré ce qu'elle touchait.

4. *Italia!* Aucun passage de Childe Harold ne donne mieux que

A funeral dower of present woes and past,
On thy sweet brow is sorrow plough'd by shame,
And annals graved in characters of flame.
Oh, God! that thou wert in thy nakedness
Less lovely or more powerful, and couldst claim
Thy right, and awe the robbers back[1], who press
To shed thy blood, and drink the tears of thy distress;

XLIII

Then might'st thou more appal; or, less desired,
Be homely and be peaceful, undeplored
For thy destructive charms; then, still untired
Would not be seen the armed torrents pour'd
Down the deep Alps; nor would the hostile horde
Of many-nationed spoilers from the Po
Quaff blood and water; nor the stranger's sword
Be thy sad weapon of defence, and so,
Victor or vanquish'd, thou the slave of friend or foe.

XLIV

Wandering in youth, I traced the path of him[2],
The Roman friend of Rome's least-mortal mind,
The friend of Tully : as my bark did skim

celui-ci l'idée du travail et de la manière de travailler de lord Byron. Parcourant l'Italie et la Grèce, il voyage tour à tour dans les ruines et dans les livres. Il lit Filicaja, et imite de ce poète du dix-septième siècle le sonnet célèbre qui commence ainsi : *Italia! Italia! o tu...* Il va de même lire, traduire et citer le Poggo et la lettre de Sulpicius.

1. *Awe...back*. Faire reculer d'épouvante et de respect, même sens que plus bas *appal*.
2. *Of him*. De Sulpicius, l'ami de Tullius (de Cicéron). Byron rappelle la lettre de Sulpicius à Cicéron, page célèbre, devenue et restée classique, dans laquelle Sulpicius, parlant de la mort de la fille de Cicéron, parle aussi de la mort des villes et des peuples.

The bright blue waters with a fanning wind,
Came Megara before me, and behind
Ægina lay, Piræus on the right,
And Corinth on the left; I lay reclined
Along the prow, and saw all these unite
In ruin, even as he had seen the desolate sight;

XLV

For Time hath not rebuilt them, but uprear'd
Barbaric dwellings on their shatter'd site,
Which only make more mourn'd and more endear'd
The few last rays of their far-scatter'd light,
And the crush'd relics of their vanish'd might.
The Roman saw these tombs in his own age,
These sepulchres of cities, which excite
Sad wonder, and his yet surviving page
The moral lesson bears, drawn from such pilgrimage.

XLVI

That page is now before me, and on mine [1]
His country's ruin added to the mass
Of perish'd states he mourn'd in their decline,
And I in desolation [2] : all that *was*
Of then destruction *is;* and now, alas!
Rome— Rome imperial, bows her to the storm,
In the same dust and blackness, and we pass
The skeleton [3] of her Titanic form,
Wrecks of another world, whose ashes still are warm.

« J'ai fait le même voyage que Sulpicius, dit ici Byron. J'avais derrière moi Egine... » etc.

« *Post me erat Ægina* », écrivait Sulpicius. Byron a traduit, d'abord en prose, puis en vers, et mot pour mot, l'auteur latin.

1. *On mine.* Sur ma page s'ajoute le nom de Rome.
2. *In desolation.* Dans *leur* désolation.
3. *The skeleton.* Sulpicius avait dit : *Oppida prostrata jacent,* puis *oppidum cadavera.* Le Pogge

XLVII

Yet, Italy! through every other land
Thy wrongs[1] should ring, and shall, from side to side;
Mother of Arts! as once of arms; thy hand
Was then our guardian, and is still our guide;
Parent of our religion! whom the wide
Nations have knelt[2] to for the keys of heaven!
Europe, repentant of her parricide,
  Shall yet redeem thee, and, all backward driven[3],
Roll the barbarian tide, and sue to be forgiven.

Florence. — La vallée de l'Arno. La Toscane. — La Vénus de Médicis. — Santa-Croce. — Les cendres des poètes toscans exilées. (Str. XLVIII à LX.)

XLVIII

But Arno wins us to the fair white walls,
Where the Etrurian Athens claims and keeps
A softer feeling for her fairy halls.
Girt by her theatre of hills, she reaps
Her corn, and wine, and oil, and Plenty leaps
To laughing life, with her redundant horn.
Along the banks where smiling Arno sweeps
  Was modern Luxury of Commerce born,
And buried Learning rose[4], redeem'd to a new morn.

---

avait répété le mot en y ajoutant une image : *Et nunc prostrata jacet, instar gigantei cadaveris corrupti.*

1. *Thy wrongs*. Tes injures.

2. *Knelt for...*, demandèrent genoux.

3. *Driven... tide*. Le flot repoussé.

4. *Learning rose*, la Renaissance.

XLIX

There, too, the Goddess loves in stone[1], and fills
The air around with beauty; we inhale
The ambrosial aspect, which, beheld, instils
Part of its immortality; the veil
Of heaven is half undrawn; within the pale
We stand, and in that form and face behold
What Mind can make, when Nature's self would fail;
And to the fond idolaters of old
Envy the innate flash which such a soul could mould:

L

We gaze and turn away, and know not where,
Dazzled and drunk with beauty, till the heart
Reels with its fulness; there—for ever there[2]—
Chain'd to the chariot of triumphal Art,
We stand as captives, and would not depart[3].
Away!—there need no words, nor terms precise[4],
The paltry jargon of the marble mart,
Where Pedantry gulls Folly—we have eyes:
Blood, pulse, and breast confirm the Dardan Shepherd's prize.

LI

Appear'd'st thou not to Paris in this guise?
Or to more deeply blest Anchises? or,

---

1. *Loves in stone.* Dans le marbre elle respire l'amour. Il s'agit ici de la Vénus de Médicis.
2. *For ever there.* C'est là qu'il faut rester à jamais.
3. *Would not depart.* Ce passage rappelle la belle page de Lucien racontant que les Gaulois représen- taient le dieu de l'éloquence enchaînant ses auditeurs : ils auraient été fâchés si leurs chaines s'étaient rompues. Raphaël a composé un dessin sur ce sujet.
4. *Nor terms precise.* Point de mots techniques ! Lord Byron ne se livre point ici à une boutade capri-

In all thy perfect goddess-ship, when lies
Before thee thy own vanquished Lord of War[1],
And gazing in thy face as toward a star,
Laid on thy lap, his eyes to thee upturn,
Feeding on thy sweet cheek! while thy lips are
With lava kisses melting while they burn,
Showered on his eyelids, brow, and mouth, as from an urn!

LII

Glowing[2], and circumfused in speechless love,
Their full divinity inadequate
That feeling to express, or to improve,
The gods become as mortals, and man's fate
Has moments like their brightest; but the weight
Of earth recoils upon us; let it go[3]!
We can recall such visions, and create,
From what has been, or might be, things which grow
Into thy statue's form, and look like gods below.

LIII

I leave to learned fingers[4], and wise hands,
The artist and his ape, to teach and tell
How well his connoisseurship understands
The graceful bend, and the voluptuous swell :

cieuse. Le beau, dit-il, est le beau, il charme, nous le contemplons. Les pédants et les faiseurs de dupes ont leurs raisons pour employer un jargon savant. *Away!*

1. *Lord of war*. Le dieu de la guerre, Mars.

2. *Glowing*. Réunissez *the gods glowing*. Les dieux, embrasés d'amour pour cette beauté suprême.

3. *Let it go*. Ne pensons pas a cette argile.

4. *Learned fingers*. Les doigts qui écrivent savamment. Byron se raille du jargon prétentieux des gens qui singent les artistes (*his ape*). Connaisseurs italiens ou métaphysiciens allemands, ils font des théories esthétiques et pédantes, pour prouver que le beau est le beau.

Let these describe the undescribable :
 I would not their vile breath should crisp the stream
 Wherein that image shall for ever dwell :
 The unruffled mirror of the loveliest dream
That ever left the sky on the deep soul to beam.

LIV

In Santa Croce's [1] holy precincts lie
Ashes which make it holier, dust which is
Even in itself an immortality,
 Though there were nothing save the past, and this,
 The particle of those sublimities
 Which have relapsed to chaos : here repose
 Angelo's [2], Alfieri's bones, and his,
 The starry Galileo, with his woes;
Here Machiavelli's earth returned to whence it rose.

LV

These are four minds, which, like the elements,
 Might furnish forth creation :—Italy!
Time, which hath wronged thee with ten thousand rents
Of thine imperial garment, shall deny,
And hath denied, to every other sky,
 Spirits which soar from ruin : thy decay
 Is still impregnate with divinity,
 Which gilds it with revivifying ray;
Such as the great of yore, Canova [3] is to-day.

---

1. *Santa Croce.* L'église de Santa-Croce, bâtie en 1294 par Arnolfo di Lapo.

2. *Angelo.* Michel-Ange.

3. *Canova.* Sculpteur célèbre, né en 1757, mort en 1822.

LVI

But where repose the all Etruscan three—
Dante, and Petrarch, and, scarce less than they,
The Bard of Prose[1], creative spirit! he
Of the Hundred Tales of love—where did they lay
Their bones, distinguished from our common clay
In death as life? Are they resolved to dust,
And have their country's marbles nought to say?
Could not her quarries furnish forth one bust?
Did they not to her breast their filial earth entrust?

LVII

Ungrateful Florence[2]! Dante sleeps afar,
Like Scipio, buried by the upbraiding shore :
Thy factions, in their worse than civil war,
Proscribed the bard whose name for evermore
Their children's children would in vain adore
With the remorse of ages; and the crown
Which Petrarch's laureate brow supremely wore,
Upon a far and foreign soil had grown,
His life, his fame, his grave, though rifled—not thine own.

---

1. *The Bard of Prose.* Boccace, dont la prose toscane a le charme de la poésie. Réunissez *creative of the Hundred Tales*, créateur du *Décaméron*.

2. *Ungrateful Florence!* Pour comprendre les allusions contenues dans les strophes LVII, LVIII et LIX, il faut se rappeler l'histoire des quatre personnages cités. On ne trouve pas à Rome, dit Byron, les restes de Scipion, qui fut enseveli à Laternum. On ne trouve pas à Florence la tombe de Dante, qui, proscrit en 1302, fut enterré à Ravenne (*happier Ravenna*); ni celle de Pétrarque, qui vécut à l'étranger, à Vaucluse, et eut sa tombe à Arqua (on essaya de reprendre son cadavre qui fut enlevé, *rifled*); ni celle de Boccace, qui eut un moment son sépulcre à Certaldo, village originel de sa famille, mais qui en fut expulsé par le chapitre. D'où cette insulte au chapitre, *the hyæna bigot!*

LVIII

Boccaccio to his parent earth bequeathed
His dust, — and lies it not her great among [1],
With many a sweet and solemn requiem breathed
O'er him who formed the Tuscan's siren tongue?
That music in itself, whose sounds are song,
The poetry of speech? No;—even his tomb
Uptorn, must bear the hyæna bigot's wrong,
No more amidst the meaner dead find room,
Nor claim a passing sigh, because it told for *whom!*

LIX

And Santa Croce wants their mighty dust;
Yet for this want more noted, as of yore
The Cæsar's pageant, shorn of Brutus' bust,
Did but of Rome's best Son remind her more:
Happier Ravenna! on thy hoary shore,
Fortress of falling empire, honoured sleeps
The immortal exile:—Arqua, too, her store
Of tuneful relics proudly claims and keeps,
While Florence vainly begs her banished dead and weeps.

LX

What is [2] her pyramid of precious stones?
Of porphyry, jasper, agate, and all hues

---

1. *Her great among.* Parmi ses grands hommes, comme plus loin, *her dead*, ses morts.
2. *What is...* Qu'est-ce que cette pyramide? Byron parle rapidement, dans cette strophe et dans la suivante, des autres merveilles de Florence, 'c'est-à-dire du tombeau des Médicis, à San-Lorenzo, et des palais célèbres devenus des musées, le palais Pitti et celui des Uffizi (*princely shrine*). Il dit, avec trop de légèreté, le médiocre intérêt qu'il y attache.

Of gem and marble, to encrust the bones
Of merchant-dukes? the momentary dews
Which, sparkling to the twilight stars, infuse
Freshness in the green turf that wraps the dead,
Whose names are mausoleums of the Muse,
Are gently prest with far more reverent tread
Than ever paced the slab which paves the princely head.

De Florence à Rome. — Le lac de Pérouse, la bataille de Trasimène et le Sanguinetto. — Le temple de Clitumnus. — Le Velino et la cataracte de Terni. — Les Apennins et le Soracte. — Boutade contre Horace. (Str. LXI à LXXVII.)

LXI

There be more things to greet the heart and eyes
In Arno's dome of Art's most princely shrine,
Where sculpture with her rainbow sister vies;
There be more marvels yet—but not for mine;
For I have been accustomed to entwine
My thoughts with Nature rather in the fields,
Than Art in galleries : though a work divine
Calls for my spirit's homage, yet it yields[2]
Less than it feels, because the weapon which it wields

LXII

Is of another temper, and I roam
By Thrasimene's lake, in the defiles
Fatal to Roman rashness, more at home[2];

---

1. *It yields.* Mon esprit ne rend pas.

2. *More at home.* En pleine campagne, mon esprit est chez lui.

For there the Carthaginian's warlike wiles
Come back before me, as his skill beguiles
The host between the mountains and the shore,
Where Courage falls in her despairing files,
And torrents, swollen to rivers with their gore,
Reek through the sultry plain, with legions scattered o'er.

LXIII

Like to a forest felled by mountain winds;
And such¹ the storm of battle on this day,
And such the frenzy, whose convulsion blinds
To all save carnage, that, beneath the fray,
An earthquake reeled unheededly away!
None felt stern Nature² rocking at his feet,
And yawning forth a grave for those who lay
Upon their bucklers for a winding sheet
Such is the absorbing hate when warring nations meet!

LXIV

The Earth to them was as a rolling bark
Which bore them to Eternity; they saw
The Ocean round, but had no time to mark
The motions of their vessel; Nature's law,
In them suspended, recked not of the awe
Which reigns when mountains tremble, and the birds
Plunge in the clouds for refuge, and withdraw
From their down-topling nests; and bellowings herds
Stumble o'er heaving plains, and man's dread hath no words.

---

1. *Such.* Tel fut, such (*was*)... flexible dans ses lois. Tout ce pas-
2. *Stern nature,* la nature in- sage est inspiré de Tite-Live.

LXV

Far other scene is Thrasimene now :
Her lake a sheet of silver, and her plain
Rent by no ravage save the gentle plough ;
Her aged trees rise thick as once the slain[1]
Lay where their roots are; but a brook hath ta'en —
A little rill of scanty stream and bed —
A name of blood from that day's sanguine rain ;
And Sanguinetto[2] tells ye where the dead
Made the earth wet, and turned the unwilling waters red.

LXVI

But thou, Clitumnus[3]! in thy sweetest wave
Of the most living crystal that was e'er
The haunt[4] of river nymph, to gaze and lave
Her limbs where nothing hid them, thou dost rear
Thy grassy banks whereon the milk-white steer
Grazes; the purest god of gentle waters !
And most serene of aspect, and most clear;
Surely that stream was unprofaned by slaughters—
A mirror and a bath for Beauty's youngest daughters!

LXVII

And on thy happy shore a Temple still,
Of small and delicate proportion, keeps,
Upon a mild declivity of hill,

---

1. *Thick as the slain.* La végétation est aussi épaisse aujourd'hui que l'hécatombe autrefois.
2. *Sanguinetto.* Le ruisseau du Sang nous dit où ils moururent.
3. *Clitumnus.* « Aucun voyageur, dit Byron, ne manque de consacrer un long chapitre au temple de Clitumne, situé entre Foligno et Spolète. »
4. *The haunt.* Le séjour fréquenté par...

Its memory of thee; beneath it sweeps
Thy current's calmness; oft from out it leaps
The finny darter[1] with the glittering scales,
Who dwells and revels in thy glassy deeps;
While, chance, some scatter'd water lily sails
Down where the shallower wave still tells its bubbling
tales.

LXVIII

Pass not unblest[2] the Genius of the place!
If through the air a zephyr more serene
Win to the brow, 'tis his; and if ye trace
Along his margin a more eloquent green,
If on the heart the freshness of the scene
Sprinkle its coolness, and from the dry dust
Of weary life a moment lave it clean
With Nature's baptism,—'tis to him ye must
Pay orisons for this suspension of disgust.

LXIX

The roar[3] of waters!—from the headlong height
Velino[4] cleaves the wave-worn precipice;
The fall of waters! rapid as the light
The flashing mass foams shaking the abyss,
The hell of waters! where they howl and hiss,

---

1. *The darter.* Le poisson qui s'élance.
2. *Unblest*, sans qu'il soit béni.
3. *The roar.* Voici le mugissement.
4. *Velino.* Le Velino forme la célèbre cataracte de Terni ou de la Marmora, chute de 165 mètres, fort admirée des voyageurs. Byron a voulu l'étudier de plusieurs points, la voir à deux reprises et la signaler par une description spéciale. C'est pour lui la cataracte sans rivale, *matchless cataract.* Le Velino se jette dans la Nera, sur laquelle était située la ville d'Interamna (aujourd'hui Terni, comme l'indique la ressemblance des deux noms).

And boil in endless torture; while the sweat
Of their great agony, wrung out from this
Their Phlegethon, curls round the rocks of jet
That gird the gulf around, in pitiless horror set,

LXX

And mounts in spray the skies, and thence again
Returns in an unceasing shower, which round,
With its unemptied cloud of gentle rain,
Is an eternal April to the ground,
Making it all one emerald :—how profound
The gulf! and how the giant element
From rock to rock leaps with delirious bound,
Crushing the cliffs, which, downward worn and rent
With his fierce footsteps, yield in chasms a fearful vent[1].

LXXI

To the broad column which rolls on, and shows
More like the fountain of an infant sea
Torn from the womb of mountains by the throes
Of a new world, than only thus to be
Parent of rivers, which flow gushingly,
With many windings, through the vale :—Look back!
Lo! where it comes like an eternity,
As if to sweep down all things in its track,
Charming the eye with dread,—a matchless cataract,

LXXII

Horribly beautiful! but on the verge,
From side to side, beneath the glittering morn,

---

1. *Yield in chasms a fearful vent* (to...). Les rochers brisés ouvrent un abîme et une route (à la masse d'eau qui semble une mer naissante). Mot à mot : Ouvre dans les abîmes une issue.

An Iris[1] sits, amidst the infernal surge,
Like Hope upon a death-bed, and, unworn :
Its steady dyes, while all around is torn
By the distracted waters, bears serene
Its brilliant hues with all their beams unshorn :
Resembling, 'mid the torture of the scene,
Love watching Madness with unalterable mien.

LXXIII

Once more upon the woody Apennine[2],
The infant Alps, which—had I not before
Gazed on their mightier parents, where the pine
Sits on more shaggy summits, and where roar
The thundering lauwine[3]—might be worshipp'd more;
But I have seen the soaring Jungfrau rear
Her never-trodden snow, and seen the hoar
Glaciers of bleak Mont Blanc both far and near,
And in Chimari heard the thunder-hills of fear,

LXXIV

Th' Acroceraunian mountains of old name;
And on Parnassus seen the eagles fly
Like spirits of the spot, as 't were for fame,

---

1. *An Iris.* Un arc-en-ciel se dessine au-dessus de la tempête infernale. Ici Byron nous renvoie à Pline qui en a parlé et à son propre poème de *Manfred*, dans lequel il a inséré une nouvelle note sur ce sujet.

2. *Apennine.* Les Apennins n'ont pas fourni au poète un sujet sérieux d'observation. Il reprend le ton méprisant de la strophe LX, dit qu'il a vu mieux et s'attaque à Horace comme tout à l'heure il s'attaquait à Boileau. Il faut lire ces strophes comme elles ont été écrites.

3. *Lauwine.* C'est le nom que l'on donne en Suisse à l'avalanche. Byron l'emploie ici comme plus haut il empruntait à l'allemand le nom des sapins des Alpes (*tannen*).

For still they soared unutterably high :
I've look'd on Ida with a Trojan's eye;
Athos, Olympus, Ætna, Atlas, made
These hills seem things of lesser dignity,
  All, save the lone Soracte's [1] height, display'd
Not *now* in snow, which asks the lyric Roman's aid

LXXV

For our remembrance, and from out the plain
Heaves like a long-swept wave about to break,
And on the curl hangs pausing : not in vain
May he, who will, his recollections rake,
And quote in classic raptures, and awake
The hills with Latian echoes; I abhorr'd
Too much, to conquer for the poet's sake,
  The drill'd dull lesson, forced down word by word
In my repugnant youth, with pleasure to record

LXXVI

Aught that recalls the daily drug which turn'd
My sickening memory; and, though Time hath taught
My mind to meditate what then it learned,
Yet such the fixed inveteracy wrought
By the impatience of my early thought,

---

1. *Soracte.* Le Soracte, à 50 kilomètres au nord de Rome, dépasse le autres pics des Apennins dans cette partie de la chaîne. Horace l'a rendu classique, et Byron, à la seule idée d'un souvenir *classique*, s'abandonne à une boutade contre Horace, les traductions en devoir et le mot à mot sévère. Sa colère est un jeu qui l'amuse. Si l'on voulait lui répondre, pour prouver combien il a lu et aimé les poètes antiques, il faudrait citer tout *Childe Harold*, et aussi la note dans laquelle il atténue l'effet de ces strophes, disant : « Le temps que j'ai passé à Harrow fut le plus heureux de ma vie. »

That, with the freshness wearing out before
My mind could relish what it might have sought
If free to choose, I cannot now restore
Its health; but what it then detested, still abhor.

LXXVII

Then farewell, Horace; whom I hated so,
Not for thy faults, but mine; it is a curse
To understand, not feel thy lyric flow,
To comprehend, but never love thy verse;
Although no deeper Moralist rehearse
Our little life, nor Bard prescribe his art,
Nor livelier Satirist the conscience pierce,
Awakening without wounding the touch'd heart,
Yet fare thee well—upon Soracte's ridge we part.

Rome, la Niobé des nations. — Patrie des ruines et des cœurs ruinés. — Génies qui la ressuscitent. — Coup d'œil jeté sur l'histoire du génie politique romain et sur celle de la Liberté. — Sylla, César, Pompée. Leurs successeurs modernes : Cromwell, Bonaparte. Au-dessus d'eux Washington. (Str. XXVII à XCVIII).

LXXVIII

Oh Rome[1]! my country! city of the soul!
The orphans of the heart must turn to thee,

---

1. *Oh Rome!* Byron a dit en prose : « Je suis dans Rome, la merveille... J'y crois revoir la Grèce, Constantinople, tout enfin ; mais je ne saurais vous la décrire... Quant au Colisée, au Panthéon, à Saint-Pierre, au Vatican, au mont Palatin, etc., ils passent toute conception : il faut les voir. » Rome est la métropole de l'histoire.

CANTO THE FOURTH. 215

Lone mother of dead empires! and control [1]
In their shut breasts their petty misery —
What are our woes and sufferance? Come and see
The cypress, hear the owl, and plod your way
O'er steps of broken thrones and temples, Ye!
Whose agonies are evils of a day—
A world is at our feet as fragile as our clay.

LXXIX

The Niobe of nations! there she stands,
Childless and crownless, in her voiceless woe;
An empty urn within her wither'd hands,
Whose holy dust was scatter'd long ago;
The Scipios' tomb contains no ashes now;
The very sepulchres lie tenantless
Of their heroic dwellers: dost thou flow,
Old Tiber! through a marble wilderness?
Rise, with thy yellow waves, and mantle her distress.

LXXX

The Goth, the Christian, Time, War, Flood, and Fire,
Have dealt upon [2] the seven-hill'd city's pride;
She saw her glories star by star expire,
And up the steep barbarian monarchs ride,
Where the car climb'd the capitol; far and wide
Temple and tower went down, nor left a site [3] :
Chaos of ruins! who shall trace the void,
O'er the dim fragments cast a lunar light,
And say, « here was, or, is », where all is doubly night?

---

1. *Control.* Ils doivent comprimer.
2. *Dealt upon.* Ont fait leur œuvre sur son orgueil.
3. *A site.* N'ont pas laissé le souvenir de leur emplacement même. C'est pourquoi les fouilles durent toujours.

LXXXI

The double night of ages, and of her,
Night's daughter, Ignorance, hath wrapt and wrap[1]
All round us; we but feel our way to err:
The ocean hath his chart, the stars their map,
And Knowledge spreads them on her ample lap;
But Rome is as the desert, where we steer
Stumbling o'er recollections; now we clap
Our hands, and cry « Eureka! » it is clear—
When but some false mirage of ruin rises near.

LXXXII

Alas! the lofty city! and alas!
The trebly hundred triumphs[2]! and the day
When Brutus made the dagger's edge surpass[3]
The conqueror's sword in bearing fame away!
Alas, for Tully's voice, and Virgil's lay,
And Livy's pictured page!—but these shall be
Her resurrection; all beside—decay.
Alas, for Earth, for never shall we see
That brightness in her eye she bore when Rome was free!

LXXXIII

Oh thou[4], whose chariot roll'd on Fortune's wheel,
Triumphant Sylla! Thou, who didst subdue

---

1. *Hath wrapt and wrap.* Il faudrait *wraps*; mais on peut sous-entendre *does* devant *wrap*, ce qui permet au poète de faire rimer *wrap* et *map*.

2. *The trebly hundred triumphs.* Il y eut trois cents triomphes à Rome d'après Orose, Panvinio et Gibbon. (Note de Byron.)

3. *Surpass.* Le poignard surpasse l'épée du maître et remporte la victoire.

4. *O thou.* O toi, Sylla! Sans transition, le poète passe aux ques-

Thy country's foes ere thou wouldst pause[1] to feel
The wrath of thy own wrongs, or reap the due
Of hoarded vengeance till thine eagles flew
O'er prostrate Asia;—thou, who with thy frown
Annihilated senates—Roman, too,
With all thy vices, for thou didst lay down
With an atoning smile a more than earthly crown—

LXXXIV

The dictatorial wreath—couldst thou divine
To what would one day dwindle that which made
Thee more than mortal? and that so supine[2]
By aught than[3] Romans Rome should thus be laid?
She who was named Eternal, and array'd
Her warriors but to conquer—she who veiled
Earth with her haughty shadow, and display'd,
Until the o'er-canopied horizon fail'd,
Her rushing wings— Oh! she who was Almighty hail'd!

LXXXV

Sylla was first of victors; but our own,
The sagest of usurpers, Cromwell!—he
Too swept off senates while he hew'd the throne
Down to a block—immortal rebel! See
What crimes it costs to be a moment free,

tions éternelles que soulève l'histoire de Rome, au jugement qu'il faut porter sur les luttes politiques dont les Sylla et les César furent les héros.

1. *Ere thou wouldst pause... till...* Sylla attendit qu'il eût écrasé es ennemis de Rome en Asie avant de songer à ses ennemis personnels à Rome.

2. *And that so supine.* Contruisez : et (que) cette Rome si orgueilleuse.

3. *By aught than,* par autre chose que... par quoi que ce soit. *Aught* a le sens indéfini.

And famous through all ages! but beneath
His fate the moral[1] lurks of destiny;
His day[2] of double victory and death
Beheld him win two realms, and, happier, yield his breath.

LXXXVI

The third of the same moon whose former course
Had all but crown'd him, on the self-same day
Deposed him gently from his throne of force,
And laid him with the earth's preceding clay.
And show'd not Fortune thus how fame and sway,
And all we deem delightful, and consume
  Our souls to compass through each arduous way,
Are in her eyes less happy then the tomb?
Were they but so[3] in man's, how different were his doom!

LXXXVII

And thou, dread statue[4]! yet existent in
The austerest form of naked majesty,
Thou who beheldest, 'mid the assassins' din,
At thy bathed base the bloody Cæsar lie,
Folding his robe in dying dignity,
An offering to thine altar from the queen

---

1. *The moral.* Construisez : la morale du destin.
2. *His day.* Cromwell gagna, le 3 septembre 1650, la bataille de Dunbar; il gagna le 3 septembre 1651 la bataille de Worcester; il mourut le 3 septembre 1658. Le rapport de ces dates qui a l'air d'être établi par la destinée, forme un exemple tout trouvé pour ceux qui croient aux dates fatales.
3. *Were they but so.* Si pour l'homme la gloire et la puissance n'étaient que cela.
4. *Dread statue!* Statue terrible, au pied de laquelle tomba César. Le dictateur tomba au pied de la statue de Pompée.

CANTO THE FOURTH. 219

Of gods and men, great Nemesis! did he die,
And thou, too, perish, Pompey? have ye been
Victors of countless kings, or puppets[1] of a scene?

LXXXVIII

And thou, the thunder-stricken nurse of Rome!
She-wolf[2], whose brazen-imaged dugs impart
The milk of conquest yet within the dome
Where, as a monument of antique art,
Thou standest: — Mother of the mighty heart[3],
Which the great founder suck'd from thy wild teat,
Scorch'd by the Roman Jove's ethereal dart,
And thy limbs black with lightning — dost thou yet
Guard thine immortal cubs, nor thy fond charge forget?

LXXXIX

Thou dost; but all thy foster-babes are dead —
The men of iron; and the world hath rear'd
Cities from out[4] their sepulchres: men bled
In imitation of the things they fear'd,
And fought and conquer'd, and the same course steer'd,
At apish distance; but as yet none have,

---

1. *Puppets.* Ils ont joué le rôle de vainqueurs des rois et, (sous un autre aspect), celui de marionnettes de théâtre, de poupées. La mode d'aujourd'hui dirait de *pupazzi.*

2. *Thunder-stricken... she-wolf.* La louve de la tradition, laquelle avait été frappée de la foudre. C'est ce qui inspire à Byron les trois derniers vers de la fin, vers peu naturels.

3. *Of the heart.* Mère au grand cœur, qui a donné son cœur avec son lait.

4. *Reared from out...* Ils ont bâti des cités avec les pierres des tombes. Les villes du moyen âge construisaient leurs remparts avec les pierres tombales des Romains. Il en fut de même jusque dans notre pays. On peut voir à Sens tout un musée, formé par M. Julliot et composé de pierres romaines extraites des remparts.

Nor could, the same supremacy have near'd,
Save one vain man[1], who is not in the grave,
But, vanquish'd by himself, to his own slaves a slave —

XC

The fool of false dominion — and a kind
Of bastard Cæsar, following him of old[2]
With steps unequal; for the Roman's mind
Was modell'd in a less terrestrial mould,
With passions fiercer, yet a judgment cold,
And an immortal instinct which redeem'd
The frailties of a heart so soft[3], yet bold,
Alcides with the distaff now he seem'd
At Cleopatra's feet, — and now himself he beam'd,

XCI

And came — and saw — and conquer'd! But the man
Who would have tamed his eagles[4] down to flee,
Like a train'd falcon, in the Gallic van,
Which he, in sooth, long led to victory,
With a deaf heart which never seem'd to be
A listener to itself, was strangely framed;
With but one weakest weakness — vanity,
Coquettish in ambition, still he aim'd —
At what? can he avouch or answer what he claim'd?

---

1. *One vain man*. Napoléon, qui était alors à Sainte-Hélène. Byron revient toujours à lui. Dans *Childe Harold* il écrit contre lui les strophes sur la guerre d'Espagne (chant I). Il l'admire dans le passage sur Waterloo (chant III). Ici il en fait un César bâtard, imitateur des Romains, un vaniteux. cobuet dans l'ambition (*coquettish*).

2. *Him of old*. Le César de l'antiquité.

3. *So soft...* Construisez : Il avait le cœur tout à la fois si tendre et si viril, que tour à tour c'était Hercule, aux pieds d'Omphale, ou le Génie rayonnant.

4. *His eagles*. Ses aigles à lui devaient paraître (et voler dans le ciel) avant l'armée française.

XCII

And would be all or nothing — nor could wait
For the sure grave to level him; few years
Had fix'd[1] him with the Cæsars in his fate,
On whom we tread : For *this*[2] the conqueror rears
The arch of triumph; and for this the tears
And blood of earth flow on as they have flow'd,
An universal deluge, which appears
Without an ark for wretched man's abode,
And ebbs but to reflow! — Renew thy rainbow, God!

XCIII

What from[3] this barren being do we reap?
Our senses narrow, and our reason frail,
Life short, and truth a gem which loves the deep,
And all things weigh'd in custom's falsest scale;
Opinion an omnipotence, — whose veil
Mantles the earth with darkness, until right[4]
And wrong are accidents, and men grow pale[5]
Lest their own judgments should become too bright,
And their free thoughts be crimes, and earth have too much light.

---

1. *Had fixed.* Quelques années de plus l'auraient installé parmi les Césars.
2. *For this.* Voilà pourquoi on fait la guerre, le déluge de sang.
3. *What from...* Que recueillons-nous de ces longues luttes ? Byron lui-même déclare que dans les vers qui suivent, il répète ce que Cicéron écrivait il y a dix-huit cents ans. « *Imbecilles animos, brevia curricula vitæ, in profundo veritatem demersam*, etc. » Telles sont les expressions de l'auteur latin.
4. *Until right.* Si bien que le droit... Au point que le bien et le mal ne sont plus que des accidents.
5. *Grow pale lest...* Ont peur que...

XCIV

And thus they plod in sluggish misery,
Rotting from sire to son, and age to age,
Proud of their trampled nature, and so die,
Bequeathing their hereditary rage
To the new race of inborn slaves, who wage
War[1] for their chains, and rather than be free,
Bleed gladiator-like, and still engage
Within the same arena where they see
Their fellows fall before, like leaves of the same tree.

XCV

I speak not of men's creeds — they rest between
Man and his Maker — but of things allow'd,
Averr'd, and known, and daily, hourly seen —
The yoke that is upon us doubly bow'd,
And the intent of tyranny avow'd,
The edict of Earth's rulers, who are grown
The apes of him who humbled once the proud,
And shook them from their slumbers on the throne;
Too glorious[2], were this all his mighty arm had done.

XCVI

Can tyrants but by tyrants conquer'd be,
And Freedom find no champion and no child
Such as Columbia saw arise when she
Sprung forth a Pallas, arm'd and undefiled?

---

1. *Who wage war*... qui réengagent la bataille. Sens général : La guerre recommence toujours et jamais pour a liberté.

2. *Too glorious.* Il serait trop grand (Bonaparte), s'il se fût arrêté après avoir secoué les rois du haut de leur trône.

Or must such minds be nourished in the wild,
Deep in the unpruned forest 'midst the roar
Of cataracts, where nursing Nature smiled
On infant Washington[1]? Has Earth no more
Such seeds within her breast, or Europe no such shore?

XCVII

But France got drunk[2] with blood to vomit crime,
And fatal have her Saturnalia been
To Freedom's cause, in every age and clime;
Because the deadly days which we have seen
And vile Ambition, that built up between
Man and his hopes an adamantine wall,
And the base pageant last[3] upon the scene,
Are grown the pretext for the eternal thrall
Which nips life's tree, and dooms man's worst — his second fall.

XCVIII

Yet, Freedom! yet thy banner, torn, but flying,
Streams like the thunder-storm *against* the wind;
Thy trumpet voice, though broken now and dying,
The loudest still the tempest leaves behind;
Thy tree[4] hath lost its blossoms, and the rind,
Chopp'd by the axe, looks rough and little worth,

---

1. *Washington*. Le poète termine cette grande page sur la tyrannie et la liberté par l'éloge du seul homme qui ait renversé la tyrannie pour fonder la liberté. Washington venait de mourir au seuil du dix-neuvième siècle, en 1799.

2. *Got drunk*, s'enivra. Une fois encore on peut comparer ici Gœthe et Byron : l'un et l'autre, ils ont opposé la Révolution à la Terreur.

3. *Last*. Le spectacle d'hier.

4. *Tree*. L'arbre de la liberté garde sa sève. Cette strophe dément les précédentes.

But the sap lasts, — and still the seed we find
Sown deep, even in the bosom of the North;
So shall a better spring less bitter fruit bring forth.

La tombe de Cécilia Metella. — Qui était-elle? — Méditation sur le néant et l'orgueil de l'humanité. (Str. XCIX à CVI.)

XCIX

There is a stern round tower [1] of other days,
Firm as a fortress, with its fence of stone,
Such as an army's baffled strength delays,
Standing with half its battlements alone
And with two thousand years of ivy grown;
The garland of eternity, where wave
The green leaves over all by time o'erthrown : —
What was this tower of strength? within its cave
What treasure lay so lock'd, so hid? — A woman's grave.

C

But who was she, the lady of the dead [2],
Tomb'd in a palace? Was she chaste and fair?
Worthy a king's, or more — a Roman's bed?
What race of chiefs and heroes did she bear?
What daughter of her beauties was the heir?
How lived, how loved, how died she? Was she not

---

1. *Tower.* Le tombeau de Cécilia Metela, en forme de tour, est situé sur la voie Appienne. C'était la femme du triumvir Crassus.
2. *The lady of the dead.* La reine des morts.

So honoured — and conspicuously there,
Where meaner relics must not dare to rot,
Placed to commemorate a more than mortal lot?

CI

Was she as those who love their lords, or they
Who love the lords of others [1]? such have been
Even in the olden time, Rome's annals say.
Was she a matron of Cornelia's mien,
Or the light air of Egypt's graceful queen,
Profuse of joy — or 'gainst it did she war,
Inveterate in virtue? Did she lean
Tothe soft side of the heart, or wisely bar
Love from amongst her griefs? — for such the affections are.

CII

Perchance she died in youth : it may be, bow'd
With woes far heavier than the ponderous tomb
That weigh'd upon her gentle dust, a cloud
Might gather o'er her beauty, and a gloom
In her dark eye, prophetic of the doom
Heaven gives its favourites — early death [2]; yet shed
A sunset charm [3] around her, and illume
With hectic light, the Hesperus of the dead,
Of her consuming cheek the autumnal leaf-like red.

---

1. *The lords of others.* Ici le poète, cherchant à deviner les traits et le caractère de la femme disparue, écrit des strophes qui seraient mieux placées dans *Don Juan* que dans *Childe Harold*.

2. *Early death*, une mort venue de bonne heure. On se rappelle le proverbe grec : « Celui que les dieux aiment meurt jeune. »

3. *A sunset charm.* Même dans la maladie, sa figure devait avoir le charme du soleil couchant, l'éclat de la fièvre ; sa joue mourante devait avoir le ton rouge de la feuille d'automne.

CIII

Perchance she died in age — surviving all,
Charms, kindred, children — with the silver gray
On her long tresses, which might yet recall,
It may be, still a something of the day
When they were braided, and her proud array
And lovely form were envied, praised, and eyed
By Rome — But whither would Conjecture stray?
Thus much alone we know — Metella died,
The wealthiest Roman's wife : Behold his love or pride!

CIV

I know not why — but standing thus by thee
It seems as if I had thine inmate known,
Thou Tomb! and other days come back on me
With recollected music, though the tone
Is changed and solemn, like the cloudy groan
Of dying thunder on the distant wind;
Yet could I[1] seat me by this ivied stone
Till I had bodied forth the heated mind
Forms from the floating wreck which Ruin leaves behind;

CV

And from the planks, far shatter'd o'er the rocks,
Built me a little bark of hope, once more
To battle with the ocean and the shocks
Of the loud breakers, and the ceaseless roar
Which rushes on the solitary shore

---

1. *Yet could I.* Et quand même je pourrais (m'arrêter, refaire ma nacelle, etc.). *Could I* domine la construction des deux strophes.

Where all lies founder'd that was ever dear :
But could I gather from the wave-worn store
Enough for my rude boat, where should I steer?
There woos[1] home, nor hope, nor life, save what is here.

CVI

Then let the winds howl on! their harmony
Shall henceforth be my music, and the night
The sound shall temper[2] with the owlets' cry,
As I now hear them, in the fading light
Dim o'er the bird of darkness' native site[3],
Answering each other on the Palatine,
With their large eyes, all glistening gray and bright,
And sailing pinions.—Upon such a shrine[4]
What are our petty griefs?—let me not number mine.

Nouvelle promenade parmi les ruines et les souvenirs de Rome. — Tout change et se mêle. — Le Palatin, la colonne Trajane, la roche Tarpéienne. — Le Forum. — Cicéron. — Rienzi. — Les drames de la liberté ou de l'anarchie. (Str. CVII à CXIV).

CVII

Cypress and ivy[5], weed and wallflower grown
Matted and mass'd together, hillocks heap'd

---

1. *There woos*, Rien ne me séduit, ni le lieu natal, ni l'espoir, ni la vie. Le mot *woos* ne peut pas être remplacé par *was* comme on l'a quelquefois proposé (*woos* est la 3ᵉ pers. sing. du prés. indicatif de *to woo*).
2. *Temper*, entremêler de...
3. *O'er the site.* Construction difficile. Le crépuscule qui répand sa lumière obscure sur la demeure des oiseaux de nuit, lesquels se répondent...
4. *Shrine.* Ailleurs c'est l'autel ; ici c'est le reliquaire ou l'ossuaire.
5. *Cypress and ivy... behold the Imperial mount.* Ce fouillis d'her-

On what were chambers, arch crush'd, column strown
In fragments, choked up vaults, and frescos steep'd
In subterranean damps, where the owl peep'd,
Deeming it midnight : — Temples, baths, or halls ?
Pronounce who can; for all that Learning reap'd
From her research hath been, that these are walls —
Behold the Imperial Mount ! 't is thus the mighty falls.

CVIII

There is the moral of all human tales;
'T is but the same rehearsal of the past,
First Freedom, and then Glory—when that fails,
Wealth, vice, corruption,—barbarism at last,
And History, with all her volumes vast,
Hath but *one* page—'t is better written here,
Where gorgeous Tyranny hath thus amass'd
All treasures, all delights, that eye or ear,
Heart, soul could seek, tongue ask—Away with words draw near,

CIX

Admire, exult, despise, laugh, weep,—for here
There is such matter for all feeling :—Man!
Thou pendulum [1] betwixt a smile and tear,
Ages and realms are crowded in this span [2],
This mountain, whose obliterated plan
The pyramid of empires pinnacled,

---

bes folles et de ruines, c'est le mont impérial, c'est le Palatin. Byron dit qu'on n'y trouve plus un vestige, et se moque (dans une note) des antiquaires romains qui en rapportent des briques. Depuis on a creusé et trouvé le vrai pavé des antiques palais.

1. *Pendulum*. Une chose qui oscille.

2. *Span*. Ce petit espace (vieux mot *empan*).

Of Glory's gewgaws shining in the van
Till the sun's rays with added flame were fill'd!
Where are its golden roofs? where those who dared to build?

CX

Tully was not so eloquent as thou,
Thou nameless column[1] with the buried base!
What are the laurels of the Cæsar's brow?
Crown me with ivy from his dwelling-place.
Whose arch or Trajan's? No—'t is that of Time:
Triumph, arch, pillar, all he doth displace
Scoffing; and apostolic statues[2] climb
To crush the imperial urn, whose ashes slept sublime,

CXI

Buried in air, the deep blue sky of Rome,
And looking to the stars: they had contained
A spirit[3] which with these would find a home,
The last of those who o'er the whole earth reign'd,
The Roman globe, for after none sustain'd,
But yielded back his conquests:—he was more
Than a mere Alexander, and, unstain'd
With household blood and wine, serenely wore
His sovereign virtues—still we Trajan's name adore.

CXII

Where is the rock of Triumph, the high place
Where Rome embraced her heroes? where the steep

---

1. *Column.* La colonne Trajane.
2. *Apostolic statues.* On a placé sur la colonne Trajane la statue de saint Pierre, et sur la colonne de Marc-Aurèle la statue de saint Paul.
3. *A spirit.* Un esprit, Trajan.

Tarpeian? fittest goal[1] of Treason's race,
The promontory whence the Traitor's Leap
Cured all ambition. Did the conquerors heap
Their spoils here? Yes; and in yon field below
A thousand years of silenced factions sleep—
The Forum, where the immortal accents glow,
And still the eloquent air breathes—burns with Cicero!

CXIII

The field of freedom, faction, fame, and blood:
Here a proud people's passions were exhaled,
From the first hour of empire in the bud
To that when further worlds to conquer fail'd;
But long before had Freedom's face been veil'd,
And Anarchy assumed her attributes;
Till[2] every lawless soldier who assail'd
Trod on the trembling senate's slavish mutes[3],
Or raised the venal voice of baser prostitutes[4].

CXIV

Then turn we to her latest tribune's name,
From her ten thousand tyrants turn to thee,
Redeemer of dark centuries of shame—
The friend of Petrarch—hope of Italy—
Rienzi[5]! last of Romans! While the tree

---

1. *Goal.* La roche Tarpéienne est e vrai terme de la carrière du traître.

2. *Till.* Au point que... (comme plus haut, strophe CIX).

3. *Mutes.* Les sénateurs qui n'osent pas parler.

4. *Prostitutes.* Ceux qui prostituent leur suffrage.

5. *Rienzi.* Au quatorzième siècle, Nicolas Rienzi joua à Rome le rôle de tribun que rappellent à Byron et la vue du Forum et ses lectures de Gibbon.

Of freedom's wither'd trunk puts forth a leaf,
Even for thy tomb a garland let it be—
The forum's champion, and the people's chief—
Her new-born Numa thou—with reign, alas! too brief.

Égérie. — Numa. — L'amour illusion sublime que l'homme se forge à lui-même, et qui n'est qu'un mirage. (Str. CXV à CXXVII.)

CXV

Egeria! sweet creation of some heart
Which found no mortal resting-place so fair
As thine ideal breast; whate'er thou art
Or wert,—a young Aurora of the air,
The nympholepsy [1] of some fond despair;
Or, it might be, a beauty of the earth,
Who found a more than common votary there
Too much adoring; whatsoe'er thy birth,
Thou wert a beautiful thought, and softly bodied forth.

CXVI

The mosses of thy fountain still are sprinkled
With thine Elysian water-drops; the face [2]
Of thy cave-guarded spring, with years unwrinkled,
Reflects the meek-eyed genius of the place,
Whose green, wild margin now no more erase
Art's works; nor must the delicate waters sleep,

---

1. *Nympholepsy.* Rêve et délire.
2. *The face.* La surface de tes ondes.

Prison'd in marble; bubbling from the base
Of the cleft statue, with a gentle leap
The rill runs o' er, and round, fern, flowers, and ivy creep,

CXVII

Fantastically tangled : the green hills
Are clothed with early blossoms, through the grass
The quick-eyed lizard rustles, and the bills
Of summer-birds sing welcome as ye pass;
Flowers fresh in hue[1], and many in their class,
Implore the pausing step[2], and with their dyes
Dance in the soft breeze in a fairy mass;
The sweetness of the violet's deep blue eyes,
Kiss'd by the breath of heaven, seems colour'd by its skies.

CXVIII

Here didst thou dwell[3], in this enchanted cover,
Egeria! thy all heavenly bosom beating
For the far footsteps of thy mortal lover;
The purple Midnight veil'd that mystic meeting
With her most starry canopy, and seating
Thyself by thine adorer, what befell?
This cave was surely shaped out for the greeting
Of an enamour'd Goddess, and the cell
Haunted by holy Love—the earliest oracle!

---

1. *Fresh in hue.* De couleurs fraîches et d'espèces variées.
2. *The pausing step.* Elles vous prient d'arrêter vos pas.
3. *Here didst thou dwell.* C'était ici ta demeure. Byron, mêlant dans la même description la retraite d'Égérie et la nymphe elle-même, reprend le thème qu'il a développé en parlant de Clarens et de Rousseau : il traite de l'amour comme d'une puissance qui se développe dans la nature et dans l'imagination créatrice.

CXIX

And didst thou not, thy breast to his replying,
Blend a celestial with a human heart;
And Love, which dies as it was born, in sighing,
Share with immortal transports? could thine art
Make them indeed immortal, and impart
The purity of heaven to earthly joys,
Expel the venom[1] and not blunt the dart—
The dull satiety which all destroys —
And root from out the soul the deadly weed which cloys?

CXX

Alas! our young affections run to waste,
Or water but the desert; whence arise
But weeds of dark luxuriance, tares of haste[2],
Rank at the core, though tempting to the eyes,
Flowers whose wild odours breathe but agonies,
And trees whose gums are poison; such[3] the plants
Which spring beneath her steps as Passion flies
O'er the world's wilderness, and vainly pants
For some celestial fruit forbidden to our wants.

CXXI

Oh Love! no habitant of earth art thou
An unseen seraph, we believe in thee,—
A faith[4] whose martyrs are the broken heart, —
But never yet hath seen, nor e'er shall see

---

1. *The venom.* Le venin, à savoir, la satiété.
2. *Tares of haste.* Ivraies qui poussent tout à coup.
3. *Such.* Telles (sont) les plantes.
4. *A faith.* Tu es une religion dont le cœur est le martyr.

The naked eye, thy form, as it should be;
The mind hath made thee, as it peopled heaven,
Even with its own desiring phantasy,
And to a thought such shape and image given,
As haunts the unquench'd soul—parch'd, wearied, wrung and riven.

CXXII

Of its own beauty [1] is the mind diseased,
And fevers into false creation:—where,
Where are the forms the sculptor's soul hath seiz'd?
In him alone.—Can Nature show so fair?
Where are the charms and virtues which we dare
Conceive in boyhood and pursue as men,
The unreach'd Paradise of our despair,
Which o'er-informs the pencil and the pen,
And overpowers the page where it would bloom again?

CXXIII

Who loves, raves—'t is youth's frenzy—but the cure
Is bitterer still, as charm by charm [2] unwinds
Which robed our idols, and we see too sure
Nor worth nor beauty dwells from out the mind's
Ideal shape [3] of such; yet still it binds
The fatal spell, and still it draws us on,
Reaping the whirlwind from the oft-sown winds;
The stubborn heart, its alchemy [4] begun,
Seems ever near the prize—wealthiest when most undone.

---

1. *Of its own beauty.* L'esprit souffre de la beauté qu'il a créée lui-même. C'est la pensée de toutes ces strophes. L'idéal nous donne des visions trop supérieures (*o'er-informs*).

2. *Charm by charm.* Locution analogue à la nôtre, quand nous disons *tomber* feuille à feuille.

3. *Ideal shape.* Nos idoles n'ont d'autre beauté que la forme idéale des idoles de l'esprit.

4. *Alchemy.* Nos illusions sont faites dans l'alambic de l'esprit.

CXXIV

We wither from our youth, we gasp away—
Sick—sick; unfound the boon[1], unslaked the thirst,
Though to the last, in verge of our decay,
Some phantom lures, such as we sought at first—
But all too late,—so are we doubly curst.
Love, fame, ambition, avarice—'t is the same,
Each idle, and all ill, and none the worst—
For all are meteors with a different name,
And Death the sable smoke where vanishes the flame.

CXXV

Few—none—find what they love or could have loved,
Though accident, blind contact[2], and the strong
Necessity of loving, have removed
Antipathies—but to recur, ere long,
Envenom'd with irrevocable wrong;
And Circumstance, that unspiritual god
And miscreator, makes and helps along
Our coming evils with a crutch-like rod,
Whose touch turns Hope to dust,—the dust we all have trod.

CXXVI

Our life is a false nature : 't is not in
The harmony of things,—this hard decree[3],

---

1. *Unfound the boon.* Ellipse ou forme absolue. Rien de trouvé !

2. *Accident... contact... circumstance.* Une rencontre nous fait croire à une sympathie ; mais ceux qui ont cru s'aimer sont souvent séparés par des torts irrévocables (*irrevocable wrong*).

3. *'T is not... this decree.* Cette condamnation de l'homme, elle est contre nature ; elle n'est pas dans l'harmonie des choses.

This uneradicable taint of sin,
This boundless upas[1], this all-blasting tree,
Whose root is earth, whose leaves and branches be
The skies which rain their plagues on men like dew—
Disease, death, bondage—all the woes we see,
And worse, the woes we see not—which throb through
The immedicable soul, with heart-aches ever new.

CXXVII

Yet let us ponder boldly[2]—'t is a base
Abandonment of reason to resign
Our right of thought— our last and only place
Of refuge; this, at least, shall still be mine :
Though from our birth the faculty divine
Is chain'd and tortured—cabin'd, cribb'd, confined,
And bred in darkness, lest the truth should shine
Too brightly on the unprepared mind[3],
The beam[4] pours in, for time and skill will couch the blind.

---

1. *Upas.* Arbre empoisonné dont les voyageurs et les poètes du dix-huitième siècle avaient beaucoup parlé.

2. *Yet let us ponder boldly.* Malgré tout (pensons) et pesons les choses. La vérité viendra ; elle nous éclairera ; la science abattra (ce qui fait) les aveugles (notre cécité) : *will couch the blind.*

3. *Unprepared mind.* Notre esprit qu'on n'a pas dressé à la vérité.

4 *The beam.* Le rayon du vrai pénètre en nous.

Le Colisée. — Le Temps l'a marqué de sa main. Le Temps embellit la mort. Il amène la justice. C'est lui et Némésis, qui vengeront Byron calomnié. (Str. CXXVIII à CXXXVIII.)

CXXVIII

Arches on arches[1]! as it were that Rome,
Collecting the chief trophies of her line[2],
Would build up all her triumphs in one dome,
Her Coliseum stands; the moonbeams shine
As 't were its natural torches, for divine
Should be the light which streams here, to illume
This long-explored but still exhaustless mine
Of contemplation; and the azure gloom
Of an Italian night, where the deep skies assume

CXXIX

Hues which have words, and speak to ye of heaven,
Floats o'er this vast and wondrous monument,
And shadows forth[3] its glory. There is given
Unto[4] the things of earth, which Time hath bent,
A spirit's feeling, and where he hath leant
His hand, but broke his scythe, there is a power
And magic in the ruin'd battlement,
For which the palace of the present hour
Must yield its pomp, and wait till ages[5] are its dower.

1. *Arches on arches!* Arcades sur arcades! Le poète parle ici de ces arcades superposées qui forment le mur même du Colisée, à travers lesquelles on aperçoit la nuit d'azur (*azure gloom*).

2. *Her line.* Sa généalogie; toutes ses générations.

3. *Shadows forth.* La nuit d'azur dessine et ombre la gloire de Rome (*adumbrat*).

4. *Given unto.* Il est donné à...

5. *Ages.* Attendre l'effet pittoresque des siècles, ce qu'on appelle la pâtine du temps.

CXXX

Oh Time! the beautifier of the dead,
Adorner of the ruin, comforter
And only healer when the heart hath bled;
Time! the corrector where[1] our judgments err,
The test of truth, love—sole philosopher,
For all beside are sophists—from thy thrift,
Which never loses though it doth defer—
Time, the avenger! unto thee I lift
My hands, and eyes, and heart, and crave of thee a gift.

CXXXI

Amidst this wreck, where thou hast made a shrine
And temple more divinely desolate,
Among thy mightier offerings[2] here are mine,
Ruins of years, though few, yet full of fate:
If thou hast ever seen me too elate,
Hear me not; but if calmly I have borne
Good, and reserved my pride[3] against the hate
Which shall not whelm me, let me not have worn
This iron in my soul in vain—shall *they*[4] not mourn?

CXXXII

And thou, who never yet of human wrong
Left the unbalanced[5] scale, great Nemesis!

---

1. *The corrector where*. Le correcteur de nos jugements, là où ils se trompent.
2. *Offerings*. Parmi les victimes qui te sont offertes.
3. *Reserved my pride*, gardé ma fierté.
4. *Shall they...?* N'est-ce pas à eux (à mes ennemis) de pleurer.
5. *Unbalanced*, inégale.

Here, where the ancient paid thee homage long—
Thou, who didst call the Furies from the abyss,
And round Orestes[1] bade them howl and hiss
For that unnatural retribution—just,
Had it but been from hands less near—in this
Thy former realm, I call thee from the dust!
Dost thou not hear my heart?—Awake! thou shalt, and must

CXXXIII

It is not that I may not have incurr'd
For my ancestral faults or mine the wound
I bleed withal, and had it been conferr'd
With a just weapon, it had flowed unbound;
But now my blood shall not sink[2] in the ground:
To thee I do devote it—*thou* shalt take
The vengeance, which shall yet be sought and found.
Which if I have not taken for the sake[3]—
But let that pass—I sleep, but thou shalt yet awake.

CXXXIV

And if my voice break forth, 't is not that now
I shrink from what is suffer'd: let him speak
Who hath beheld decline upon my brow,
Or seen my mind's convulsion leave it weak;
But in this page a record will I seek.
Not in the air shall these my words[4] disperse,

---

1. *Orestes.* Némésis a châtié Oreste et la famille dans laquelle on se frappait les uns les autres, vengeance contre nature.

2. *Sink.* Mon sang ne doit pas se perdre dans la terre. C'est à toi que je le consacre, c'est toi qui...

3. *For the sake.* Je ne me suis pas vengé à cause (d'elle, de ma fille).

4. *Shall these my words.* Dans cette strophe, *will* et *shall* ont leur sens premier. Je *veux* laisser un souvenir et cela *sera* (*shall*); mes paroles resteront, l'heure viendra où elles seront entendues.

Though I be ashes; a far hour shall wreak
The deep prophetic fulness of this verse,
And pile on human heads the mountain of my curse!

CXXXV

That curse shall be Forgiveness.—Have I not—
Hear me, my mother Earth! behold it, Heaven!—
Have I not had to wrestle with my lot?
Have I not suffer'd things to be forgiven?
Have I not had my brain sear'd, my heart riven,
Hopes sapp'd, name blighted, Life's life lied away?
And only not to desperation driven,
Because not altogether of such clay
As rots into the souls of those whom I survey.

CXXXVI

From mighty wrongs to petty perfidy
Have I not seen what human things could do?
From the loud roar of foaming calumny
To the small whisper of the as paltry few[1],
And subtler venom of the reptile crew,
The Janus glance of whose significant eye,
Learning to lie with silence, would *seem* true,
And without utterance, save the shrug or sigh,
Deal round to happy fools its speechles obloquy.

---

1. *As paltry few*. Quelques personnages aussi lâches, des Janus à double visage, qui ont l'*air* sincère (*seem*). Byron souligne, voulant dans ce mot faire éclater son indignation. On peut pardonner les fautes qui sont des passions ou des faiblesses, jamais l'hypocrisie des gens qui font semblant de ne pas y toucher. Leur regard ment en silence, avec l'air loyal. Tout ce passage est vibrant de colère.

CXXXVII

But I have lived, and have not lived in vain:
My mind may lose its force, my blood its fire,
And my frame perish even in conquering pain [1];
But there is that within me which shall tire
Torture and Time, and breathe when I expire;
Something unearthly, which they deem not of,
Like the remember'd tone [2] of a mute lyre,
Shall on their softened spirits sink, and move
In hearts all rocky now the late remorse of love.

CXXXVIII

The seal is set. — Now welcome, thou dread power!
Nameless, yet thus omnipotent, which here
Walk'st in the shadow of the midnight hour
With a deep awe [3], yet all distinct from fear;
Thy haunts are ever where the dead walls rear
Their ivy mantles, and the solemn scene
Derives from thee a sense so deep and clear
That we become a part of what has been,
And grow unto [4] the spot, all-seeing but unseen.

---

1. *In conquering pain.* En triomphant de la douleur.
2. *Like the remembered.* Comme le souvenir des accents d'une lyre devenue muette.

3. *With a deep awe.* Répandant la crainte et le respect.
4. *Grow unto.* Nous vivons de la vie de ce lieu, nous ne faisons qu'un avec cette ruine.

Le Gladiateur mourant. — Suite et fin de la description du Colisée. (Str. CXXXIX à CXLV.)

CXXXIX

And here the buzz of eager nations ran,
In murmur'd pity, or loud-roar'd applause,
As man was slaughtered by his fellow man.
And wherefore slaughter'd? wherefore, but because
Such were the bloody Circus' genial laws,
And the imperial pleasure. — Wherefore not?
What matters where we fall to fill the maws
Of worms — on battle-plains or listed spot [1]?
Both are but theatres where the chief actors rot.

CXL

I see before me [2] the Gladiator lie:
He leans upon his hand — his manly brow
Consents to death, but conquers agony,
And his droop'd head sinks gradually low —
And through his side the last drops [3], ebbing slow
From the red gash [4], fall heavy, one by one,
Like the first of a thunder-shower; and now
The arena swims [5] around him — he is gone,
Ere ceased the inhuman shout which hail'd the wretch who won.

---

1. *Listed spot.* Que ce soit sur la plaine ouverte d'un champ de bataille ou dans la lice d'un cirque.

2. *I see before me.* J'ai sous les yeux... La statue qui inspire ces vers magnifiques est la célèbre statue du *Gladiateur mourant*, conservée au musée du Capitole, et si expressive.

3. *Last drops*, les dernières gouttes de sang.

4. *Gash*, la blessure, l'entaille béante.

5. *Swims*, flotte autour de lui.

CXLI

He heard it, but he heeded not — his eyes
Were with his heart, and that was far away;
He recked not of the life he lost nor prize,
But where his rude hut by the Danube lay,
There were his young barbarians all at play,
There was their Dacian mother — he, their sire,
Butcher'd to make a Roman holiday —
All this rush'd with his blood — Shall he expire
And unavenged? Arise! ye Goths, and glut your ire!

CXLII

But here, where Murder breathed her bloody steam;
And here, where buzzing nations choked the ways[1],
And roar'd or murmur'd like a mountain stream
Dashing or winding as its torrent strays;
Here, where the Roman million's blame or praise[2]
Was death or life, the playthings of a crowd,
My voice sounds much — and fall the stars' faint rays
On the arena void — seats crush'd — walls bow'd —
And galleries, where my steps seem echoes strangely loud.

CXLIII

A ruin — yet what ruin! from its mass[3]
Walls, palaces, half-cities, have been rear'd;

---

1. *Choked the ways*; envahissait les issues, les *vomitoires*.
2. *Blame or praise*. Un signe, favorable ou hostile, c'était la vie ou la mort. On sait qu'il suffisait au peuple de montrer le sol en renversant le pouce (*pollice verso*) pour prononcer la mort du gladiateur vaincu.
3. *From its mass*. On enleva les pierres et le marbre du Colisée pour construire les palais de la Rome moderne. Comparez à cette strophe la strophe LXXXIX.

Yet oft the enormous skeleton ye pass,
And marvel[1] where the spoil could have appear'd.
Hath it indeed been plunder'd, or but clear'd?
Alas! developed, opens the decay,
When the colossal fabric's form is near'd:
It will not bear the brightness of the day,
Which streams too much on all years[2], man, have reft away.

CXLIV

But when the rising moon begins to climb
Its topmost arch, and gently pauses there;
When the stars twinkle through the loops of time,
And the low night-breeze[3] waves along the air
The garland-forest, which the gray walls wear,
Like laurels on the bald first Cæsar's[4] head;
When the light shines serene but doth not glare,
Then in this magic circle raise the dead:
Heroes have trod this spot — 't is on their dust ye tread.

CXLV

" While stands the Coliseum, Rome shall stand;
" When falls the Coliseum, Rome shall fall,
" And when Rome falls—the World." From our own land
Thus spake the pilgrims o'er this mighty wall

---

1. *Marvel.* Et vous, soyez surpris.
2. *All years.* Tout (ce que) les ans.
3. *Low night breeze*, la brise de nuit qui souffle tout bas.
4. *The bald first Cæsar.* Le premier César, qui était chauve. Là-dessus Byron nous renvoie à Suétone. Le Sénat décréta que César aurait le droit de porter toujours une couronne de laurier. César la porta surtout pour cacher qu'il était chauve. « On n'aurait pas deviné ce motif, dit Byron, si l'historien ne nous l'indiquait pas. »

In Saxon times, which we are wont to call
Ancient; and these three mortal things are still
On their foundations, and unalter'd all;
Rome and her Ruin past Redemption's skill [1],
The World, the same wide den—of thieves, or what ye will.

Le Panthéon. — Sanctuaire commun de l'art, du génie et de la piété. (Str. CXLVI et CXLVII.)

CXLVI

Simple, erect, severe, austere, sublime —
Shrine of all saints and temple of all gods,
From Jove to Jesus — spared and blest by time;
Looking tranquillity, while falls or nods
Arch, empire, each thing round thee, and man plods
His way through thorns [2] to ashes — glorious dome!
Shalt thou not last? Time's scythe and tyrants' rods
Shiver upon thee — sanctuary and home
Of art and piety — Pantheon! — pride of Rome!

CXLVII.

Relic of nobler days, and noblest arts!
Despoiled yet perfect [3], with thy circle spreads

---

1 *Past skill.* Dépassant le savant mystère de la Rédemption, c'est-à-dire en dépit de la Rédemption.

2. *Through thorns.* A travers les épines (de la vie) pour arriver aux cendres (de la mort).

3. *Despoiled yet perfect.* Parfait encore quoique dépouillé. Le Panthéon, rotonde où l'on avait groupé toutes les divinités, eut à souffrir des incendies, des inondations, des ravages du temps. On enleva les lames d'or qui le recouvraient, on fit des canons avec le bronze des bas-reliefs; on remplaça les dieux par des hommes célèbres. Malgré tout, dit le poète, le dôme

A holiness appealing to all hearts —
To art a model [1]; and to him who treads
Rome for the sake of ages, Glory sheds
Her light through thy sole aperture; to those
Who worship, here are altars for their beads;
And they who feel for genius may repose
Their eyes on honoured forms, whose busts around them
    close.

Saint-Nicolas in carcere. — La jeune Romaine. — Le lait de la vie. — Le môle d'Adrien. (Str. CXLVIII à CLII.)

CXLVIII

There is a dungeon [2], in whose dim drear light
What do I gaze on? Nothing : Look again!
Two forms are slowly shadowed on my sight —
Two insulated phantoms of the brain :
It is not so; I see them full and plain —
An old man, and a female young and fair,
Fresh as a nursing mother, in whose vein
The blood is nectar : — But what doth she there,
With her unmantled neck, and bosom white and bare?

---

reste un modèle de l'art, et l'effet de la lumière tombant d'en haut par une seule ouverture (voir le sixième vers de cette strophe) est toujours saisissant.

1. *To art o model.* Pour l'art tu es un modèle.

2. *There is a dungeen.* Voici un cachot. Selon une tradition, il y eut, à l'endroit où se trouve aujourd'hui l'église Saint-Nicolas *in carcere*, une prison qui avait été le théâtre d'une vieille légende, rapportée par les écrivains anciens : ce serait là qu'un homme, enfermé et condamné à mourir de faim, fut sauvé par sa fille, qui le nourrit de son lait.

CXLIX

Full swells¹ the deep pure fountain of young life,
Where *on* the heart and *from* the heart we took
Our first and sweetest nurture, when the wife,
Blest into mother², in the innocent look,
Or even the piping cry of lips that brook
No pain, and small suspense, a joy perceives
Man knows not, when from out its cradled nook
She sees her little bud put forth its leaves —
What may the fruit be yet? I know not—Cain was Eve's.

CL

But here youth offers to old age the food,
The milk of his own gift : it is her sire
To whom she renders back the debt of blood
Born with her birth. No; he shall not expire
While in those warm and lovely veins the fire
Of health and holy feeling can provide
Great Nature's Nile³, whose deep stream rises higher
Than Egypt's river : rom that gentle side
Drink, drink and live, old man! Heaven's realm holds no such tide.

CLI

The starry fable of the milky way
Has not thy story's purity; it is
A constellation of a sweeter ray,

---

1. *Full swells.* La source pure est toute gonflée.
2. *Blest into mother.* Qui a ce bonheur de devenir une mère.
3. *Great Nature's Nile.* Comme le Nil, qui nourrit l'Égypte, le lait nourrit l'humanité. — Alfred de Musset a traité le même sujet.

248 CHILDE HAROLD'S PILGRIMAGE.

And sacred Nature triumphs more in this
Reverse of her decree, than in the abyss
Where sparkle distant worlds :—Oh, holiest nurse!
No drop of that clear stream its way shall miss
To thy sire's heart, replenishing its source
With life, as our freed souls rejoin the universe.

CLII

Turn to the mole¹ which Hadrian rear'd on high,
Imperial mimic of old Egypt's piles,
Colossal copyist of deformity,
Whose travell'd phantasy from the far Nile's
Enormous model, doom'd the artist's toils
To build for giants, and for his vain earth,
His shrunken ashes, raise this dome : How smiles
The gazer's eye with philosophic mirth,
To view the huge design which sprung from such a birth !

Saint-Pierre. — Œuvre colossale; effet toujours grandissant.
— Éducation des sens par l'art. (Str. CLIII à CLIX.)

CLIII

But lo! the dome ²—the vast and wondrous dome,
To which Diana's marvel³ was a cell—

1. *The mole.* Le môle d'Adrien ou château Saint-Ange. Ce fut un pastiche, une construction imitée des pyramides d'Égypte par le caprice d'un empereur. Adrien voulut se faire une tombe à la manière des Pharaons.
2. *The dome.* L'église de Saint-Pierre, appelée le Dôme, comme ces grandes *coupoles* italiennes que les artistes de la Renaissance essayaient d'élever le plus haut possible. Elle fut élevée dit-on, sur l'emplacement même où saint Pierre subit le martyre (*martyr's tomb*).
3. *Diana's marvel.* Le temple prodigieux de Diane à Éphèse

Christ's mighty shrine above his martyr's tomb!
I have beheld the Ephesian's miracle;—
Its columns strew the wilderness, and dwell
The hyæna and the jackal in their shade;
I have beheld Sophia's[1] bright roofs swell
Their glittering mass i' the sun, and have survey'd
Its sanctuary the while the usurping Moslem pray'd;

CLIV

But thou, of temples old, or altars new,
Standest alone, with nothing like to thee—
Worthiest of God, the holy and the true.
Since Zion's desolation, when that[2] He
Forsook his former city, what could be,
Of earthly structures, in his honour piled,
Of a sublimer aspect? Majesty,
Power, Glory, Strength, and Beauty all are aisled
In this eternal ark of worship undefiled.

CLV

Enter: its grandeur overwhelms thee not;
And why? it is not lessen'd; but thy mind,
Expanded by the genius of the spot,
Has grown colossal, and can only find

(*Ephesian's miracle*); celui même que brûla Érostrate.

1. *Sophia*. La mosquée de Sainte-Sophie, jadis église chrétienne.

2. *When that*, lorsque. C'est la forme ancienne de la locution primitive qui, plus tard, a été réduite à un mot. Jusqu'au seizième siècle *when*, *though* et quelques autres conjonctions étaient considérées comme des *adverbes*, et lorsqu'on voulait leur donner le sens conjonctif, on était obligé d'y joindre la conjonction *that*. On trouve dans Shakespeare de nombreux exemples de ce fait, qui a des analogues dans toutes les langues.

A fit abode wherein appear enshrined
Thy hopes of immortality; and thou
Shalt one day, if found worthy, so defined,
See thy God face to face, as thou dost now
His Holy of Holies, nor be blasted by his brow.

CLVI

Thou movest, but increasing[1] with the advance,
Like climbing some great Alp, which still doth rise,
Deceived by its gigantic elegance;
Vastness which grows, but grows to harmonise—
All musical in its immensities;
Rich marbles, richer painting—shrines where flame
The lamps of gold—and haughty dome which vies
In air with Earth's chief structures[2], though their frame
Sits on the firm-set ground, and this the clouds must claim.

CLVII

Thou seest not all; but piecemeal thou must break[3],
To separate contemplation, the great whole;
And as the ocean many bays will make
That ask the eye—so here condense thy soul
To more immediate objects, and control
Thy thoughts until thy mind hath got by heart

---

1. *But increasing*. Vous avancez; mais, en avançant, vous grandissez avec l'édifice, parce qu'il n'est pas seulement gigantesque, il a des proportions élégamment colossales (*gigantic elegance*).

2. *Chief structures*. Les chefs-d'œuvre de l'architecture.

3. *Break*. Il faut décomposer l'édifice. Byron, admirant les dimensions de Saint-Pierre, a peint ici l'effet grandissant du temple, puis de chaque détail. La perspective, prodigieusement savante, de cet édifice en rend peu à peu toutes les parties plus grandioses.

Its eloquent proportions, and unroll
　In mighty graduations, part by part,
The glory which at once upon thee did not dart,

CLVIII

Not by its fault—but thine : Our outward sense
Is but of gradual grasp [1]—and as it is
That what we have of feeling most intense
Outstrips our faint expression : even so this
Outshining and o'erwhelming edifice
Fools our fond gaze, and greatest of the great
Defies at first our Nature's littleness,
　Till, growing with its growth, we thus dilate
Our spirits to the size of that they contemplate.

CLIX

Then pause, and be enlighten'd [2]; there is more
In such a survey than the sating gaze
Of wonder pleased, or awe which would adore
The worship of the place, or the mere praise
Of art and its great masters, who could raise
What former time, nor skill, nor thought could plan;
The fountain of sublimity displays
　Its depth, and thence may draw the mind of man
Its golden sands, and learn what great conceptions can.

---

1. *Grasp.* Nos sens (notre perception extérieure) ne peuvent saisir que graduellement.

2. *Be enlightened.* Que la clarté lui arrive. Au lieu de trouver là un sujet ou de plaisir, ou de recueillement, ou d'éloges esthétiques, reconnaissez le sublime dans sa source, c'est-à-dire la puissance de l'Idéal.

Le Vatican. — Le groupe du *Laocoon.* — *L'Apollon du Belvédère.*
(Str. CLX à CLXIII.)

CLX

Or, turning to the Vatican[1], go see
Laocoon's torture dignifying pain—
A father's love and mortal's agony
With an immortal patience blending : Vain
The struggle; vain, against[2] the coiling strain
And gripe, and deepening of the dragon's grasp,
The old man's clench; the long envenom'd chain
Rivets the living links,—the enormous asp
Enforces pang on pang, and stifles gasp on gasp.

CLXI

Or view the Lord[3] of the unerring bow,
The God of life, and poesy, and light—
The sun in human limbs array'd, and brow
All radiant from his triumph in the fight;
The shaft hath just been shot—the arrow bright
With an immortal's vengeance; in his eye
And nostril beautiful disdain, and might
And majesty, flash their full lightnings by,
Developing in that one glance the Deity.

1. *Vatican.* On a placé au Vatican le célèbre groupe de *Laocoon,* chef-d'œuvre antique retrouvé au seizième siècle.

2. *Vain against.* Construisez : contre l'étreinte du serpent.., l'effort est vain.

3. *The Lord of...* Il s'agit de *l'Apollon du Belvédère,* d'Apollon le maître dont l'arc est certain, le dieu de la vie. Au Vatican encore se trouve cette statue que le seizième siècle restitua également à l'histoire de l'art.

CLXII

But in his delicate form—a dream of Love,
Shaped¹ by some solitary nymph, whose breast
Long'd for a deathless lover from above,
And madden'd in that vision—are exprest
All that² ideal beauty ever bless'd
The mind with in its most unearthly mood,
When each conception was a heavenly guest—
A ray of immortality—and stood,
Starlike, around, until they gathered to a god!

CLXIII

And if it be³ Prometheus stole from Heaven
The fire which we endure⁴, it was repaid
By him to whom the energy was given
Which this poetic marble hath array'd
With an eternal glory—which, if made
By human hands, is not of human thought⁵;
And Time himself hath hallow'd it, nor laid
One ringlet in the dust—nor hath it caught
A tinge of years, but breathes⁶ the flame with which
't was wrought.

---

1. *Shaped.* Auquel une nymphe donna sa forme.

2. *All that... with.* Tout ce avec quoi le beau idéal remplit si heureusement notre esprit.

3. *If it be.* S'il est vrai que...

4. *We endure*, dont nous nous sentons brûlés.

5. *Not of human thought.* L'œuvre est d'un homme, la pensée est d'un dieu, s'il est vrai que l'idée du beau absolu soit une parcelle de l'intelligence divine. (Voy. la strophe CLIX de ce chant.)

6. *But breathes.* Mais ce marbre respire...

254 CHILDE HAROLD'S PILGRIMAGE.

Fin du poème. — Byron abandonne Childe Harold et fait rentrer ce fantôme dans le néant où tout doit rentrer. — La Mort. — Bonheur de ne pas recommencer la vie. — Chant de deuil sur une jeune princesse et une jeune mère. (Str. CLXIV à CLXXII.)

CLXIV

But where is he, the Pilgrim of my song,
The being who upheld[1] it through the past?
Methinks he cometh late and tarries long.
He is no more — these breathings are his last;
His wanderings done, his visions ebbing fast,
And he himself as nothing : — if he was
Aught but a phantasy, and could be class'd
With forms which live and suffer — let that pass —
His shadow fades away into Destruction's mass,

CLXV

Which gathers[2] shadow, substance, life, and all
That we inherit in its mortal shroud,
And spreads the dim and universal pall
Through which all things grow phantoms; and the cloud
Between us sinks and all which ever glow'd,
Till Glory's self is twilight, and displays
A melancholy halo scarce allow'd
To hover on the verge of darkness; rays
Sadder than saddest night, for they distract the gaze.

CLXVI

And send us prying into the abyss,
To gather what we shall be when the frame

---

1. *Upheld*, qui a soutenu mon chant jusqu'à l'heure présente.

2. *Which gathers.* La Destruction ; elle enveloppe tout.

Shall be resolved to something less than this
Its wretched essence; and to dream of fame,
And wipe the dust from off the idle name
We never more shall hear, — but never more,
Oh, happier thought! can we be made the same:
It is enough in sooth that *once* we bore
These fardels of the heart — the heart whose sweat was gore.

CLXVII

Hark! forth from the abyss a voice proceeds,
A long low distant murmur of dread sound,
Such as arises when a nation bleeds
With some deep and immedicable wound;
Through storm and darkness yawns the rending ground,
The gulf is thick with phantoms, but the chief
Seems royal[1] still, though with her head discrown'd,
And pale, but lovely, with maternal grief
She clasps[2] a babe, to whom her breast yields no relief.

CLXVIII

Scion of chiefs and monarchs, where art thou?
Fond hope of many nations, art thou dead?
Could not the grave forget thee, and lay low
Some less majestic, less beloved head?

---

1. *But the chief seems royal.* Dans le gouffre où se pressent les morts, voici un fantôme royal. Il s'agit de la princesse Charlotte, mariée au prince de Saxe-Cobourg, qui devint roi des Belges. Elle était fille du prince de Galles, le futur George IV, et fort aimée de la nation anglaise.

2. *She clasps a babe.* Elle serre dans ses bras un enfant. La princesse venait d'accoucher d'un enfant mort-né, et elle mourut presque aussitôt.

In the sad midnight, while thy heart still bled[1],
The mother of a moment, o'er thy boy,
Death hush'd that pang for ever : with thee fled
The present happiness and promised joy
Which fill'd the imperial isles so full it seem'd to cloy.

CLXIX

Peasants bring forth[2] in safety. — Can it be,
Oh thou that wert so happy, so adored!
Those who weep not[3] for kings shall weep for thee,
And Freedom's heart, grown heavy, cease to hoard
Her many griefs for ONE! for she had pour'd
Her orisons for thee, and o'er thy head
Beheld her Iris. — Thou, too, lonely lord,
And desolate consort — vainly wert thou wed!
The husband of a year! the father of the dead!

CLXX

Of sackcloth was thy wedding garment made;
Thy bridal's fruit is ashes : in the dust
The fair-hair'd Daughter of the Isles is laid,
The love of millions! How we did entrust
Futurity to her! and, though it must
Darken above our bones[4], yet fondly deem'd
Our children should obey her child, and bless'd
Her and her hoped-for seed, whose promise seem'd
Like stars to shepherd's eyes : — 't was but a meteor
  beam'd.

---

1. *Bled*. Ton cœur saignait encore de la mort de ton enfant.
2. *Bring forth*. Accouche.
3. *Those who weep not*. Ceux qui (comme moi) ne pleureraient pas pour les rois... Il s'agit des libéraux (*freedom's heart*).
4. *Our bones*, nos cadavres. Nous serions morts, nous, mais nos enfants auraient aimé le tien.

CLXXI

Woe unto us, not her! for she sleeps well :
The fickle¹ reek of popular breath, the tongue
Of hollow counsel, the false oracle,
Which from the birth of monarchy hath rung
Its knell in princely ears, till the o'erstrung
Nations have arm'd in madness, the strange fate
Which tumbles mightiest sovereigns, and hath flung
Against their blind omnipotence a weight
Within the opposing scale, which crushes² soon or late,—

CLXXII

These might have been her destiny; but no,
Our hearts deny it : and so young, so fair,
Good without effort, great without a foe :
But now a bride and mother — and now *there!*
How many ties did that stern moment tear!
From thy Sire's to his humblest subject's breast
Is link'd the electric chain of that despair,
Whose shock was as an earthquake's, and opprest
The land which loved thee so that none could love thee best.

---

1. *The fickle.* Tous les vers qui suivent dépendent grammaticalement du premier vers de la strophe suivante: (Sa destinée aurait été de voir les mensonges de l'opinion ou des cours, les révolutions, etc.)

2. *Which crushes.* Ici Byron rappelle en note la mort de quelques souverains, depuis Marie Stuart montant à l'échafaud, jusqu'à Napoléon s'éteignant sur le rocher de Sainte-Hélène.

Byron achève son voyage en saluant le lac de Nemi, l'Albano, le Latium ; puis il s'arrête, et, embrassant du regard les pays qu'il a parcourus, il contemple, au milieu de la terre pleine de ruines, l'Océan immortel. (Str. CLXXIII à la fin.)

CLXXIII

Lo, Nemi! navell'd in the woody hills
So far [1], that the uprooting wind which tears
The oak from his foundation, and which spills
The ocean o'er its boundary, and bears
Its foam against the skies, reluctant spares
The oval mirror of thy glassy lake;
And calm as cherish'd hate, its surface wears
A deep cold settled aspect nought can shake,
All coil'd into itself and round, as sleeps the snake.

CLXXIV

And near, Albano's [2] scarce divided waves
Shine from a sister valley; — and afar
The Tiber winds, and the broad ocean laves
The Latian coast where sprung the Epic war,
"Arms and the man," whose re-ascending star
Rose o'er an empire : — but beneath thy right

---

1. *So far*. Dans une telle profondeur. Le lac Nemi est encaissé dans des montagnes boisées, si bien (*so far that*) que le vent n'atteint pas la surface : elle reste polie comme un miroir. C'est le « miroir de Diane ».

2. *Albano*, le lac d'Albano. Byron est là au milieu des origines de l'empire romain. Il embrasse du regard le Latium, la place où fut Albe, le théâtre de *l'Énéide* (dont il rapporte le premier vers : *Arma virumque cano*); il se rappelle toute la descendance impériale d'Énée, puis le Tusculum de Cicéron, et la ferme d'Horace dans la Sabine ; il est plus classique que jamais.

Tully reposed from Rome; — and where yon bar
   Of girdling mountains intercepts the sight
The Sabine farm was till'd, the weary bard's delight.

CLXXV

But I forget. — My Pilgrim's shrine is won[1],
And he and I must part, — so let it be, —
His task and mine alike are nearly done;
Yet once more let us look upon the sea[2];
The midland ocean breaks on him and me,
And from the Alban Mount we now behold
Our friend of youth, that Ocean, which when we
Beheld it last by Calpe's rock unfold
Those waves, we follow'd on till the dark Euxine roll'd.

CLXXVI

Upon the blue Symplegades[3] : ong years —
Long, though not very many — since have done
Their work on both[4]; some suffering and some tears
Have left us nearly where we had begun :
Yet not in vain our mortal race hath run;
We have had our reward, and it is here, —

---

1. *Shrine is won.* Mon pèlerin a gagné son reliquaire et terminé son voyage.
2. *The sea.* Transition au morceau final du poème, à la belle page sur la Méditerranée qu'il appelle *the broad Ocean.*
3. *Upon the blue Symplegades.* Byron, résumant ses voyages, se plaît à mesurer le chemin parcouru de Gibraltar (Calpé) à la mer Noire (Pont-Euxin), à l'entrée de laquelle se trouvaient et s'entrechoquaient les îles Symplegades ou Cyanées. Le navire Argo passa entre ces îles qui devinrent fixes. Childe Harold est aussi un Argonaute, qui a vu les roches *bleues* (*Cyanées*).
4. *Both,* tous deux. Childe Harold et moi.

That we can yet feel gladden'd by the sun,
And reap from earth, sea, joy almost as dear
As if there were no man to trouble what is clear.

CLXXVII

Oh! that the Desert[1] were my dwelling-place,
With one fair Spirit for my minister,
That I might all forget the human race,
And, hating no one, love but only her!
Ye elements! — in whose ennobling stir
I feel myself exalted — Can yet not
Accord me such a being? Do I err
In deeming such inhabit many a spot?
Though with them to converse can rarely be our lot.

CLXXVIII

There is a pleasure in the pathless woods,
There is a rapture on the lonely shore,
There is society, where none intrudes,
By the deep Sea, and music in its roar :
I love not Man the less, but Nature more,
From these our interviews, in which I steal[2]
From all I may be, or have been before,
To mingle with the Universe, and feel
What I can ne'er express, yet can not all conceal.

CLXXIX

Roll on[3], thou deep and dark blue Ocean — roll!
Ten thousand fleets sweep over thee in vain;

---

1. *The Desert.* Le désert avec une compagne, c'est ce que je désire. Ce vœu rappelle sur un autre ton le *Ah! si...* (*Oh! that*) de La Fontaine.

2. *I steal.* Je me dérobe à ce que je puis être ou avoir été.

3. *Roll on!...* Cette description de l'Océan, restée célèbre, faisait l'admiration de Lamartine et son

CANTO THE FOURTH.

Man marks the earth with ruin — his control
Stops with the shore; upon the watery plain
The wrecks are all thy deed, nor doth remain
A shadow of man's ravage, save his own,
When, for a moment, like a drop of rain,
He sinks[1] into thy depths with bubbling groan,
Without a grave, unknell'd, uncoffin'd, and unknown.

CLXXX

His steps are not upon thy paths, — thy fields
Are not a spoil for him, — thou dost arise
And shake him from thee; the vile strength he wields
For earth's destruction thou dost all despise,
Spurning him from thy bosom to the skies,
And send'st him, shivering[2] in thy playful spray
And howling, to his Gods, where haply lies
His petty hope in some near port or bay,
And dashest him again to earth : — there let him lay[3].

CLXXXI

The armaments[4] which thunderstrike the walls
Of rock-built cities, bidding nations quake,

---

envie. Il voyait toujours Byron debout sur le mont Albano « découvrant l'abîme et le saluant d'un « adieu sublime ».

1. *He sinks...* Il disparaît. Comparez à ce passage les vers dans lesquels le Dante nous montre l'homme dévoré par les flots sous la figure d'Ulysse, qui périt pour avoir voulu franchir les barrières de l'Océan.

2. *Shivering.* Lui qui tremble au milieu de tes vagues qui jouent.

3. *Lay.* Il faudrait *lie*, puisque *lay* est actif et veut dire *poser*, tandis que le neutre *lie* veut dire *être posé, rester là*. Nous avons signalé plus haut la tendance de Byron à mêler, parmi des strophes lyriques, une locution énergiquement vulgaire. Celle-ci est une faute populaire.

4. *The armaments*, la marine. Lord Byron, selon son habitude mêle ici deux sentiments contraires. Il raille la prétention de l'homme

And monarchs tremble in their capitals,
The oak leviathans, whose huge ribs make
Their clay creator the vain title take
Of lord of thee, and arbiter of war —
These are thy toys, and, as the snowy flake,
They melt into thy yeast of waves, which mar
Alike the Armada's pride or spoils of Trafalgar.

CLXXXII

Thy shores are empires, changed in all save thee —
Assyria, Greece, Rome, Carthage, what are they?
Thy waters washed them power while they were free,
And many a tyrant since; their shores obey
The stranger, slave, or savage; their decay
Has dried up realms to deserts: not so thou; —
Unchangeable, save to thy wild waves' play,
Time writes no wrinkle on thine azure brow
Such as creation's dawn beheld, thou rollest now.

CLXXXIII

Thou glorious mirror, where the Almighty's [1] form
Glasses itself in tempests; in all time, —
Calm or convulsed, in breeze or gale or storm,
Icing the pole, or in the torrid clime
Dark-heaving — boundless, endless, and sublime,
The image of eternity, the throne

---

qui se dit roi des mers : or c'est l'Angleterre qui a cette prétention (voy. strophe XVII, *Ocean queen*). Puis il cite *l'Armada* et *Trafalgar*, c'est-à-dire les désastres subis en divers temps par les adversaires de l'Angleterre.

1. *Almighty*. Le Tout-Puissant et plus bas l'Invisible. En terminant son poème, Byron parle de Dieu sur un ton différent de celui qu'il prenait au début.

Of the Invisible; even from out thy slime
The monsters of the deep are made; each zone
Obeys thee; thou goest forth, dread, fathomless, alone.

CLXXXIV

And I have loved thee, Ocean! and my joy
Of youthful sports was on thy breast to be
Borne, like thy bubbles, onward : from a boy
I wanton'd[1] with thy breakers — they to me
Were a delight; and if the freshening sea
Made them a terror — 't was a pleasing fear,
For I was as it were a child of thee,
And trusted to thy billows far and near,
And laid my hand upon thy mane — as I do here.

CLXXXV

My task is done, my song hath ceased, my theme
Has died into an echo[2]; it is fit
The spelll should break of this protracted dream.
The torch shall be extinguished which hath lit
My midnight lamp — and what is writ, is writ;
Would it were worthier! but I am not now
That which I have been — and my visions flit
Less palpably before me — and the glow
Which in my spirit dwelt is fluttering, faint, and low.

---

1. *I wantoned.* J'ai joué avec tes vagues. Le poète se targuait d'être excellent nageur. Il a longuement raconté comment il avait traversé l'Hellespont à la nage, pour vérifier la légende dont le héros était un nageur, Léandre allant trouver Héro.

2. *Has died into an echo.* Vient de mourir dans un dernier écho.

CLXXXVI

Farewell! a word that must be, and hath been —
A sound which makes us linger[1]; — yet — farewell!
Ye! who have traced the Pilgrim to the scene
Which is his last, if in your memories dwell
A thought which once was his, if on ye swell
A single recollection, not in vain
He wore his sandal-shoon, and scallop-shell[2];
Farewell! with *him* alone may rest the pain,
If such there were — with *you*, the moral of his strain.

1. *Linger.* Le mot adieu retarde l'adieu ; pourtant il faut le dire.
2. *Sandal-shoon.* Byron termine son poème, son *romaunt*, par une image et des expressions archaïques qui en rappellent le début et la donnée : *shoon* pour *shoes* ; *scallop-shell*, la coquille que le pèlerin mettait à son chapeau. Et ce pèlerin lui-même qui emporte ses douleurs en nous laissant une leçon morale fait songer à une comparaison entre Childe Harold et le *Pilgrim's Progress* de Bunyan.

FIN

www.ingramcontent.com/pod-product-compliance
Lightning Source LLC
Chambersburg PA
CBHW070538160426
43199CB00014B/2288